Bind

A CRITICAL ESSAY
ON THE
ANCIENT INHABITANTS
Of the *Northern Parts* of
BRITAIN, or *SCOTLAND*.

CONTAINING
An ACCOUNT of the *Romans*, of the *Britains* betwixt the Walls, of the *Caledonians* or *Picts*, and particularly of the *Scots*.

WITH
An APPENDIX of ancient MS. Pieces.

VOL. II.

By *THOMAS INNES*, M. A.

LONDON:
Printed for WILLIAM INNYS, at the West-End of St. *Paul's*. MDCCXXIX.

SECTION II.

An enquiry into the antiquity of the first settlement of the Scots *in* Ireland, *and in the northern parts of* Britain.

HAVING in the preceding section on the *Scots* considered their settlement and government in *Britain*, on the supposition of their having been, long before the incarnation, settled in *Ireland*; my design in this is to examine the truth of this ancient settlement of the *Scots* in *Ireland*, that being a necessary preliminary towards the discovery of the time of the first coming and settlement of the *Scots* in *Britain*, and of the beginning of their monarchy in the *Scotish* line in this island. This double enquiry shall make the subject of the two dissertations, into which I shall divide this last section.

IN the first dissertation, I shall enquire into the grounds of the remote antiquities of *Ireland*; and particularly into the time of the first settlement of the *Scots* in that island.

IN the second, after a short account of the writers in general, and of some historical monuments of *Scotland*, I ſhall endeavour to fix the time of the firſt ſettlement, and of the beginning of the monarchy of the *Scots* in *Britain*.

DISSERTATION I.

On the accounts that the Iriſh *give of the remote antiquities of* Ireland, *and of the firſt ſettlement of the* Scots *in that iſland.*

IT is with very great reluctancy that I enter upon this ſubject; which, if I could have avoided, I certainly had not meddled with it, but it being generally agreed on, that the *Scots* of *Britain* came in from *Ireland*, there was no treating of the ſubject, nor any poſſibility of fixing the time of their ſettlement in *Britain*, without firſt examining into the antiquity of their ſettlement in *Ireland*. And having ventured in this eſſay to call in queſtion the common traditions of my own country, ſupported by the authority of all our modern hiſtorians, concerning the firſt forty kings, and other points of antiquity, it ought not to appear ſtrange, that I take the like freedom with the ſettlement of the *Scots* in *Ireland*, eſpecially ſince the diſcuſſion of this laſt is ſo neceſſary to give light into what concerns their ſettlement in *Britain*. But having in this enquiry into the remote antiquities of *Ireland*, nothing in my view but to endeavour to diſcover the truth of hiſtory, and to ſeparate what is uncertain and conteſted, from what is more certain, and generally agreed on; I think I may ſo much the more juſtly hope that none of the learned of the *Iriſh* nation will take offence at it, that my intention is to treat the ſubject with that moderation and candour that becomes a ſincere enquirer after truth, without preſuming to decide in ſo intricate and obſcure queſtions as may be made about thoſe remote antiquities: that being a task to which I muſt acknowledge I am very unequal, and which none but ſome of the learned natives, skilled in their ancient language, with the helps of the remains of what is more authentick in their hiſtory, could with any hopes of ſucceſs undertake.

AND indeed I have often wondered, that among ſo many truly learned and capable men, who have diſtinguiſhed themſelves in all kinds of learning, that *Ireland* hath produced during the laſt, and in this age, none of them have ever applied to ſeparate what is certain of their hiſtory, and grounded upon ſolid monuments of antiquity, written in times of light and learning, from what is uncertain, and hath no other foundation but the traditions or writings of their *Seanachies* and bards, in order to give a true hiſtory of the country ſince the times of St. *Patrick* and king *Leogaire*; both civil and ſacred; whilſt others, ſuch as *Keating*, *O Flaherty*, &c. render all uncertain, by putting on an equal level, and delivering, and that on the ſole credit of the bards, the accounts of their hiſtory from almoſt the deluge of *Noah*, with as much assurance as they do the transactions of *Ireland* after St. *Patrick*'s time.

But in order to give a true history of *Ireland*, and for a solid foundation to it, the first thing to be done, were that according to the example of all countries of *Europe*, who pretend to have any ancient chronicles, annals, or other historical monuments, some of the learned men of *Ireland*, skilled in their ancient language, would publish, as all other nations have done, and are daily doing, the most authentick historical monuments of their country, I mean those chiefly which contain the transactions of *Ireland* since the time of St. *Patrick*; since which they had, without doubt not only the use of letters and learning; but in some ages, such as the seventh, eighth, and ninth, *Ireland* appears to have been more famous for learning and learned men, than most other nations; and by consequence, it is natural to expect that they should have had as good monuments of history, civil and ecclesiastical, as any other country. And though by the *Danish* invasions, and other accidents, many valuable pieces of that kind may have perished, there are, no doubt, still enough remaining to make some volumes of collections of historical monuments; such, among others, are the chronicles of *Tigernach*, the annals of *Ulster*, the synchronisms of *Flannus*, the annals of *Inisfall*, &c. and the loss which they (*a*) complain they

(1) Colgan. Præfat. Vit. Sanctorum Hyberniæ.

have

have already suffer'd of so many others, by different accidents, should be a new motive to engage them to publish what as yet remains, to hinder them from having the same fate. And I cannot but add, that it is extremely surprizing to see, that though there are very few nations that pretend to so ancient monuments of history, as the *Irish* do; yet they should be the only people in *Europe* that have never as yet published any original history or chronicle of their country, written before these two or three last ages: but leaving that to the consideration of the learned natives of *Ireland*, zealous for its honour, I return to the enquiry into the remote antiquities of that island, and the time of the first settlement of the *Scots* in it.

THERE are two opposite opinions concerning the time of the first coming in, and settlement of the *Scots* in *Ireland*: the one is that of the generality of the modern *Irish* writers, who relying on the authority of their bards, seanachies, and poets, (which are but different names of the same kind of men) make no distinction betwixt the ancient inhabitants of *Ireland*, or *Milesians*, that came into it after the four first colonies, and the *Scots*; and pretend, that these *Milesians*, or *Milesian Scots*, came into *Ireland*, some say ten, some twelve, some fourteen centuries before the incarnation; and that at the same time they set up a monarchy, whereof *Heremon* son to *Milesius*, was the first king.

THE

THE other opinion is that of *Camden*, and other learned men, who make a great distinction betwixt the ancient inhabitants of *Ireland* and the *Scots*: and as they are persuaded, that *Ireland* was first planted from *Britain* in the earliest times, so they hold that the *Scots* were not of the number of the ancient inhabitants of that island, but originally a foreign people, distinct from the ancient inhabitants, and who came not into it till after the times of the incarnation. And I myself have known some of the most learned and judicious of the *Irish* nation, that I ever was acquainted with, of the same opinion: and after all the enquiry I could make into this matter, by all the best authority and reasons I could discover, I cannot but be of the same sentiment, that the *Scots* were not of the number of the ancient inhabitants of *Ireland*, but a foreign people that came not into it till about the times of the incarnation, or after it, as I shall endeavour to shew in its proper place.

NOW because the greatest objection that is made against this opinion, of the *Scots* not being the ancient inhabitants of *Ireland*, nor the same with the *Milesians*, is drawn chiefly from the histories accompanied with chronologies, genealogies of the *Irish* kings, and great men of the *Milesian* race, continued down from *Milesius* till St. *Patrick*'s time, and forwards, that have been published by *Keating*, *O Flaherty*, and other modern *Irish*

Irish writers, taken, as they tell us, from the poems and other pretended ancient writings of their bards and ſeanachies: I ſhall therefore begin by enquiring into the grounds of the accounts of theſe remote antiquities delivered by them; but I ſhall do it, as I ſaid before, with the reſervedneſs that becomes a candid enquirer, and content myſelf to propoſe the objections and difficulties that occur to me about the authority of them, and the reaſons that hinder me to give credit to them, after I ſhall, in the firſt place, for greater clearneſs, have ſet down certain heads that generally all agree upon, as to the firſt plantation and ancient inhabitants of *Ireland*.

THAT *Ireland* was inhabited in the earlieſt times there is no doubt: and I think it can be as little doubted, that the firſt inhabitants of it came from *Britain* in its neighbourhood, as thoſe of *Britain* came from the neareſt coaſts of the *Gauls*, and of other countries of the continent oppoſite to it. For thus, from place to place, the world was at firſt planted by degrees after the deluge: men as they multiplied, being obliged to march forward to the new habitations in the *neighbourhood*, and therefore to advance not only on the ſame continent over rivers, but to tranſport themſelves over the narrow paſſages of ſeas into the neighbouring iſlands or lands; but at firſt, and in the earlieſt times, for want of ſkill of navigation, only to ſuch lands or iſlands as they could diſcern from their own coasts, before they durst venture upon sea-voyages out of the sight of land.

THIS, and the conformity of languages and customs betwixt the *British* and *Irish* in ancient times, makes it much more (*a*) probable, that the first inhabitants of *Ireland* came from *Britain*, than from *Spain*, or any other great distance: and these same reasons prove, that the first and most ancient inhabitants of *Ireland* must have come from the northern parts of *Britain*, that is, either from the point of land called the *Mull of Galloway*, or from *Cantyre* by the lesser islands, that lie betwixt it and *Ireland*, all in sight one of another; and the more remote of them in sight of *Ireland*, and at no great distance from it. And in effect we are told, that the *Irish* seanachies (*b*) bring some of their first colonies after the deluge from the north of *Britain*, that being the nearest coast. In process of time, when men became more used to navigation, 'tis not unlike there might come to *Ireland* new colonies from *Spain*, as well as from the vast continent of the north.

I conceive also, that it cannot be doubted, but that before the times of the incarnation, there was some kind of government in *Ireland*; and by consequence, as the most ancient of all governments, and that of which a rude people is only capable,

(*a*) Camden Britan. edit. Lond. in 4to. Tom. II. p. 356.
(*b*) Flaherty Ogygia — Keating, &c.

is

is that of a king, or a ſingle chief or leader, that kind of government was in uſe in *Ireland*; not that they had one monarch of all the iſland, but many little kings, as we ſee there were in *Britain*, and meet with among all nations in the earlieſt times, and among the people found out in later ages at their firſt diſcovery. There were probably alſo among them, as among the *Gauls* and *Germans*, ſome uncertain traditions of more memorable tranſactions. All this may be allowed to the ancient inhabitants of *Ireland*, before the times of chriſtianity, or to any other uncultivated nation, before they had policy or the uſe of letters among them; provided always that no particulars be alledged to have been preſerved of the dates or circumſtances of old tranſactions, no more than any ſure ſeries or ſucceſſion of kings, or of their deſcents or genealogies, at any diſtance of time, paſt the memory of men, before the introduction of the uſe of letters.

As to the ſettlement of the *Scots* in *Ireland*, 'tis generally agreed on alſo, that they were already come into that iſland, and ſettled in the firſt ages of chriſtianity, and perhaps a little before, or at leaſt about theſe times, as I ſhall have occaſion to obſerve; though (*a*) *Camden* places the coming in of the *Scots* into *Ireland* later, becauſe there is no word of them in ancient writers, till the ſecond or third age.

(*a*) Camden Britan. edit. Lond. 4to. p. 759.

THIS

This being premised, I shall in this first dissertation propose, 1°. The difficulties that I meet with, or objections that may be made against the remote antiquities of *Ireland*, containing the different reasons and authorities that hinder learned men from giving credit to them; and that seem rather to prove that, as the learned (*a*) *Waræus* says, those circumstantial accounts, which their modern writers give of their ancient history, are the workmanship or invention of writers of later ages. 2°. I shall endeavour to shew, that though we should grant that these remote antiquities, and even what is related of the *Milesian* race in general were probable, that would not prove that these *Milesians* were properly the *Scots*; but that it seems rather certain, that the *Scots* were not settled in *Ireland* till about the times of the incarnation, or even after it.

(*a*) Waræus de Antiq. Hybern. Præf. p. 1.

CHAP.

CHAP. I.

Containing the difficulties and doubts which occur in the particular accounts that the modern Iriſh *writers, ſuch as* Keating, O Flaherty, *and others give on the credit of their* Bards *and* Seanachies, *of the remote or high antiquities of* Ireland.

I MEAN by the remote or high antiquities of *Ireland*, as I have already obſerved, all thoſe particular and circumſtantiated details that theſe, and other *Iriſh* writers have ſet down, not only of the firſt plantations and four firſt colonies after the flood of *Noah*, but in particular of that of the *Mileſians* coming in from *Spain* to *Ireland*, and there ſetting up a monarchy above ten or twelve centuries before the incarnation; with the details they give of the names, genealogies, chronology, ſucceſſions, reigns, and actions of thoſe *Iriſh* monarchs, from *Heremon* their firſt king, till *Leogaire*, who lived in the fifth century, when St. *Patrick* preached the goſpel in that iſland.

MY intention is to propoſe in this chapter the difficulties and doubts that occur in theſe remote antiquities, and the reaſons which ſeem to render the opinion of *Waræus*, and of other learned men, very

very probable; who pretend that all, or most of these particular accounts, especially of what past in *Ireland* before the incarnation, are the inventions of writers of posterior ages.

In order to put this matter in a better light, I shall reduce these doubts or difficulties, and reasons to the following heads.

The first occasion of doubt is the particular detail of these antiquities, such as their modern authors assure us are contained in what they call their most ancient writers.

The second arises from the account that they give us, of the means by which their antiquities were preserved and conveyed down; and of the ancient polity and literature of the *Irish*.

3°. Some testimonies of the most ancient writers that mention the *Irish*, and of the most learned among the modern; by which it appears, that the inhabitants of *Ireland* were unpolished, barbarous, and without the use of letters in the first ages of christianity.

4°. That in all appearance the use of letters was not introduced into *Ireland*, till the preaching of the gospel among them in the fifth century of christianity.

5°. That

5°. THAT even supposing, against what hath been said, that the *Irish* had received the use of letters before the fifth age, the character of the authors of their remote antiquities, to wit, of the bards, suffices to raise doubts against what they might have written.

6°. THE uncertainty of the remote antiquities of *Ireland*, appears by the several alterations that have been made in them at different times.

7°. THEIR continuing to avoid the publication of their pretended original ancient histories, chronicles, poems, *&c.* in literal and faithful transactions, such as they are, without adding or retrenching, gives new grounds to suspect the credit of them.

ART. I. *A short account of the* Irish *remote antiquities.*

THE first difficulty against the credit of these antiquities, is the detail in which they are delivered, with particular facts, names of persons and places, and dates of time, all pretended to be taken from what they esteem their best records of ancient history. For from this we may easily learn the characters of the writers of these pretended ancient monuments, and be able to judge what credit

credit is due to men, that had the confidence to deliver the most remote antiquities in a circumstantiated detail; that none, except the sacred writers, inspired by God, ever pretended to. Hence (*a*) *Camden* says pleasantly enough of them, *That if what the* Irish *writers relate of their antiquities be true, those of all other nations, if compared with them, are but new, and as of yesterday. For they tell us that* Cæsarea, *niece to* Noah, *&c.*

THE *Irish* writers begin their history, not only from the coming of *Cæsarea* (*Ceasrach*) niece to *Noah*, into *Ireland*, before the deluge, which is all the antiquity that *Camden* remarks; but their most approved writers, such as *Leabhuir Dromnasnachta*, or book with the white cover, inform us, according to (*b*) *Keating*, that *Cain*'s three daughters had long before *Noah* taken possession of *Ireland*; and that the eldest of these ladies, called *Bamba*, gave her name to that island. It is true, *Keating* in relating this, and such other anti-diluvian accounts of *Ireland*, treats them as fabulous;

(*a*) Camden Hybernia, *p.* 32 *edit. Amsterdam.* Si verum sit quod Hybernici tradunt historici non immerito hæc Insula Ogygia, *i. e.* perantiqua Plutarcho dicta fuit. A profundissima enim antiquitatis memoria historias suas auspicantur, adeo ut præ illis omnis omnium Gentium antiquitas sit novitas & infantia. Cæsaream enim quidam Noachi neptim ante-diluvium hanc incoluisse tradunt, &c.

(*b*) Keating, *p.* 17. *edit. London*, 1723. from Leabhuir Dromsasnachta.

bulous; but a late *Irish* (*a*) writer, assuring us that the *Leabhuir Dromnasnachta*, is quoted by all their antiquaries, as a most ancient and very authentick piece of antiquity, written in the time of their *Pagan* anceſtors; it is no rash judgment to suspect the credit of the ordinary writers of their antiquities, since one of *their most ancient* and *authentick* books contains, even in *Keating*'s judgment, the most *fabulous and romantick relations*.

THE (*b*) story of *Ceasrach*, niece to *Noah*, though related by the *Psaltar Cashel*, together with the other particulars of the anti-diluvian inhabitants of *Ireland*, is rejected, says *Keating*, by their best antiquaries, and with reason: but what becomes then of the credit of *Psaltar Cashel*, and by consequence of that of *Psaltar Teambrach*, or *Tara*, whereof we are (*c*) told, *Psaltar Cashel* was a transcript made by authority.

BUT the *Irish* (*d*) writers are much more particular in their accounts of the first four colonies that came to *Ireland* after the deluge. The first colony was that of *Partholan*, who landed at *Inverskene* on a *Tuesday*, the fourteenth of the moon

(*a*) D. Kenedy's genealogy, *præf. pag.* 25.

(*b*) Keating, *p.* 20.

(*c*) D. Ken. præf. *pag.* 18, 19.

(*d*) Keating, from *p.* 23. to *p.* 53. and O. Flaherty, Ogyg. from p. 163. to *p.* 182.

moon, in *May* just 312 years, according to *Flaherty*, after the deluge: the rest of the particulars may be seen at length in *Keating* and *O Flaherty*; as also those of the second colony of *Nemedius* and his sons, of the *Clanbolg*, who made the third colony; and of the fourth, called *Tuadadanan*. What is most partiular is, that of all these colonies (whereof the latest, according to *Flaherty*, came to *Ireland* before the taking of *Troy*) these late *Irish* writers confidently give us an historical detail, with as particular an enumeration of facts, as if they had been transactions of three or four ages ago. In a word, they tell us the names of the chief leaders of each colony, the precise time and place of their landing in *Ireland*; the names, succession, and reigns of their kings, and their memorable actions, each one with its date; the precise time each *Lough* broke out in *Ireland*, (a circumstance not to be matched in other histories) the genealogies of their great men down from *Noah*; the year in which each colony expired, or was destroyed; the precise number of years that *Ireland* was desert, betwixt the *Exit* of one colony, and the coming in of the following one; and this when there was no body there, neither bard nor other, to mark them down: and all this account of these four colonies above two thousand years before the incarnation: of which the detail may be seen in *Keating* and *Flaherty* above quoted, and said to be taken from their

psalters,

Psaltars, *Poets*, and other surest antiquaries, not as yet published.

As to the *Milesian* colony, they pretend to give of it as yet more circumstantial accounts: and that not only from their settlement in *Spain*, and next in *Ireland*; but of all the pilgrimages of their predecessors, down from *Fenius Farsaidh* (who, they say, was great grandson to *Japhet*, one of *Noah*'s sons) of his son *Niul*, and all his posterity; whose circuits, twice backward and forward, from *Scythia* to *Egypt*, from thence to *Spain*, and up and down thro' *Europe*, *Asia*, and *Africa*, may be seen at large in (*a*) *Keating*, taken, as he assures us, from the best *Irish* antiquaries.

They (*b*) assure us, that *Heremon*, with the *Milesian* colony, arrived in *Ireland* precisely the first day of *May*, on a *Thursday*, and the seventh of the moon: they give us account of all the leaders of that colony; of the harbours where each of them landed; of the *Loughs* that broke out the night of their landing. In a word, from *Heremon* the first king of the *Milesians*, they give a distinct series, or chronological history of all their kings, down till *Leogare* (who began his reign *Anno Christi* 427. and during whose time the christian faith was preached in *Ireland* by St. *Patrick*) with the number, names, genealogies, chronology of

(*a*) Keating, from *pag.* 57. to *pag.* 89.
(*b*) O Flaherty, *pag.* 84, 85, 182, &c.

their kings, the years of their reigns, their chief battles and actions, the manner and time of each of their deaths: and all this they deliver from about two thousand years before the incarnation with an equal assurance, as they do the history of *Ireland* since St. *Patrick*.

THIS prospect alone of the *Irish* antiquities suffices to breed violent suspicions in all impartial persons conversant in true ancient history; that the whole is an invention of later ages: and these suspicions are still increased by the detailed accounts of these antiquities, that *Keating* himself (as he is lately published) hath, the most warily he could, selected out of their more ancient writers, as more likely and less absurd than the most of what they contain: and especially if it be considered that they have no other vouchers for the *Milesian* antiquities; but those very writers who recount with an equal confidence the stories of the peopling of *Ireland* before the deluge, as they do those after: so that even *Keating* himself is forced to abandon them in this, tho' they be their writers of the first rate, such as (*a*) *Psaltar Cashel*, the (*b*) book with the white cover, and their poets.

(*a*) V. Keating, *p.* 20.
(*b*) V. Keating, *p.* 17.

ART.

ART. II. *The second objection drawn from the means by which the* Irish *pretend their high antiquities were preserved and conveyed down; and of their ancient literature and polity, before the times of christianity.*

As all ancient histories depend upon the credit of their vouchers, so, besides other qualities, the more the transactions related in a history are ancient and extraordinary, the more ancient must also be the vouchers that attest them, and of a more extraordinary character. Hence the *Irish Seanachies*, that relate the story of the ante-diluvian inhabitants of *Ireland*, furnish us with ante-diluvian authors, and tell us of four of those ancient inhabitants that lived before and after the deluge, as *Keating* says some ancient MSS. of *Ireland* record: but since *Keating* informs us, that these ante-diluvian authors, with their stories, are rejected by their best antiquaries, I shall pass them over, and come to what they relate seriously, as the true account of the antiquity of letters and learning among their predecessors.

As the accounts of their antiquities far surpassed those of all other nations, except what is recorded in the scriptures: so their bards, as if they had had it in their choice when to begin the literature among the *Irish* and their predecessors, thought fit to fix on the highest antiquity, and at the

the very origine of the different languages ſoon after the flood of *Noah*: and the following inſtances of it are ſeriouſly related by thoſe that they eſteem their moſt genuine antiquaries, and received by *Keating*, and others of their modern writers.

(*a*) THEY tell us then 1°. That one *Fenius Farſaidh*, great-grand-child to *Japhet Noah*'s ſon, and predeceſſor of the *Mileſians*, ſet up a ſchool of learning in the plains of *Senaar*, about one hundred and fifty years after the deluge; and having two tutors under him, *Gaodel* and *Jar*, he there formed the *Iriſh* tongue, and firſt invented the *Hebrew*, *Greek*, *Latin*, and *Iriſh* letters. A particular detail of this ſchool may be ſeen in *Keating* at length, from *pag.* 59. to *pag.* 64.

BUT what at firſt would ſeem very ſurprizing is, that this ſtory of *Fenius Farſaidh*'s having formed the firſt *Hebrew*, *Greek*, and *Latin* alphabets, with the *Beth-luis-nion*, an *Ogum*, or *Iriſh* alphabet, is ſeriouſly related as an hiſtorical fact by (*b*) *Toland*, another *Iriſh* writer, ſo famous for his incredulity in regard of other facts, the beſt atteſted that ever were recorded. It is true, *Toland* endeavours to mend the matter; and being ſenſible of the abſurdity of this *Fenius*'s having formed the *Greek* and *Latin* alphabets, ſo many ages before the

(*a*) Keating, *p.* 59, &c.
(*b*) Toland's poſthumous works, *Tom.* I. *pag.* 38.

Greeks

Greeks and *Latins* were a people, he reforms the bard *Forchern*'s story of it (according to the usual custom of posterior bards, who, as they happened to live in times of more light and learning, reformed the traditions of their ignorant predecessors) and would have us believe that *Forchern*'s meaning was only that *Fenius invented the first letters, in imitation of which the alphabets of these nations were made.* And doth not the giving credit even to that, on the bare testimony of a bard, whose absurdities he is forced to explain away, seem at first very surprizing in a person of so noted incredulity as *Toland.*

But the surprize will be less, when it is considered that *Toland*'s incredulity was chiefly in regard of revealed facts, or the objects of faith: for it being a property of faith, according to the (a) apostle, *to cast down all imaginations* or reasonings, *and every thing that exalts itself against the knowledge of God, and to bring into captivity every thought to the obedience of Christ*; this seems an intolerable yoke to men of *Toland*'s principles, there being nothing more opposite to that unlimited liberty of *Free-thinking*, upon which he chiefly valued himself: whereas all that could raise a sublime notion of the engine of meer man, without any extraordinary assistance of Almighty God, served admirably to the purpose of *Free-thinkers*:

(a) II Cor. x. 5.

and nothing appearing a ſtronger evidence of the natural extent of man's capacity, than to find out merely, by his own application and ſtudy, ſo ſurprizing an art as that of painting (if I may ſo ſay) or of rendring ſenſible and laſting, by figures or characters, bare thoughts or ſounds of articulate words, ſo as to convey them to any diſtance of time or place: the ſtory of *Fenius Farſaidb*'s having made this wonderful diſcovery, and being the firſt inventor of letters, was more eaſily ſwallowed down by *Toland*, though he had no other ground to believe it, nor that there ever was ſuch a man as *Fenius Farſaidb* in being, but the relation of this *Forchern*, a bard: and though he himſelf (*a*) acknowledges, that the bards in general were a ſet of men *both partial and mercenary, to a ſcandalous degree.*

Besides, that *Toland*, who ſet up ſo much for a man verſed in all kind of literature, could not, I ſuppoſe, be ignorant, that the moſt judicious among ancient writers, after *Eupolemus*, quoted by *Clement* of *Alexandria* and *Euſebius*, looked upon the invention of alphabetical letters as having been at firſt communicated by God himſelf to *Moſes* and the *Iſraelites*, and from them derived to the *Phœnicians*, from whom the *Greeks* at firſt received it.

(*a*) Toland, *ibid. pag.* 50.

A

A new proof that the invention of letters was no ancienter than *Moses*; and that the *Pentateuch* is the most ancient book in the world, may be drawn from the ignorance we are in of all past transactions, not only before *Moses*'s time (except what is contained in the *Pentateuch*) but of all certainty of history before the siege of *Troy*, about three hundred years after *Moses*; which answers the time that *Cadmus* (who is believed to be contemporary to king *David*) is supposed to have brought the first letters from *Phœnicia* to *Greece*. And since it cannot be doubted of, but that the desire to perpetuate their memory was no less natural and vehement in men before *Moses*'s time, than after it, how comes it that we have no remains of any certain account of what past in these times, besides what is in the scripture?

I do not pretend here to enter upon *Toland*'s principles as to what concerns religion, but leave that to the divines, who have abundantly discussed his principles on those matters: I am only concerned at present in historical facts, and cannot but observe the strange bent of the reasonings of this person, who pretends to be wholly governed by reason, and yet could believe, or seem to believe, that *Fenius Farsaidh* was the first inventor of letters, without any other ground but that of the bards, whom he looked upon, as we have seen, as venal souls; and this in opposition to the solid arguments, which prove the first use of letters to have been a particular gift of Almighty God to mankind, in the person of *Moses*.

But it is very likely, that the chief reason that determined *Toland* to vouch the story of *Fenius*, and other bardish inventions of the same kind, that suppose the ancient use of letters among the *Irish*, was to put in credit the pretended writings of the ancient *Irish Druids* in times of *paganism*, in order to make a handle of them to rally and run down what he calls *priestcraft*. And so we shall meet him again more than once chiming in with the bards, for the ancient use of *letters among the Irish*.

(a) The second instance of learning among the *Irish* is placed about an age after the settlement of the *Milesians* in *Ireland*, to wit, that twelve hundred years before the incarnation, they had publick professors of learning in king *Tigernma*'s time; and those already in so great esteem, that they were allowed the precedency next to their kings, and only one colour less in their robes: this was about one hundred years before the taking of *Troy*, and four hundred years before the first *Olympiad*, the two most ancient *Epochs* of profane history. So it is no wonder that a late *Irish* (b) writer falls in a rapture at the thought of such a distinguish-

(a) Keating, p. 127. D. Ken. p. 20. pref.
(b) D. Ken. Gen. pref. p. 21.

ing character of his country. *Could a nation*, says he, *be called barbarous, that, so many ages before Christ, set such a value upon learning?* &c.

The third proof of ancient literature among the *Irish*, and of the care they had of preserving the memory of past transactions, is according to their modern writers, and (a) *Toland* among others, that about nine hundred sixty-seven years before the birth of Christ, king *Eocha Ollam-Fodla*, order'd all the transactions of his royal ancestors, from *Fenius Farsaidh* to his own time, to be review'd; and in order to digest them, he appointed a committee of nine, or an assembly of three kings, three druids, and three poets or bards, to meet every third year at a parliament at *Tara*, to examine and digest them for the benefit of posterity. An account of this parliament and assemblies at *Tara* may be seen at length in *Keating*, from *pag.* 132, to *pag.* 143. where the curious reader will be, no doubt, surprized to find, among other things, an order, discipline, politeness, and especially a progress of learning; but above all, a singular care of the annals and histories among the *Irish*, about two hundred years before the founding of *Rome*, that will scarce be met with in most other nations in the most polished ages.

(a) Toland's hist. of *Druids*, p. 50.
(b) Keating, p. 132.

I omit

I omit other inſtances that they (*a*) give of the progreſs and encouragement of learning in *Ireland*, in times, when other nations were generally in ignorance and barbarity, and refer my reader to their own writers, but I cannot forbear to mention that, in order to confirm the matter, and to canonize theſe *Pagan* antiquities; we (*b*) are told, that they were judged of that importance by St. *Patrick* apoſtle of *Ireland*, that contrary to the cuſtom of all other apoſtolical preachers, amidſt his labours in the goſpel, he thought it became him to liſt himſelf in the committee of nine, with two other biſhops, amidſt their bards and kings, and digeſt the hiſtorical and genealogical collections of their *Pagan* antiquities.

THE firſt thing that is to be remarked on theſe high pretenſions to ſo ſurprizingly antient literature and polity is, that the invention proves that the *Iriſh* were conſcious to themſelves, that an early literature and polity were abſolutely neceſſary to gain credit to their high antiquities: ſo that if they were deprived of that ſupport, it would ſeem, that even in their own judgment the credit of their antiquities would be quite ſunk.

(*a*) Keating, *p.* 147. *cap.* 217, 252. D. Ken. *pref. pag.* 19, 20, &c.

(*b*) Keating, *p.* 335.

(*c*) D. Ken. *pref. pag.* 118.

AND

AND yet in the ſecond place it is evident, that all theſe inſtances that they give of the early ſettlement of learning and polity among them, are yet more incredible if they be well conſidered, and more liable to exceptions, and ſo ſtand as yet more in need of new proofs to ſupport them, than thoſe very antiquities which they are brought to ſupport and authorize, and indeed ſerve only to prove the fertility of the bards imaginations in invention.

FOR however the high antiquities of *Ireland*, or the detailed accounts they give of the ſettlement and hiſtory of their ſeveral ancient colonies, and among others of that of the *Mileſians*, muſt be all looked upon abſolutely as uncertain; whilſt hitherto no ancient writer appears within two thouſand years of the time, to atteſt or ſupport them; yet they have at leaſt this advantage, above the accounts that the *Iriſh* give in ſo many inſtances of their having been ſo anciently poliſhed with learning, that theſe inſtances of learning being equally deſtitute of all credible teſtimonies from ancient authors or records to ſupport them, can be more plainly ſhewn to be groundleſs, as well by the concurrent teſtimonies of ancient writers, and by the moſt learned among the modern, that have examined into them, as by the terms that the *Iriſh* make uſe of in learning, and by the proper characters of their letters, ſuch as have hitherto been

been publiſhed. By all which it appears, that *Ireland*, far from having the advantage over the *Greeks* and *Romans*, of a more early ſettlement of learning and polity, as a late *Iriſh* (*a*) writer boaſts; on the contrary, it remained much longer in ignorance, and without the uſe of letters, than moſt of the other weſtern countries, who acknowledged they were beholden for their being civilized to the *Romans*.

ART. III. *That the inhabitants of* Ireland *were ſtill unpoliſhed and barbarous; and by conſequence, without the uſe of letters in the firſt ages of chriſtianity, according to all the accounts we have of them from the moſt ancient writers, and in the opinion of the moſt learned among the modern.*

THE only credible accounts we can have of any country, in ancient times, is from thoſe ancient writers that deſcribe the ſeveral nations as they came to be known, and had taken their accounts from theſe on the place, or in the neighbourhood. We have nothing of *Ireland* in the more ancient geographers, but its bare ſituation or poſition. *Strabo* (who wrote under *Auguſtus* and *Tiberius*) is the firſt that gives ſome particulars of the inhabitants of that iſland. The firſt account he gives of their manners and cuſtoms in his time, is juſt the ſame that the firſt diſcoverers of *America*, and of the remoteſt coaſts of *Africa*, give of theſe new-found

(*a*) Ken. geneal. pref. p. 26.

inha-

inhabitants in their natural ſtate; to wit, *that they were barbarous and wild men. Thoſe,* ſays (*a*) *Strabo, that now-a-days make a ſurvey of the different countries of the world, find nothing to relate of any country beyond* Ireland, *which lies to the north, and near* Britain, *and is inhabited by men entirely wild.* (ἀγρίων τελέως ἀνθρώπων.)

THE ſame author ſpeaking afterwards of the *Britains*, tells us, that in his time the *Britans* were, as to their manners and way of living, partly like to the inhabitants of the *Gauls*, partly more rude and barbarous than the *Gauls*. And then adds, (*b*) As to *Ireland*, all I know of certainty is, that its inhabitants are more barbarous and ſavage (ἀγριώτεροι) than thoſe of *Britain*; and by conſequence, of theſe three nations the *Gauls* or *Celtes*, the *Britains* and the *Iriſh*, theſe laſt were, in *Strabo*'s time, reputed the moſt barbarous. He adds ſome inſtances of their barbarous cuſtoms; but as to thoſe I ſhall not inſiſt upon them, becauſe *Strabo* ſays he had them not well enough atteſted.

THE next ancient writer from whom we have account of the manners of the *Iriſh* in thoſe times, is (*c*) *Pomponius Mela*, who wrote not long after *Strabo* in the firſt age of chriſtianity; and gives

(*a*) Strabo, p. 114, 115.
(*b*) Strabo, l. 4. p. 201.
(*c*) Pomp. Mela, c. 3. c. 6.

this

this account of them; *The inhabitants of* Ireland *are unpolished, barbarous and ignorant of all virtues.* Thus we see *Ireland* still esteemed unpolished and barbarous, and that more than a thousand years after the times that the modern writers tell us of its being so civilized.

All that they (*a*) answer to this is, that *Strabo* or *Mela* had no opportunities to be informed of the condition and manners of the *Irish*: but for this I refer them to a modern writer (*b*) of their own, who assures us, after *Tacitus* (*c*) in the life of *Agricola*, *that the ports of* Ireland *were better known, and more frequented by the merchants, than those of* Britain; as being much the more numerous, and the more safe, and perhaps not inferior to any in *Europe*. Now *Strabo* and *Mela* had a fair occasion to be informed of the state of *Ireland*, by the resort of the *Britains* to *Rome*, who could not but know the condition of *Ireland* in their neighbourhood, as well as others that frequented their ports: and *Strabo* makes particular mention of the *Britains* coming to *Rome*. Now it doth not seem likely, that *Strabo* and *Mela* having such opportunities, could be so grosly mistaken, as to impute so great barbarity to *Ireland* in the first age of christianity, if it had been then, and for so long a tract of time before, polished with

(*a*) Pref. to Keating, p. 2, 3.
(*b*) Ken. pref. p. 27.
(*c*) Tacit. p. 233.

arts and ſciences, as the late *Iriſh* writers pretend it was; for it cannot be doubted, but thoſe *Roman* writers, having for their peculiar deſign in their books, to give an account of the ſeveral foreign countries, and to remark what was more rare and ſingular in them, would uſe their utmoſt diligence to be rightly informed.

BUT what ſhall be ſaid of *Tacitus*'s account of the manners of the *Iriſh* in his time; for he is the next author that mentions them. He had his informations from *Agricola* his father-in-law; and *Agricola* had his account of *Ireland* from no leſs an author than one of the *Iriſh* leſſer kings; and yet far from mentioning polity or learning among the *Iriſh*, *Tacitus* after deſcribing the barbarous *Britains*, ſuch the *Romans* eſteemed thoſe who had not been cultivated as yet by their diſcipline, as an unpoliſhed and rude people, *diſperſi & rudes*, tells (*a*) us the *Iriſh* in their manners were much the ſame as theſe *Britains*. *Tacitus* adds to this; that he had often heard from *Agricola*, that with one ſingle legion, and a few auxiliaries, *Ireland* might have been eaſily conquered and ſubjected to the *Roman* empire. This ſhews how mean an opinion *Agricola* had of the inhabitants of *Ireland*, in compariſon of thoſe of *Caledonia*, or the north of *Britain*, who at that very time, under their leader *Galgacus*, gave work to all the *Roman* legions and

(*a*) Ingenia cultuſque hominum [*in Hybernia*] non multum a Britannia differunt, *Tacit. p.* 233.

auxili-

auxiliaries in *Britain:* not but *Ireland* was probably much more populous than the north of *Britain*, but because the inhabitants of *Ireland* being more rude and unpolished, were more ignorant of the military art, and of all parts of polity and discipline.

We have no more ancient writers that speak of the manners of the *Irish*, before they received christianity in the fifth age, except *Julius Solinus*, who, by some, is placed in the second age after the incarnation; by others in the third: and *Solinus's* account of the manners of the *Irish* in those days, agrees with that of *Strabo* and *Mela.* The manners of the *Irish*, says (*a*) *Solinus*, are inhuman and rude. He adds to their being inhospitable, a new character which no former writer had given them, to wit, that of their being *warlike:* in all appearance, because by this time (the third age) the *Scots* were settled among them, and began to make inroads on *Britain*, tho' their name was not perhaps yet known at *Rome*; where it is thought *Solinus* wrote. What he adds of their making no difference betwixt right and wrong, is a clear proof of their being as yet entirely barbarous, and a full conviction of the fable of (*b*) *Ugane-more's* laws,

(*a*) Hybernia inhumana ritu incolarum aspera. Gens inhospita & bellicosa; fas & nefas eodem animo ducunt. *Solin.* p. 36. p. 62. *edit. Basil.* 1538.

(*b*) Ken. geneal. pref. p. 22.

laws, pretended to have been made seven or eight hundred years before *Solinus.*

THUS I have gone through all I could meet with, of ancient writers, that give any account of the state of *Ireland*, before christianity was planted in it in the fifth age: and by all of them it appears, it was still a barbarous and uncultivated nation. I come now to examine the opinion of the learned in modern times, since the revival of the study of critical learning; and we shall find, that they are no less unanimous than the ancients, in asserting that the *Irish* of old were uncultivated by polity or letters.

CAMDEN, an author, in the judgment of (*a*) one of the latest abettors of the *Irish* antiquities, *of great esteem and reputation*, and which makes more to our purpose, *one*, says this writer, *who had taken a strict, particular and full information* of the *Irish* antiquities; *Camden* (*b*), I say, after having told us that he could not think that the *Romans* ever entered *Ireland*, adds, that

(*a*) Ken. general. pref. p. 6.

(*b*) Animum vix inducere possum ut hanc regionem [*Hyberniam*] in Romanorum potestatem ullo tempore concessisse credam. Proficuum sane felixque Hyberniæ fuisset, si concessisset. certe barbariem exuisset: ubicunque enim Romani victores erant, victos humanitate excoluerunt. Nec sane alibi per Europam, humanitatis, litterarum & elegantiæ cultus, nisi ubi illi imperarunt. *Camd. Hybernia, p.* 33. *Amstelod. edit. Jansen. in fol. p.* 33.

it had been a happy thing for Ireland, *that the* Romans *had subdued it; for that had been*, says he, *a sure means to civilize it, and deliver it from barbarity: since wherever the* Romans *became masters of any nation, they cultivated and civilized it. Nor was there any where in* Europe *any knowledge of polity, of civilized manners, or of letters, but where the* Romans *governed.* That is to say, in plain terms, that since the *Romans* never ruled in *Ireland*, there was neither polished manners, nor knowledge of letters there in ancient times. In short, *Camden* looks upon the barbarity and ignorance of the *Irish* in ancient times, as a thing so certain, that he makes use of that as a proof to shew that the *Romans* had never governed in that island. Accordingly, *Camden* (*a*) looks upon the *Irish* antiquities, and in particular on the *Scots* being settled in *Ireland* before the incarnation, as fabulous; and is of opinion, that the name of the *Scots* was not heard of till the third age at soonest.

Before I proceed to the next authority, I cannot but observe, that it is no small argument against the credit of the high antiquities, and ancient learning of *Ireland*, that one so well versed in all kind of antiquities, and so perfectly acquainted with all the remains of the writers of *Ireland*, as the famous archbishop *Usher* was, and an *Irishman* by birth, hath never said one word of

(*a*) Camden. Britan. p. 50, 51. edit. Amstelod.

their high antiquities, or of their ancient monarchs before christianity, neither in his *Annales Sacri*, where he sets down the origins and successions of all ancient certain monarchies and commonwealths, nor even in his antiquities of the churches of *Britain* and *Ireland*, where he gives us at length all that he could find of ancient stories concerning the *Scots* in *Ireland* or in *Britain*; nor in any other book I could ever meet with. But he was too wise to hazard the reputation he had justly acquired among the learned, of one of the best antiquaries of his time, by countenancing any such uncertain stories as the high antiquities of *Ireland*. And far from believing the *Scots* were the ancient inhabitants of that island, he (*a*) joins in with *Camden*'s opinion, and proves that the name of *Scots* was not heard of till some ages after the incarnation.

THE next testimony I shall bring is, as yet, more evident, and of greater weight, than that of *Camden*. It is that of sir *James Ware*, or *Waræus*, one of the most learned and best skilled in the *Irish* antiquities, and at the same time one of the most diligent enquirers after them that *Ireland* hath produced these many years: as appears not only by his books published, *De Antiquitatibus Hyberniæ* (*b*), and *De Episcopis Hyberniæ* (*c*); but

(*a*) Usser. Antiq. Britan. p. 38c. fol. Lond. 1687.
(*b*) Edit. Lond. in 8vo. A. D. 1658.
(*c*) Edit. Dublin. A. D. 1665.

more by his work, *De Scriptoribus Hyberniæ* (a); and most of all by a most curious collection he made of all he could find of *Irish* MSS. relating to their history or antiquities: in the search of which it appears, he spared neither pains nor expence. The catalogue of his MSS. was first printed by itself, in *quarto*; and again in *folio*, and may be seen in the great collection of the MSS. of *England* and *Ireland*, printed at *Oxford*; and the MSS. themselves are now in the possession of the duke of *Chandos*.

THE judgment of a gentleman of so great a capacity, as *Waræus*, and so versed in the antiquities of his country, will be, no doubt, of incomparably greater weight in this debate, with impartial and learned men, than the accounts that are given of these remote antiquities by more credulous writers copying one after another, and ofttimes at second hand; and who appear to have had neither the opportunities which this learned man had, nor his skill in discerning authentick monuments of history from the inventions of bards.

THE first place where *Waræus* gives his opinion of the *Irish* writers, and of the learning and antiquities of *Ireland* before the conversion of *Ireland* to christianity, is in the preface of his book *De Antiquitatibus Hyberniæ*, in these words:

(a) Edit. Dublin. A. D. 1639.

(*a*) *It is most certain, that there remains very little knowledge of what passed in* Ireland *before the preaching of the gospel there: neither am I ignorant that the most part of what is delivered by writers, concerning those ancient times before St.* Patrick's *coming to* Ireland, *is rejected by several learned men as fictions and fables. And it is to be remarked, that almost all the descriptions or particular accounts that are extant, of matters transacted in these ancient times, are of the fabrick or invention of late ages. Therefore, in this enquiry I have spoken very sparingly of them,* &c.

In this passage of *Waræus* it may be remarked, 1°. That he acknowledges, several learned men rejected the remote antiquities of *Ireland* as fictions and fables: and accordingly he owns, 2°. himself, that most of all the accounts we have of these ancient times, are the productions of modern writers; and by consequence, that there remains extreme little knowledge of what passed in *Ireland* before St. *Patrick* preached the gospel there in the fifth age: for this reason he begins his accounts of the

(*a*) Perexiguam superesse notitiam rerum in Hybernia gestarum ante exortam ibi evangelii auroram, liquido constat. Neque me latet a viris nonnullis doctis pleraque quæ de antiquioribus illis temporibus ante S. Patricii in Hyberniam adventum traduntur, tanquam figmenta esse explosa. Notandum quidem descriptiones fere omnium quæ de illis temporibus (antiquioribus dico) extant, opera esse posteriorum sæculorum. Idcirco in hac indagine de iis admodum parce locutus sum. *War. de antiq. praef. p.* 1.

Irish kings only at *Loegare*, who lived in St. *Patrick*'s time; not perhaps that he believed absolutely that all that was said of their former kings was entirely false and fabulous, but because he was persuaded (*a*) *that the most part of all that is delivered concerning them, was either fables, or so mixed with fables and anachronisms*, that there was no means left to find out truth.

The second place where *Wareus*'s opinion of the ancient learning of *Ireland* appears, is in his book (*b*) *De Scriptoribus Hyberniæ*; of the writers of *Ireland*. Certainly a person of *Wareus*'s erudition, of his skill, and diligence to be informed of all that concerned *Ireland*, could not fail to have met with, or heard of what was most ancient, most curious, and most valuable on the subject of which he treats: and his zeal for his country, as well as the design of his book, and his own reputation, equally required that he should set down all he could find of their ancient writers, worth the taking notice of, or that deserved any credit. And yet after all his searches, it appears that he could find no writer of the general history or antiquities of *Ireland*, worth the naming, more ancient than the *Psaltair. Cashel*, written

(*a*) Ad prædecessores Loegarii quod attinet, eos certe consilio omisi, quia pleraque quæ de iis traduntur (ut quod sentio dicam) vel fabulæ sunt, vel fabulis & anachronismis mire admixta. *War. de antiq. Hybern. c. 4. p.* 20.

(*b*) Edit. Dublin. A.D. 1639.

in

in the tenth age, as he (a) says in this book; but by what *Waræus* himself quotes from this *Psaltair* elsewhere (b), it must have either been written only in the eleventh age, or had additions made to it in that age. However, till this *Psaltair Cashel*, in all *Waræus*'s account of the *Irish* writers, where he passes not over the meanest biographers, there is nothing like a history of the antiquities of *Ireland*; for as to the *Liber Cuaña*, he only mentions it from the *Ulster* annals.

3°. *WARÆUS*'s judgment of the learning and polity of *Ireland*, in ancient times, doth plainly appear by many other passages of his aforesaid treatise of their antiquities; as in particular, in the fifth chapter, where he treats designedly of the ancient schools of *Ireland*, where he shews (c) indeed that schools and learning flourished in *Ireland* since the planting of christianity there; but doth not so much as insinuate, that there ever had been any such thing as a school, college, professor, or any learning, or even the use of letters in *Ireland*, (d) till the *Irish* were taught the *Alphabet* by their apostle St. *Patrick*, as we shall see presently. But what confirms this matter, as to *Waræus*'s opinion of the barbarous state in which *Ireland*

(a) Lib. 1. c. 10.
(b) War. de præsul. Hybern. p. 10, 11.
(c) War. de antiq. Hyber. c. 15. p. 74.
(d) War. de scriptor. Hyber. l. 2. c. 1. p. 103.

was in ancient times, (*a*) *Waræus* joins iſſue with *Camden*, and tells us, *that it had been happy for* Ireland, *that it had been ſubdued by the* Romans; *for by that means it had been ſooner delivered from its barbarouſneſs.*

We may now, I think, conclude, that by the joint teſtimonies of the moſt ancient authors, who mention the ſtate of *Ireland* before it received the goſpel, and of the moſt learned among modern writers, who treat of its ancient ſtate, it is certain that *Ireland* was as unpoliſhed and barbarous as other northern countries, and without the uſe of letters, till it received them with chriſtianity in the fifth age. But this will yet farther appear, by what we have to ſay in the next article.

Art. IV. *That in all appearance the uſe of letters was not introduced into* Ireland, *till the preaching of the goſpel among them in the fifth century of chriſtianity.*

That the *Iriſh* received the firſt uſe of letters with the preaching of the goſpel, is proved by *Waræus*, from the authority of (*b*) *Nennius*, a

(*a*) Et ego quidem Camdeno aſſentior, quod felix fauſtumque Hyberniæ fuiſſet, ſi in Romanorum poteſtatem conceſſiſſet, nam citius tunc barbariem exuiſſet. *War. Antiq. Hybern. c.* 20. *p.* 103.

(*b*) S. Patricius ſcripſit Abietoria 365, & eo amplius numero. Eccleſias quoque eod. numero fundavit. *Nennius, c.* 59. p. 113. *edit. Oxon. Gale.*

writer

writer of the ninth age, compared with the most ancient life we have of St. *Patrick*, by *Tirechanus*, who, as (*a*) *Waræus* supposes, lived in the seventh age. *Nennius* says that St. *Patrick*, whilst he preached the gospel in *Ireland*, wrote above three hundred and sixty A, B, C's, or alphabets. *Nennius* calls them *Abgetoria*, or *Abietoria*. That by these were meant alphabets, for the use of the new converts in *Ireland*, is plainly shewn by *Waræus*, from the aforesaid life of St. *Patrick* by *Tirechanus*. These are the words of *Waræus*: [*Tirechanus*, an ancient writer of St. *Patrick*'s life, not yet published, explains to us, in the following citations compared together, what is meant by the word *Abgetoria*. St. *Patrick*, says *Tirechan*, *baptized men daily, and taught, or read to them letters or Abgetories*; and again, *he wrote elements or letters for the use of* Cerpanus: likewise, after he had baptized one *Macerca*, *he wrote elements or letters for him, and blessed him*, &c. and having baptized one *Hina*, *he wrote for him Abgetories, and blessed him with the blessing of a bishop*. By all this I think it is certain, says (*b*) *Waræus*, that by the word *Abgetoria* is meant the alphabet, or first elements of letters, which St. *Patrick* wrote and taught his new converts in *Ireland*.]

(*a*) War. de scriptor. Hyber. l. 2. c. 1. p. 103.

(*b*) Unde constat, opinor, Nennii Abgetoria significare, alphabetum sive elementa quæ scripsit & docuit S. Patricius. *War. de scriptor. Hyber.* p. 103.

THE

THE learned *Du Cange* (a) in his glossary shews, by many authorities, that the authors of the middle ages made use of the words *Abgatorium*, *Abcturium*, *Abecenarium*, *Abecedarium*, made up of the three first letters of the alphabet A, B, C, to express it; each one according to his way of pronouncing. So the *Irish*, who pronounce the C as a K, or G, called the alphabet *Abgatorium*, or *Abketorium*.

FROM the authorities brought by *Waræus*, the learned *Bollandus* (b) having concluded naturally, that the *Irish* had not the use of letters till they were taught it by St. *Patrick*, and confirmed his opinion with good reasons: (c) *Flaherty* falls very warmly upon him, as if he had been the first that had advanced that opinion, without reflecting that *Camden* had declared for it long before; and that sir *James Ware*, from whom *Bollandus* had it, proves it by the most ancient legend they have of St. *Patrick*'s life. As to *Flaherty*'s proofs for the ancient use of letters among the *Irish*, we shall by and by consider them. Mean time, to confirm *Bollandus*, and these other learned mens opinion, I shall farther add one proof, which I conceive will appear of weight with impartial readers.

(a) Du Cange Glossar. tom. 1. *on the words* Abcturium, Abgatoria, &c.

(b) Act. Sanctor. Bollandi, tom. 2. Martij ad diem 17. in Not. ad vitam S. Patricii.

(c) Ogyg. Domest. c. 30. p. 214.

I de-

I desire then it may be considered, that in the same manner, as tho' we had no other argument from ancient history, to prove that the *Latins* or *Romans* had the first use and knowledge of letters and sciences from the *Greeks*, than the bare names of which the *Latins* make use in letters, arts and sciences, and by which they express them: that alone would abundantly suffice to demonstrate, that the *Latins* had originally the knowledge of letters, arts and sciences, from the *Greeks*, since they still express them in *Greek* terms, and have no other proper expression for them; as *Grammatica*, *Rhetorica*, *Philosophia*, *Logica*, *Mathematica*, *Politica*, *Chirurgia*, *Physica*, &c.

In like manner, altho' we had no other proof to shew that the *Irish* had the use of letters originally from the *Latins*, or from those that spoke the *Latin* tongue, but the proper terms by which the *Irish* in their vulgar language express them, *v. g.* *a letter*, *a book*, *to read*; *to write*, &c. This would alone suffice to convince all unprejudiced persons, that the *Irish* had the first use of letters, and were taught to read and write originally by the *Latins*, or by those that spoke that language. Now it being agreed on, that the *Romans* never entered *Ireland*, the *Irish* could not have learned these terms immediately from them, but must needs have been taught them, with the things meant by them, by St. *Patrick*, and the other

ther first preachers of the gospel; who all of them knowing the *Latin* tongue, and finding no expressions or terms in the *Irish* language for letters, book, reading, writing, *&c.* as being all things of which the *Irish* had never any use before, they naturally expressed them in *Latin* terms, the only ones they had for them themselves, giving them only an *Irish* inflexion: so they called *Littera*, *Lietar*; *Liber*, *Leabar*; *Lego*, *Leagmi*; *Scribo*, *Scriabmi*; *Leagham*, to read, *Scriobám*, to write, *&c.* in the same manner as they were forced to make use of *Latin* terms with an *Irish* inflexion: for all sacred things belonging to christianity, whereof the first preachers of christianity brought in the first use to *Ireland*; such as *Criosd*, *Christus*; *Crosh*, *Crux*; *Eagluish*, *Ecclesia*; *Ceile*, *Cella*; *Espic* or *Easbug*, *Episcopus*; *Baisteadh*, *Baptisma*; and the like.

We come now to examine the proofs that *Flaherty* brings, of the ancient use of letters among the *Irish*, before they received christianity. The first is, that they have or had many books, poems, and histories (*a*), written in their *Pagan* ancestors times. But all that is nothing but to beg the question, and to suppose what is under debate, till these books, or some of them, be published to the world, with fair literal translations and documents to prove their authority and age, and to shew

(*a*) Ogygia Domestica, c. 30.

how,

how, and where they have been preserved during so many ages.

2°. *FLAHERTY*, for a proof that the *Irish* had not the use of letters from the *Latins*, and by consequence that their letters were much ancienter than the preaching of the gospel among them, and peculiar to the *Irish*, tells us, that their letters differred from those of the *Latins*, and all others in name, order, character, number, and pronunciation and force: to shew this, he gives from the book of *Lecan*, (an *Irish* MS. about three hundred years old) the copy of the *Latin* alphabet, inverted and digested in a new arbitrary order, with the names of trees attributed to each letter, beginning with the three letters B, L, N; and from thence called *Beth-luis-nion*. And this he pretends was the ancient *Irish* alphabet, before they had communication with the *Latins* and *Romans*.

BUT when *Flaherty* sets about to prove the antiquity of this *Beth-luis-nion*, he brings for proofs stories more incredible than the facts themselves, which he intends to prove by them. *Flaherty* tells us then the story we made mention of already from *Keating* and *Toland*: that the first author of this alphabet was *Fenius-Farsaidh*, *who composed*, says *Flaherty*, *the alphabets of the* Hebrews, Greeks *and* Latins; *the* Bethluisnion, *and the* Ogum. This *Fenius Farsaidh* (as we said before) was, according

4 to

to the *Irish Seanachies*, great grand-child to *Jafeth*, son to *Noah*, and lived in *Noah*'s own time, about one hundred years after the deluge. For this piece of antiquity, *Flaherty* (*a*) quotes one *Forcherne* an *Irish* poet, who, as a late *Irish* (*b*) writer informs us, lived one hundred years before the incarnation. Now, not to ask how this poet *Forcherne*, or *Feirtcherne*, as old as he is placed, knew so distinctly things past above two thousand years before the time in which he is classed: it may at least be enquired, by what spirit of prophecy this *Fenius Farsaidh* composed the *Greek* alphabets so long before *Cecrops* and *Cadmus*, and that of the *Romans*, some 1700 years before the *Romans* were a people. And will the authority of *Lecan*, a MS. of about three hundred years, convince the learned of so rare a discovery, as that of an *Irish* writer one hundred years before the birth of Christ?

But to let that paradox pass, there needs no great skill of the *Irish* language, to shew that the *Beth-luis-nion* is nothing else but an invention of some of the *Irish Seanachies*; who, since they received the use of letters, have put the *Latin* alphabet into a new arbitrary order, and assigned to each letter a name of some tree; and that this was not the genuine alphabet of the *Irish* in anci-

(*a*) Ogyg. Domest. p. 221.
(*b*) D. Ken. geneal. p. 29.

ent

ent times, or peculiar to them; but a bare inversion of the *Latin* alphabet.

FOR, 1°. The genuine *Irish* alphabet consists only of eighteen letters; for so (*a*) many only they make use of in that tongue, *viz.* A, B, C, D, E, F, G, H, I, L, M, N, O, P, R, S, T, U; whereas in *Flaherty*'s *Beth-luis-nion* there are twenty-six letters, that is, eight supernumerary, *viz.* Q, X, Y, Z, *oi*, *io*, *ng*, and *ea*: of these eight there are four which are never used in the genuine *Irish*, *viz.* Q, X, Y and Z; at least in such *Irish* books or MSS. as I could hitherto ever meet with, or hear of: but they are in use in the *Latin* tongue, and with the other eighteen letters make up the *Latin* alphabet: which therefore the *Irish* bard must have had before him when he invented the *Beth-luis-nion.* As to the syllables *oi*, *io*, *ea*, and double letter *ng*, which are the other four letters in the *Beth-luis-nion*, they have no one proper character in the *Irish*, distinct from the common alphabet, but are express'd by two of the usual letters of it; and nothing but meer fancy could have placed them in this new alphabet as distinct letters from the other eighteen. So, I think, it is plain that this *Beth-luis-nion* was neither the genuine *Irish* alphabet, nor was in use among them till after the times of christianity, when they received the use of the *Latin* letters, whereof this is but a bare transposition.

(*a*) *Irish* Gram. p. 299. Archæolog. Britan. Edit. Lhugd.

As

As to the names of trees attributed to each letter, it ſeems viſibly the work of meer fancy, without any reaſon or motive, there being no reſemblance in the character of theſe letters to theſe trees, from whence this bard hath named them: whereas in the languages where the names of the letters are ſignificative, as generally thoſe of the *Hebrew*, the thing meant by theſe letters hath often ſome reſemblance to the figure of the letter. And as for the term *Feadha*, *Woods*, which they gave to this alphabet, it was natural to call by the name of a foreſt or wood; an alphabet whereof each letter was metamorphoſed into a tree.

Another proof which the *Iriſh* modern writers bring for the antiquity of their letters, is from the form of their characters, as being peculiar to the *Iriſh* (*a*), and *not agreeing with the* Greek *or* Latin *characters, or perhaps any other now in the world.* But ſuch arguments as theſe are only fit to impoſe upon thoſe that never ſaw any *Latin* books or characters, but in vulgar print; and never had occaſion to ſee any MS. but *Iriſh*: for if they had ſeen any ancient *Latin* MSS. or characters, they would have in the firſt place found, by peruſing thoſe of the ſixth, ſeventh, eighth, and following ages, down to the times of printing, as great differences betwixt the figures of letters, and form of the writing in MSS. of all countries, and the com-

(*a*) D. Ken. pref. p. 27.

mon

mon print, as betwixt the usual characters in printed books, and those of the *Irish*; and yet originally all of them derived from the ancient *Roman* or *Latin* characters or letters.

In the second place, the inspection of old *Latin* MSS. or charters will furnish new proofs to demonstrate, that the *Irish* had their letters originally from the *Latins*, or those that used the *Latin* characters; for all the characters of the *Irish* letters, (without excepting the *Saxon* (*a*) *f*, *g*, *r*, *s*, which seem more extraordinary to vulgar readers), are generally to be met with in the same form in ancient MSS. and charters, not only of *Britain*, but none of them but are in MSS. of other foreign countries, who had nothing to do with *Ireland*. And in many countries, where no body doubts they had the first use of letters from the *Latins*, the characters of old MSS. differ much more from the vulgar printed characters of the *Latin* than the *Irish* do. Such are the *Merovingian* and *Longobardick* characters: for a proof of this I refer the reader to the schemes of characters, and of old writ, which he will find in the learned *F. Mabillon's* book, *De Re Diplomatica*, in case he have not the opportunity to inspect *Latin* MSS. where he will generally find, even in MSS. of the twelfth, thirteenth, and fourteenth ages,

(*a*) ƒ, ᵹ, ꞃ, ꞅ.

much the ſame characters, or forms of letters, that are made uſe of in the *Iriſh* tongue; and little or no difference, but in the forms of abbreviations: for which, not only the people of different languages, but every different writer, may invent ſuch characters, or forms of contractions, as he fancies will moſt abridge.

THE ſame thing may be ſaid as to the notes for writing ſecrets, called by the *Iriſh Ogum*; of which *Waræus* ſays he had ſome copies; and one *Donald Forbis* mentions others: for no body doubts but the *Iriſh* had their notes or cyphers for writing ſhort hand, and keeping their ſecrets; eſpecially the *Druids*, for preſerving from the knowledge of chriſtians the ſecret of their profane myſteries, made uſe, no doubt, of ſecret characters or letters, from the time that once the uſe of letters was introduced in *Ireland*. All other nations, and every private man, may have the ſame, for keeping ſecrets, and thoſe entirely different from their uſual letters: ſuch among the *Romans* were the *Notæ Tironis*, whereof a ſpecimen may be ſeen in *F. Mabillon*'s diplomaticks. *Tritbemius* alſo hath written a book on the ſubject, *De Steganographia*: ſo I do not well conceive for what this ſerves towards proving the antiquity of the *Iriſh* letters; or that they were not originally the ſame as the *Roman* or *Latin* character. Since *Waræus*, who is brought in to prove

that

that the *Irish* had such characters, (*a*) tells us, that the *Ogum* did not contain the *Irish* vulgar character, but a hidden way of writing for preserving their secrets.

AND thus far as to the arguments brought by *Flaherty*, and other modern *Irish* writers, against the opinion of the learned *Bollandus*, concerning the ancient use of letters in *Ireland*; with which subject, tho' (*b*) *Flaherty* fills up about thirty pages of his *Ogygia*; yet the far greatest part is spent in useless flourishes on the origine of letters in general, and on the use and new order of the *Irish* new invention of *Bethluisnion*, there being little in his book, besides what we have mentioned, that looks like proofs of their having had the use of letters before christianity, unless we call proofs citations of legends of St. *Patrick's* life, written long after his time.

AFTER all, I do not pretend that no private person among the *Irish* had the use of letters before the coming in of St. *Patrick*, and the preaching of the gospel to them: for it may have very well happened, that some of the *Irish*, before that time, passing over to *Britain*, or other parts of the *Roman* empire, where the use of letters was

(*a*) Præter caracteres vulgares utebantur etiam veteres Hyberni variis occultis scribendi formulis, seu artificiis *Ogum* dictis, quibus secreta sua scribebant. *War. antiq. Hyb. cap.* 2. *pag.* 12.

(*b*) Ogyg. domest. from *p.* 214 to *p.* 245.

common, might have *learned to read and write.* It might alſo have happened that the *Druids*, who were the magicians of theſe times, might have had certain hieroglyphick characters to expreſs their diabolical myſteries; and that the remains of thoſe are what *Toland* and others make ſuch a noiſe about. But if the *Iriſh* had any diſtinct character or form of alphabetical letters different from thoſe which we have above mentioned, and which were introduced to *Ireland* by St. *Patrick*, how comes it that all this time, eſpecially within theſe laſt fifty or ſixty years, that the matter hath been agitated, and the diſpute warm about it, none of them have ever publiſhed any ſpecimen of theſe peculiar *Iriſh* letters, or at leaſt an alphabet of them: ſuch as *F. Mabillon* hath given of all ancient forms of letters, and Dr. *Hickes* more particularly of the *Runick*, and other northern characters?

WHAT I deſigned to ſhew in this paragraph is, that the uſe of letters was not ancient among the *Iriſh*, that they had it from the *Romans*, or thoſe that ſpoke the *Latin* tongue: and that it was ſo very rare, if at all, in *Ireland*, till after the preaching of the goſpel, that it could not be properly ſaid to have been received in that nation till then; no more than it can be properly ſaid that chriſtianity was received there before St. *Patrick*; though it is not unlikely that ſome private perſons might have been taught the goſpel, either at home or in other countries, and believed in Chriſt before the preaching of St. *Patrick*. Now

'Now if the uſe of letters was not received in *Ireland* till the coming of this ſaint, which was during the reign of king *Leogaire*; how was it poſſible that any certain account of hiſtory of the former ages could have been preſerved? Accordingly the more famous and authentick chronicles or annals of *Ireland*, that have hitherto appeared, tho' never as yet printed, generally begin the ſeries and chronology of their kings, no higher than the reign of this king *Leogaire*, and about the time of St. *Patrick*. Such are the annals of *Ulſter*, whereof there is a fair copy, with ſeveral other MSS. relating to *Ireland*, in the library of his grace the duke of *Chandos*, who was pleaſed to do me the honour to grant me acceſs to it: theſe annals which are in *Iriſh* character begin only at the year of our Lord 444. In the ſame library are the annals of *Tigernach*: theſe indeed want ſome leaves in the beginning and elſewhere, and begin only about the time of *Alexander the Great*: but till St. *Patrick*'s time they treat chiefly of the general hiſtory of the world, and contain but very little of *Ireland*: the annals of *Innisfall* are likewiſe in the ſame library, and contain a ſhort account of the hiſtory of the world in general, and very little of *Ireland*, till *A. D.* 430. where the author properly begins. a chronicle of *Ireland*, *fol.* 9. after theſe words in *Latin*, *Hic finit parva præſcriptio de principio mundi*; and then follows a little after, *Logaire Mac-Neel reg-*

navit an. 24, &c. And thenceforward contains a short chronicle of *Ireland*, continued down until about the year 1318. These three chronicles are written in *Irish* character, and in the *Irish* language, intermixed with *Latin*: they were formerly collected, with many other valuable MSS. relating to *Ireland*, by that learned antiquarian Sir *James Ware*, and came afterwards into the possession, first of the earl of *Clarendon*, and then of his grace the duke of *Chandos*. A catalogue of them, as they were in Sir *James Ware*'s time, is printed at *Oxford*, in the great collection of the MSS. of *England* and *Ireland*. And lest I may be mistaken in this account of these chronicles for want of the *Irish* language, and having as yet had only a transient inspection of them, I shall here set (*a*) down the more perfect description given of them in the printed catalogue, by one skilled in the *Irish* tongue, and who had perused

(*a*) Vol. II. Annales Ultonienses. Codex antiquissimus sermone partim Hybernico, partim Latino charactere Hybernico scriptus incipit *A. D.* 444. Explicit *A. D.* 1041. quo obiit Rodericus Cassidæus Archidiac. Clocheren qui scripsit dictorum annalium partem posteriorem.

Vol. III. Annales Tigernachi Eirenachi (juxta Waræum) Clonmacnaisensis, mutili in initio. Auctor historiam universalem attingit usque ad adventum S. Patricii, inde vero res Hybernicas usque ad *A. D.* 1088, quo obiit, describit. Liber charactere & lingua Hybernica, &c.

Vol. XXVI. Annales Cœnobii Innisfallensis, quibus auctor leviter attingit historiam universalem a mundo condito usque ad *A. D.* 430. Inde res Hybernicas usque ad *A. D.* 1215. quo vixit, satis accuratè describit.

them

them at leiſure. Theſe annals or chronicles are the moſt conſiderable monuments of *Iriſh* hiſtory that Sir *James Ware*, in the thorough ſearch which he made after ſuch pieces in *Ireland*, could meet with, moſt of them beginning no higher the regular ſucceſſion of the *Iriſh* kings, and the chronological hiſtory of *Ireland*, than about king *Leogaire*'s time. This obſervation, together with the fabulous narrations that he obſerved in thoſe MSS. pieces that pretended to give accounts of the hiſtory of that iſland, and of the ſucceſſion of their kings in the more ancient times, were, no doubt, the motives that determined this learned antiquarian to begin the chronological account of the *Iriſh* kings no higher than king *Leogaire*, and St. *Patrick*'s time: and he himſelf, as we have already obſerved, gives us this remarkable (*a*) reaſon why he began no ſooner; that the moſt part of the accounts of their kings, and other *Iriſh* matters preceding king *Leogaire*'s time, were either *fabulous, or ſtrangely mixed with fables and anachroniſms*.

I ſhall not here repeat the ſolid difficulties that the learned Dr. *Stillingfleet*, in his *Antiquities of the Britiſh churches*, raiſes againſt the accounts contained in the *Iriſh* writers of their remote antiquities, but referr the reader to the places which I have here (*b*) quoted; and in particular to the ob-

(*a*) Vel fabulæ ſunt vel fabulis & anachroniſmis mirè admixta. *Waræus de antiq. Hybern. cap.* 4. *p.* 20.

(*b*) Stillingfleet antiq. *p.* 266, 267, &c.

 ſervations

ſervations which he makes in his (*a*) *preface*, againſt their calculating ſo preciſely by the year of the world, particular facts, whilſt it appears that they could have no certain rules for regulating chronological dates in ancient times.

But I cannot but ſet down here another objection that preſents itſelf to me, and appears very conſiderable againſt the chronological part of their remote antiquities; and ſeems evidently to prove, that they have been all compoſed in much later times, and only after the *Iriſh* had communication or intercourſe with thoſe that ſpoke the *Latin* tongue.

For in the ſame manner, as it hath been already obſerved, that the proper names of which the *Iriſh*, in their language, make uſe to expreſs *letters*, *a book*, *to read*, *to write*, being all derived from the *Latin*, prove that they had the uſe of letters from thoſe that ſpoke the *Latin* tongue: ſo alſo the only proper names that the *Iriſh* in their language give to each number, being manifeſtly derived from the ſame numerical names of the *Latin*, and only altered in conformity to the *Iriſh* idiom, ſeem equally to prove, that they had not the art of calculation or numbering, much leſs that of chronology, till they received it by communication with thoſe that ſpoke the *Latin* tongue.

(*a*) Stillingfleet, *pref.* *p.* 33, 34.

Thus

THUS from *Unus* is derived *aon*, pronounced *eun*, from *Duo*, *Do*, or *Dha*, from *Tres tri*; from *quatuor*, *ceathar*, or *ceitre*; for having no Q in their language, they make uſe of C, which is always pronounced as K inſtead of Q; from *Quinque*, *Cuige*, or *Coige*; the C as we ſaid, or the G ſtanding for Q, and the *n* being ſunk to render the pronunciation more ſmooth; *Se* or *She* from *Sex*, dropping the *x*, which is not in uſe in their language; *Seacht* for *Sept* or *Septem*, the *pt* being altered to *cht*, more uſual in their tongue; *Ocht* or *Ochd*, is ſenſibly from *Octo*; and ſo is *Noi* or *Naoi* from *Novem*; and yet more, *Deic* from *Decem*. *Fichit* or *Fichid*, inſtead of *vighit* from *Viginti*, by the uſual alteration of the letters V into F, and T into D, as *Toland* (*a*) obſerves, as well as of G into C; and the *n* being ſunk to render the pronunciation more ſmooth, as we have ſeen it is in *Cuige* for *Cuinge*: ſo it is likewiſe in *Ceud* or *Cead*, inſtead of *Cent*, from *Centum*: for the D and T are reciprocal, as hath been already obſerved: the laſt number *Mil.* is yet more ſenſibly from the *Latin Mille*: and all the reſt of the intermediate numbers are compounded, or derived from theſe primitive ones.

NOW it is not eaſily to be conceived, how the *Iriſh* bards could preſerve any chronological ac-

(*a*) Toland's hiſt. of *Druids*, *pag.* 29. *note* 36.

count before they received the uſe of counting or numbering, and by conſequence that of proper names for the numbers, from one to a thouſand; for I ſuppoſe there was no *Ogum* for the numbers, as they pretend there was for the *Alphabet*; and the natural way of counting by the ten fingers, or by heaps of little ſtones, might ſerve indeed well enough for the neceſſary uſes of life in barbarous times, but could be of little or no ſervice towards regulating chronology. So that all thoſe preciſe calculations of years, of months, of the days of the month, and of the moon, in regulating their remote antiquities; and in particular, of the arrival of the *Mileſians* in *Ireland*, as it is ſet down by O *Flaherty* in his *Ogygia*, will appear rather a new objection, than a proof of the verity of their ancient hiſtory, to men verſed in antiquity, who have obſerved the great variety of calculation of time among the ancients, and the diſputes among the learned moderns concerning theſe matters.

All that we have ſaid of the uſe of numbers and calculation, derived from the *Latins*, ſerves to confirm *Waræus*'s (*a*) judgment of the remote antiquities of *Ireland*, that they were moſt part drawn up in much later times: this is alſo confirmed by the mention that is made of *Adam*, *Cain*, *Noah*, the deluge, *Moſes*, *Pharaoh*, &c. in their poems, pſaltars, and in what they call their

(*a*) Waræus de antiq. Hybern *Pref. p.* 1.

most

most ancient and most authentick monuments of history: for how could they come by the knowledge of these names, but by the holy scriptures, or by communication with those that had read them? And how could they receive either that knowledge, or have that communication, before the christian religion was preached in *Ireland?*

BEFORE I conclude this subject, I cannot but take notice of what *Toland* says farther of the ancient use of letters in *Ireland*. A great part of what he hath on this head being taken from *Keating* or *Flaherty*, or from the same sources, hath been already considered. He makes a long excursion upon a passage of *Lucian*, by which it appears, that the sirname of (*a*) *Ogmius* was given to *Hercules* in *Gaul*, and that he was named *the force of eloquence:* but that might be true, tho' the *Gauls* had not as yet the use of letters; and so might be only meant of natural eloquence, which may be found, in a great degree, in illiterate people: but *Toland* finds a relation betwixt the name of *Ogmius*, given to *Hercules*, and the *Irish Ogum*, whence he insinuates, that the use of letters, with the language and religion, came from *Gaul* to *Ireland*.

NOW, in the first place, this were to contradict all the *Irish* bards upon the origine of letters,

(*a*) *Toland*'s posthum. works, p. 33. &c.

who,

who, as we have obſerved, attribute the invention of the *Ogum*, or of the *Iriſh*, and other letters to *Fenius Farſaidh*; and pretend, that the *Iriſh* deſcended of him, brought them about with them from *Egypt* and *Spain* to *Ireland*. 2°. If the uſe of letters was in thoſe moſt ancient times received in *Gaul*, whence comes it, that in *Julius Cæſar*'s (*a*) time, the *Druids* in *Gaul* were forced to make uſe of the *Greek* letters? 3°. If before the *Roman* times the uſe of letters was in *Gaul*, how comes it that no ancient inſcription, nor any certain account of what paſt in *Gaul* in ancient times is to be found, but what is taken from the *Greek* or *Roman* writers? Are there not great actions ſaid to be performed by the *Gauls* in ancient times, and was not the deſire of perpetuating their memory as natural to them as to other men? And would they have failed to have done it, as well as the *Greeks* or *Romans*, if they had equally had the means?

But to come now to the meaning of the *Ogum* (*b*) *Waræus*, who had himſelf books concerning it, and had ſeen others, informs us, as we have already obſerved, that the *Ogum* was an artificial way of writing, different from the vulgar *Iriſh* characters, for keeping their ſecrets, a ſecret way of writing: in a word, a kind of cyphers unintelligible to all who had not the key of them.

(*a*) Cæſar. de bello Gallico, lib. 6.

(*b*) Waræus de antiq. Hybern. c. 2. p. 12.

But

But (*a*) *Toland* tells us in one place, that it was called the *ſecret of writing*; and that by *Ogum* were meant the primitive *Iriſh* characters or letters, which were of a quite different form from thoſe that St. *Patrick* afterwards introduced; and that they were afterwards, inſtead of the *ſecret of writing*, called the *ſecret writing* only by accident; becauſe St. *Patrick* having brought in the *Roman* letters, the *Ogum* began to grow obſolete, and was only intelligible to the learned, and became by degrees unintelligible to all others. This is indeed a very ingenious evaſion, and anſwer to the objection that is drawn from the account that *Waræus* gives o the *Ogum*.

BUT this conduct of St. *Patrick* would have been ſuch a ſingularity, as we meet with no where elſe; that any apoſtolical preacher ſent to convert a nation to chriſtianity, and finding the uſe of letters among them, inſtead of making uſe of that, as a means by which the goſpel and doctrine of the chriſtian religion might be more quickly and more eaſily propagated, ſhould begin by introducing among them a new form of characters or letters, entirely unknown to them, and which would take them more time and more pains to learn than all the neceſſary doctrines of chriſtianity And is it very credible, that St. *Patrick* would willingly put this new and uſeleſs obſtacle to the ſpeedy

(*a*) *Toland's* poſthum. works, p. 36.

pro-

propagation of the goſpel that he came to preach, and not rather make uſe of the advantage that the *Iriſh*, having already the uſe of letters among them, preſented to him to advance his apoſtolical work? And this ſo much the more, that St. *Patrick* (*a*) having ſpent about ſeven years of his youth in *Ireland*, had perfectly learned their language; and if they had the uſe of letters, might have learned that too.

BUT the ſame *Toland* (*b*), in another place, gives us a quite different notion of the *Ogum*; for he brings in *Will. Odonell*, afterwards a biſhop, telling king *James* I. that he had enjoined one of his aſſiſtants in tranſlating the bible into *Iriſh*, to write it according to the *Ogum*, *and the propriety of the* Iriſh *tongue*. Now I ask here, Was this *Ogum* that ancient *Iriſh* alphabet, or the *Beth-luis-nion*, which *Toland* had informed us above was become intelligible only to the learned? but that had been to render the ſcriptures abſolutely unintelligible and uſeleſs, not only to lay-people, but to miniſters. So, to be ſure, the biſhop would not make ſuch a ſhocking propoſal to the king. By the *Ogum* then, in this place, muſt be meant only the propriety of the *Iriſh* language, and ſo *Toland* himſelf explains it, or the true orthography of it, and that in the uſual *Iriſh* characters or letters. And by conſequence, no proof can be drawn from the *Ogum*,

(*a*) Uſſer. antiq. Brit. Eccleſ. fol. p. 431.
(*b*) *Toland*, ibid. p. 38.

of any peculiar characters or letters among the *Irish*, different from what we meet with in their MSS. and books printed in *Irish* character, which, as hath been already observed, was introduced by St. *Patrick*, and derived from the *Latin*.

Now whether this character, which resembles perfectly to the *Saxon*, came immediately from the *Irish* to the *Saxons*, or from the ancient *Britains* to both, as the author of the history of *Great Britain* lately published, or rather M. *Edward Lhuyd* (*a*) in his *Welch* preface to his *Archæologia*, translated and inserted into the introduction to this history, pretends; I shall determine nothing, tho' I think M. *Lhuyd*'s opinion better grounded and more probable: but whoever brought these letters or characters first into *Britain* or *Ireland*, we have (*b*) elsewhere abundantly shewn, that they came originally from the *Romans*.

But for a farther proof of the ancient use of letters in *Ireland* before St. *Patrick*'s time, *Toland* tells us (*c*), that *there flourished a great number of Druids, Bards, Vaids, and other authors in* Ireland, *long before* Patrick's *arrival*; *whose learning*, says he, (though he knew that they were all infidels) *was not only more extensive, but also more useful than*

(*a*) Hist. of *Great Britain*, in folio, by *John Lewis*. Introduction, p. 59, 60, &c.

(*b*) Supra, p. 443, &c.

(*c*) *Toland*, ibid. p. 48.

that

that of their chriſtian poſterity: this laſt ſort being almoſt wholly employed in ſcholaſtick divinity, metaphyſical or chronological diſputes, &c.

Now *Toland* knew alſo very well, that notwithſtanding any alteration that might have happened among the *Iriſh*, in the method or order of teaching the chriſtian religion; the ſubſtance and eſſentials of it were ſtill the ſame, after the eighth age, as before: and was then the learning of the *Druids*, who were truly magicians, more uſeful, in *Toland*'s judgment, than that of chriſtianity? and do all the pretenſions of this famous free-thinker, to be governed in his belief ſolely by reaſon, terminate, at laſt, in ſuch impious notions? I call the *Druids* magicians, becauſe draoi, or droiche, which is the *Iriſh* name of *Druids*, is the ſame by which, in the *Iriſh* tranſlation of the Bible, both in the old and new teſtament, a magician is expreſſed; and that in the *Latin* lives of St. *Patrick*, and in that of St. *Columba*, by *Adamnan*, the *Druids* are called *Ma*[illegible]

TOLAND, for new proofs of the ancient uſe of letters in *Ireland*, runs (*a*) out into a long digreſſion, upon the ſingular care and encouragements of learning, in that iſland, before St. *Patrick*'s time, as *Keating*, *O Flaherty*, and others had done before him; each of them, as *Toland* (*a*)

(*a*) Toland, ibid. p. 49, 50, &c.

himſelf

himself expresses elsewhere this copying one from another, *eternally serving up the same dishes at every meal*, and all of them referring to the authority of their ancient monuments, written by their bards; but never publishing any single entire piece of them, equally leave all of them in doubt. *Toland* goes on, and tells us, that there are great (*a*) numbers of MSS. of the *Druids* compositions still remaining; and for a certain proof of there having been such books of the *Druids*, extant before St. *Patrick*'s time, he quotes some modern *Irish* writers, who, from some of the many legends of St. *Patrick*'s life, relate, that he caused to be burnt many volumes of the *Druids* stuft with fables, and heathen superstitions; at which *Toland* (*b*) enters into a vehement declamation against this *book-burning and letter-murdering* humour, *which*, says he, *though far from being commanded by Christ, has prevailed in Christianity from the beginning: as in the Acts of the Apostles*, (*c*) *we read*, that many of them which believed, and used curious arts, brought their books together, and burnt them before all men; and they counted the price of them, and found it fifty thousand pieces of silver, *or, about three hundred pounds sterling. This was the first instance of burning of books among christians; and ever since that time, the example has been better followed than any precept of the Gospel.* Thus

(*a*) Toland, ibid. p. 45.
(*b*) Toland, p. 58.
(*c*) Acts xix. 19.

Toland. And one that did not know the ſate of his *chriſtianity not myſterious*, would eaſily ſuſpect, by the paſſion with which he makes mention of the Apoſtles burning wicked books, that he is himſelf a party concerned.

BUT whatever be of the legends of St. *Patrick*, which even *Toland* can believe, when they ſerve to his purpoſe; it may very well have happened, that the *Druids*, being magicians, made uſe of magical, or other hieroglyphick characters, intelligible only to themſelves, and their confederates, to expreſs their diabolical enchantments and ſuperſtitions; and that they had volumes full of theſe, which, after the example of the Apoſtles, inflamed St. *Patrick*'s zeal againſt them: but all this is no proof that they had the uſe of alphabetical letters, or that it was common in *Ireland*, before St. *Patrick* taught it the natives.

ART. V. *That even ſuppoſing that the* Iriſh *had the uſe of letters before the goſpel was preached among them, their pretended ancient writers the bards deſerve no credit.*

THE deſcription that *Cornelius Tacitus* gives us of the cuſtom uſed among the *Germans*, living in their natural ſtate, towards preſerving the memory of things paſt in old times, ſeems a lively portraiture of the more common means in uſe among the reſt of the uncultivated northern nations, towards compaſſing

ing the ſame end. He tells us, that the *Germans* of old, had no (*a*) uſe of letters among them; and that the only (*b*) means they had for preſerving the memory of paſt tranſactions, and their only annals, were rythms got by heart, which contained the elogiums of their firſt founders, and of thoſe they looked upon as their heroes: and, a little after, he tells us, that they had rythms, or verſes on this ſubject, called by them *Barditus*, by which they uſed to animate their ſoldiers to fight. Now this *Barditus* ſeems viſibly derived from the bards, authors of thoſe kind of rythms. And thus it was, in all probability, among the reſt of the northern uncultivated nations. The only records of paſt tranſactions were the rythms of the bards, not put in writing, but got by heart, and recited on ſolemn occaſions. The *Iriſh*, in particular, agree, that the bards, to whom they give ſeveral names were the recorders and preſervers of their ancient tranſactions. It is therefore of importance, to enquire into the character of the bards in general, and of thoſe of *Ireland* in particular, in order to judge of the credit of their high antiquities.

(*a*) Literarum ſecreta tam viri quam mulieres ignorant. *Tacit. de morib. German. pag.* 224. *edit. Plantin. fol. A. D.* 1585.

(*b*) Celebrant carminibus antiquis (quod unicum apud illos memoriæ & annalium genus eſt) Tuiſtonem Deum terra editum & filium Mannum, originem gentis conditoreſque. —Sunt illis hæc quoque carmina, quorum relatu, quem Barditum vocant, accendunt animos. *Tacit. ibid. p.* 221.

§. 1. *Of the bards in general.*

IN the first place it is to be remarked, that the bards, seanachies, or antiquaries, poets and genealogists frequently mentioned by the *Irish* writers, are but different names that design one and the same kind of men, called in *Celtick* (and from thence by the *Greeks* and *Latins*, and in other languages) *bards*, or, which is the same thing, *poets*, because they used to compose and chant verses, or rythms, in praise of their heroes or benefactors; called likewise *antiquaries* in *Irish seanachies*, by reason that the subject of their rythms was ordinarily the feats of ancient heroes, and of the ancestors of their patrons, or benefactors; called *genealogists*, because, in some countries, a part of their office was to make up and retain genealogies for their great men, or those that came to be in power.

As to the name of bard, it is originally *Celtick*, and so common to the *Britains* and *Irish*, as well as to the ancient *Gauls*, all these languages being originally dialects of the *Celtick*; and the word bard, in the *Celtick* tongue, signifies a poet, as a learned antiquary (*a*) observes. So we may observe, among the northern nations, the *Swedes* and *Danes*, any knowledge they pretend to of their antiquities, is ascribed by them to their ancient poets,

(*a*) Pezron. antiquitè des Gaules, p. 378.

poets, the ſame kind of men as the *Celtick* bards; and they pretend, no leſs than the *Iriſh*, to have remains and fragments of poems and rythms on their ancient heroes; and, by that means, ſet up for as high antiquities as the *Iriſh* do: witneſs *Johannes* (*a*) *Magnus*, archbiſhop of *Upſal*, his hiſtory of the *Goths*, which he begins as the *Iriſh* do, at *Magog*, the ſon of *Japhet*, and brings from him a diſtinct hiſtory of kings, ſucceeding one to another, down to his own time, to wit, to the ſixteenth age.

THE bards are entirely to be diſtinguiſh'd from the *Druids*, and from the *Evages*, or *Vates* of the ancients, whoſe characters, as well as their diſcipline was quite diſtinct, as they are ſet down by (*b*) *Cæſar* of the *Druids*, and more particularly by (*c*) *Ammian Marcellin*, both of the *Druids* and *Evages*; neither of which had any thing to do with recording paſt tranſactions or hiſtories, their whole office being employed about the religious part of the heatheniſh ſuperſtitions, or the forming their laws and manners, and deciding controverſies or debates: but none of the many ancient authors that treat of *Druids*, ever give them, for any part of their calling, the wri-

(*a*) Johan. magnus hiſtoria Goth. *edit. Baſil.* 1558.

(*b*) Cæſar de bello Gallico, *lib.* 6. *pag.* 164. *edit. Elzevir* 1651.

(*c*) Euhages ſcrutantes ſeria & ſublimia naturæ pandere conabantur. Inter hos Druidæ ingeniis celſiores, &c. *Ammian. lib.* 15. *pag.* 51. *edit. Valeſ. in* 4to.

ting or keeping records of history: and *Ammian* distinguishes them entirely from the bards.

As to the character of the bards among the ancients, *Possidonius* (one of the most ancient authors that mention them) quoted by *Athenæus*, reckons them among the parasites, that lived by their flattering great or rich men. (*a*) *Diodorus* gives much the same account of them: and *Appian* speaks of them much in the same sense. Upon these and other passages of the ancients, the learned (*b*) *Valesius*, in his notes upon *Ammian Marcellin*, gives us the following description of them. By this, says *Valesius*, it appears the bards were nothing else but parasites, and such a kind of men as the *Latins* call *Scurræ*, or buffoons: for as these buffoons, or *Scurræ*, used to follow the armies to divert the soldiers in their banquets, by their gests and mimical gestures; so likewise the bards used to do. But this character seems too hard, if literally pressed: for it appears by *Ammian*, in the place upon which *Valesius* comments here, that the bards had besides this, at least among the *Gauls*, another more honourable means to flatter great men, by

(*a*) Diod. Sicul. *lib.* 5.

(*b*) Ex his patet bardos nihil aliud fuisse quam parasitos, planeque similes eorum quos Latini scurras vocabant: ut enim scurræ exercitum sequebantur, jocis ac gesticulationibus milites inter convivia delinire soliti, ita etiam bardi. *Vales. not. in Ammian. p.* 93.

composing

composing poems on the (*a*) noble feats of the heroes, and singing them to their harps.

We are then now to consider, how far the knowledge of history, or of the antiquities of any nation, might have been preserved by men of the character of the bards. And in the first place it may be allowed, that some confused memory of the first founders, and more famous heroes of a nation, might have been preserved by their means: this may be confirmed by what we have already observed from *Tacitus*, of the custom of the ancient *Germans*: but it must be also allowed, that the accounts which the bards or poets of the ancients brought down of the origines of nations, and founders of empires, were so absolutely uncertain, and mixed with so many fables, that they can make no more faith in true history, than *Virgil*'s *Æneids* can serve to give us light into the origine of the *Latins* or *Romans*.

In the second place, some draughts of genealogies for princes or great men might also probably have been the fabrick of the bards, since that is made a part of their office: and no body fitter for it than such as they who stood at nothing to flatter their patrons, and gain favour with all that came to be in power, who could not fail to have

(*a*) Et bardi quidem fortia virorum illustrium facta heroicis composita versibus cum dulcibus lyræ modulis cantitarunt. *Ammian. l.* 15. *p.* 51.

their pedigree traced back to the first founders, or most famous men of a nation, since it cost no more than the coining a few names, or mixing them with some already in use. And these genealogies became a foundation, upon which, to build new heroes and noble exploits in after-times, when all distinct memory of past transactions being extinct, there was none who could contradict them, or who would dare to do it, when those, whose ancestors were erected into heroes, were powerful enough to crush all gainsayers. Thus the bards might have coined the first genealogies; and afterwards either they themselves, or others of the same stamp, created some of them heroes and conquerors, and attributed great exploits to them, according as it might serve to the honour of those in power at the time, whom the bards had made to descend from them: these rude draughts were polished by others, and *epochs* and dates added to them by posterior bards.

But all these rare collections of antiquities, so much valued in dark ages, came afterwards in other countries to be neglected and brought into contempt, especially in these later times; when the study of critick and true ancient history being renewed and generally received, the impartial men among the learned, in none of the northern countries of *Europe*, whether *Germans*, *French*, *Spaniards*, *Danes*, &c. do pretend to any certain history, or accounts of the origine of their people, or antiquities of their countries,

countries, but what they collect, and, as it were, glean from the *Greek* and *Roman* writers; nothing from their domestick writers in prose, or in rythm in their native tongues, before the times of the *Roman* empire. And what the ignorance or credulity of dark past ages had received of that kind, or that forgers had invented, tho' in praise of their ancestors, hath in this clear-sighted age been rejected, even by those most concerned, with disdain and contempt. Thus the *French* have rejected *Hunibaldus*, the *Spaniards*, *Berosus*, the learned among the *English*, *Geoffrey*'s inventions, and so of most other polite nations.

THUS we see how little credit hath been given of late generally in all countries, where learning hath been improved, to rythms or rhapsodies of bards or other forgers, since nothing of that kind, or very little, hath been thought fit to be transmitted to posterity, or published to the world.

§. 2. *Of the* Irish *bards.*

BUT perhaps the bards or seanachies of *Ireland* were a kind of men of greater credit and veracity, and less subject to flattering, lying, or detraction, and not so liable as the bards in other nations to the several passions, that make men swerve from the truth, that so their accounts of antiquity might deserve to be more valued.

BUT

But we need no other proofs than those we are furnished with by the *Irish* writers, and those too the greatest admirers of their high antiquities, to prove that the *Irish* bards or antiquaries, were of all others the least to be depended on.

ODONNELL, an *Irish* writer of the life of St. *Columba*, translated into *Latin*, and published by (*a*) *Colgan*, in his *Trias Thaumaturga*, informs us, that about the year 586 of Christ, it was decreed in the assembly of *Dromkeat*, by *Aidus* king of *Ireland*, that all the race of the bards or antiquaries should be banished that kingdom, and their discipline abolished; but that St. *Columba* (a very likely tale) was pleased to intercede for them: and the motive of this decree or law, against the bards or antiquaries, is very remarkable, to wit, because *they* (*b*) *used to turn their rythms or poems* (in which they delivered the accounts of antiquities or genealogies) *into excessive praises and flatteries of the great men, whose favour or presents they hunted after, or in satyrical*

(*a*) Rex Aidus statuerat bardos, seu antiquariæ rei professores tota insula pellere & disciplinam abolere. *Colgan Triad. Thaumaturga*, p. 430, 431.

(*b*) Sua sæpe poemata convertebant in excessivas laudes hominum nobilium quorum gratiam & donaria venabantur, sæpe in Satyricas invectivas in alios quibus æque affecti aut beneficiis allecti non erant. *Colgan. ibid.*

invectives

invectives against those that were not so liberal to them. This is just the character that *Diodorus Siculus* had given of the bards among the *Celtes* (*a*). *Sunt apud eos* (Celtas) *melici poetæ quos appellant bardos. Hi ad instrumenta quædam lyris similia horum laudes, illorum vituperia decantant.* This justifies (*b*) *Valesius*'s character of the bards, that their custom was *to praise and flatter their masters and princes, and those who bestowed most upon them, and to make bitter invectives against the enemies and adversaries of their patrons*, and those that were not liberal to them: so it appears, that both the *Celtish* and *Irish* bards were equally a kind of parasites in effect, but with this difference, that these ancient bards of the *Celtes* got perhaps nothing, but to fill their bellies in reward for their flatteries; whereas we are (*c*) told, that the *Irish* bards or antiquaries got for their reward lands and possessions.

Now let it be remarked, that these bards or antiquaries whom *Odonnell* says were decreed to be banished the kingdom for their impostures, flatteries, and calumnies, were probably christians: since St. *Columba* is brought in to intercede for them; and that christianity had been by this time

(*a*) Diodor. *lib.* 5. *p.* 425.

(*b*) Quippe dominos suos & reges quorum mensas sectabantur bardi laudabant: inimicos vero hostesque regum suorum conviciis incessebant. *Vales. not. in Ammian. p.* 93.

(*c*) D. Ken. geneal. pref. *p.* 78.

settled

ſettled in *Ireland* for above one hundred years: What then may be thought of the ancient bards, or antiquaries of *Ireland* in times of paganiſm? And how far would their writings, if they had left any, deſerve to be depended on, when they left the ſpirit of impoſture ſo deeply rooted in their poſterity, that even chriſtianity could not correct it? What certain hiſtory might we expect from them, if any thing had remained of their rythms to after-ages?

BUT this is not all: (*a*) we are told farther, that the bards or antiquaries of *Ireland* had been twice decreed before this to be expelled out of the iſland, their impoſtures, flatteries, and inſolence having frequently grown to that height, that even pagans had a horror of, and could not bear with them. And M. *Toland* (*b*), as hath been already obſerved, acknowledges that the *Iriſh* bards, *beſides their poetical licences, were both mercenary and partial to a ſcandalous degree.*

NOTHING ſhews a plainer proof to what a pitch thoſe pretended antiquaries of *Ireland* had carried their impoſtures and fabulous flatteries, than to conſider what the *Iriſh* (*c*) writers often repeat, of the great love and attache their countrymen had to

(*a*) D. Ken. pref. geneal. *p.* 77. 170. Keating, *pag.* 371. & alibi.

(*b*) Toland's poſthumous works, to 1. *pag.* 50.

(*c*) Keating, Flaherty, &c. D. Ken. geneal. pref. paſſim.

the

the bards and antiquaries, when they kept within tolerable bounds. To what a pitch then of lying and calumny muſt they have been arrived; when the *Iriſh*, notwithſtanding the love we are told they had for preſerving the memory of their antiquities, found themſelves obliged to come thrice, at different times, to a reſolution of baniſhing theſe only recorders and preſervers of them?

By this, I conceive, it plainly appears, that the *Iriſh* bards were at leaſt of no greater credit than thoſe of other nations; no leſs accuſtomed to meaſure their rythms and hiſtorical accounts only by love, hatred, intereſt, and ſuch other paſſions that make men ſwerve from the truth, and render their teſtimony unworthy of credit: ſo that in caſe any thing were remaining of the rythms of the bards, eſpecially antecedent to the times in which they received chriſtianity, and the uſe of letters; it may be expected that the generality of the more conſiderate men of the nation will, by degrees, look upon theſe remains of the bards, as unworthy of taking place in the body of their hiſtory, as we ſee the more learned and judicious among them do already contemn them; as the *Germans*, *Spaniards*, the *French*, and other nations have done: among whom no men of learning pretend to have any remains of their ancient bards, or any writers before the fifth or ſixth age, nor any cer-

tainty

tainty of their origines, nor of the ancient historical accounts of their countries, but what they pick out of the *Greek* and *Latin* authors.

AND so I think it may be concluded (*a*) with the learned *Wareus*, that all these pretended ancient rythms, in which we are told are contained accounts of the first founders, colonies, genealogies, and ancient kings of *Ireland*, are not pieces conveyed down from the times before christianity was received, as their modern writers would have us believe, but are almost all of them the productions of later ages.

AND from all that hath been said in this paragraph of the bards, we may likewise conclude, that tho' we should suppose (against what hath been (*b*) shewn before) that the use of letters had been received in *Ireland* in ancient times, before the preaching of the gospel there; yet the only pretended writers of the *Irish* in these early times, being the bards, no credit ought to be given to the accounts of men of such an odious character.

(*a*) Notandum descriptiones fere omnium [rerum in Hybernia gestarum] quæ de illis temporibus, (vestustioribus dico) extant, opera esse posteriorum sæculorum. *War. de antiq. Hybern, præf. pag.* 1.

(*b*) §§. 3 & 4.

ART.

ART. VI. *The uncertainty of the remote antiquities of* Ireland *appears by the contradictory accounts given of them, and the many alterations made in them by posterior writers.*

THAT very little credit ought to be given to the *Irish* bards in the accounts of their remote antiquities, even suppose it were granted, that the use of letters had been in *Ireland* before christianity, will as yet appear more evident to any that will consider in the first place the contradictions betwixt the ancient and modern writers, in the accounts they give of those antiquities: and in the next, the many additions, retrenchments, and alterations, or reformations made by degrees, in the first rude draughts of them, left by those bards who first invented them; made in them, I say, afterwards by their posterior bards or antiquaries, as they came more and more to the knowledge of the general history of the world.

WHO is there among the learned antiquaries of this critical age that can believe, for example, the detail of the accounts which we have set down from the modern *Irish* writers? ART. 1. Of the plantations of *Ireland*, even since the flood of *Noah*, and before the *Milesians*: And ART. 2. Those of the ancient literature of the *Irish* before the times of christianity, especially if compared with the accounts that the most ancient writers, and the most learned among the modern, give unanimously,

unanimously, as we have seen, of their being uncultivated, and in the ignorance of letters, common to all other northern nations of *Europe* in those early times: and yet all these accounts of their ancient plantations, with a greater detail of circumstances than I have related, as well as those of the school in the plains of *Senaar*; and other instances of their ancient literature are related, as they inform us, by their bards or seanachies, and other writers whom they value most.

BUT to go no farther up than the coming in of the *Milesians*, on the certainty of which all their following history, and succession of their ancient kings, till the times of christianity, do depend; what is more capable to bring in doubt all the detail they give of the *Milesians*, than to pretend to give us, as they do, the precise day of the week, of the month, and of the moon, on which the *Milesians* first landed in *Ireland*; when at the same time we have assured proofs, that only three or four ages ago they knew not within several hundred years the precise *Æra* of the coming in of that colony? *O. Flaherty* (*a*), one of their most learned writers, places the settlement of the *Milesians* in *Ireland* only one thousand years before the incarnation: others, as *Keating* and Dr. *Kenedy* say, one thousand three hundred years; others, one thousand four hundred: but *Donald*

(*a*) Ogyg. p. 83, 84, &c. 182, 183, &c.

Oneyl, a king of Ulster, with the other princes and inhabitants of Ireland, in their letter (a) to pope John XXII, A. D. 1317. informs the pope, (no doubt, according to the common opinions of the most learned bards or antiquaries of their time) that it was above three thousand five hundred years since the three sons of Milesius came from Spain and settled in Ireland; that is to say, that, in the opinion of the antiquaries of these times, the Milesian colony settled in Ireland about two thousand two hundred years before the incarnation: so whilst their writers pretend to give us the precise day of the week, and of the moon, of this colony's coming to Ireland, there's above one thousand years difference betwixt the date that the Irish antiquaries give to it in the fourteenth age, and that to which Flaherty hath reduced it in the seventeenth. And the same letter contains another proof of the inconsistencies of these Milesian antiquities in the number of Irish kings of that race, which the modern Irish reckon only 126 or 127, from Heremon to Leogaire; whereas king Donald Oneyl's seanachies reckoned them 136. And it is not unlikely, that if they would at last gratify the

(a) A tempore quo antiqui patres nostri, scilicet tres filii Milesii Hispani cum triginta navium classe a Cantabria—— in Hiberniam, tunc omni carentem incola, divinitus devenerunt, tres mille quingenti & amplius fluxerunt anni; & ex ipsis, sine admixtione sanguinis alieni, totius Hyberniæ cœperunt monarchiam reges centum triginta sex usque Legarium regem. Ex literis Donaldi Oneyl regis Ultoniæ, &c. ad Joannnem P. XXII. apud Fordun, edit. Tho. Hearne, pag. 908.

publick with a true edition of the ancienteſt poems, or works of their bards on this ſubject, we ſhould find that the older they are, the more they would be incredible in themſelves, and the more inconſiſtent with the new ſchemes to which they have reduced them.

But in the mean-time, until exact copies be publiſhed, with literal tranſlations, and without alterations of theſe ancient poems or works of their bards or ſeanachies, and among the reſt the (a) *book with the white cover, a very authentick piece, written*, as they ſay, *in their pagan anceſtors time*; *the* (b) *book of conqueſts*; *the Pſaltar Caſhel*, and ſuch others, which they (c) aſſure us are ſtill in being, and in their poſſeſſion, containing their remote antiquities before chriſtianity: in the mean-time, till theſe be publiſhed, ſome of their many variations and alterations in the ſcheme of their antiquities, and the inconſiſtency of their modern ſchemes of them, with the firſt draughts of them broach'd by their bards in times of ignorance, may be ſhewn, by ſetting down the different and contradictory accounts which the *Iriſh* and *Scots* give of them, tho' originally the ſame.

And firſt, it is to be obſerved that the *Iriſh* writers will by no means allow the *Scots* any knowledge of theſe high antiquities, but what they received

(a) Leabhar dromaſnacta.
(b) Leabhar gabhala.
(c) D Ken. pref. p. 25.

ceived at first from the *Irish*. The *Scots*, says a late (*a*) writer, *have no history or records* (of the high antiquities) *but what they copied or transcribed from those of* Ireland. I am truly of the same opinion, as to all that is related of the *Scots*, before they came over to *Britain*, and whilst they made as yet one people with the inhabitants of *Ireland*: and it were a great injustice to rob the *Irish* seanachies of the honour of being the first inventors and abettors of these high antiquities.

THIS supposed, it follows in course, that the stories of the *Irish* and *Scotish* seanachies concerning the origin, genealogy, and various transmigrations of the *Channagaodhall*, or *Milesian* race, were originally the same, as proceeding from the same source, to wit, the *Irish* bards or seanachies. Now it is certain, that the accounts which the *Irish* and *Scots* give of these antiquities, are become in progress of time very different, both as to the genealogy, the time of their first settlement in *Ireland*, the founders, and beginning of their monarchy there: and by consequence, either the *Irish* or the *Scotish* antiquaries must have made considerable alterations in them since the times that the *Scots* at first received them from the *Irish*. And it seems no less certain, that those alterations can be ascribed only to those that had interest to make them, towards raising their credit, and procuring honour to themselves by them.

(*a*) Geneal. D. Ken. pref. *p.* 6, 7.

In the next place it doth not appear that the *Scots* in *Britain* had any private interest or national concern in transactions which are supposed to have past long before they came to be settled in *Britain*, as a distinct people from the *Irish*: and therefore would naturally leave the genealogies, names of founders, and *Epochs* of their coming to *Ireland*, in the same case as they had at first received them from the *Irish* bards, without any alteration by design.

Whereas on the contrary, the *Irish* writers had private motives, and a national concern, as we shall just now see, for the honour of their country, to alter them: since, in order to render their history and genealogies the more likely, and to raise their settlement in *Ireland*, and beginning of their monarchy in the *Milesian* line, to a greater height of antiquity, they were under a necessity of reforming and polishing the first rude draughts of their antiquities, which their bards or seanachies had broach'd in times of darkness and ignorance, without a prospect of the large fabrick, which their posterity, by the help of a farther insight in the general history of the world, were to raise upon these rude and imperfect beginnings.

We shall now compare together the different accounts given of those antiquities, by the most ancient *Scotish* writers remaining, and those given of of them by the *Irish* of the present, and these several ages past. By the first we shall see the first originals of these antiquities, in the condition in which the *Scots* at first received them from the *Irish*. By the latter, that is, by the present scheme to which the *Irish* have reduced those antiquities, we shall easily observe, (in comparing it to the scheme which the *Scots* at first received and have preserved) what alterations the *Irish* seanachies and criticks have thought fit, in after-ages, to make in them: and at the same time, we shall endeavour to discover the motives of some of the more remarkable of these alterations.

1°. BOTH the *Scotish* and *Irish* antiquaries bring down the genealogies from (a) *Noah*'s son *Japhet*: but the first inventors of the genealogy bring the descent by *Gomer*, as being *Japhet*'s eldest son; and so it is set down by *Magraith* (b), one of the most famous *Irish* genealogists, and the *Scots* have still retained it: whereas the posterior *Irish* writers having become acquainted with ancient history, and finding that the *Scyths*, of whom the *Scots* are thought to be descended, came from *Magog*, according to *Josephus* and other historians, and not from *Gomer*; reformed the old genealogy, and brought the descent from *Magog*. It is easy to see, that this alteration is the effect of reflexion and second thoughts.

(a) Fordun, l. 5. c. 50. edit. Th. Hearne, p. 487, 488.
(b) Codex MS. biblioth. Ducis de Chandois, vol. 78.

2°. It appears, that in the firſt draughts of this genealogy there were one hundred and four deſcents (*a*) from *Adam*, that is, ninety-four from *Noah*, till *Conarc-mor*, whom the *Iriſh* place about the time of the incarnation: and the *Scots*, in their draughts of it, retain ſtill the ſame number of generations or deſcents. But it is eaſy to ſee, that the *Iriſh* antiquaries having afterwards peruſed the holy ſcriptures, and obſerving that in the ſame ſpace of time, and number of years, there were only ſixty-ſeven generations from *Noah* till Chriſt, ſet down by St. *Luke*, and according to St. *Matthew* only fifty, or fifty-four; thought fit to reform the old draught of their genealogy, containing about ninety-four generations in the ſame length of time; and by cutting off twenty of them, reduced them firſt to about ſeventy-two generations; and not ſatisfied with that, (*b*) *Flaherty* lops off nine or ten more, and reduces them exactly to the number of the longeſt ſcripture genealogy, that of St. *Luke*: and ſo on the whole, there are about 30 generations cut off; and the number, which was one hundred and four, (from *Adam* to *Conar*, placed in the time of the incarnation, according to the old draughts of the genealogy ſtill preſerved by the *Scots*) is reduced to about ſeventy-five or ſeventy-ſix; and among theſe lopt off by *Flaherty*, are *Fergus*, *Maine*, and others, reckoned

(*a*) Fordun, ſupra.
(*b*) Ogyg. p. 122.

koned among the first *Scotish* kings in their vulgar histories.

THIS freedom that *Flaherty* takes with the genealogy, shews us what the custom was of their bards in former ages, to reform their antiquities to render them more conformable to other received histories; and that the difference betwixt the numbers of descents in this genealogy, in the *Scotish* and *Irish* accounts of it, proceeds, in all appearance, from the former reductions the *Irish* had made of it, in order to render it more likely, and so gain credit to their antiquities, whereof this genealogy is the chief foundation: whereas the *Scots*, having no such interest in the remote antiquities of *Ireland*, preserved with simplicity the genealogy, in the same state that they had first received it from the *Irish* bards, before these alterations. And for a further proof that the *Scots* account of it is the more ancient and genuine, and was in ancient times that of the *Irish* also, we find the same names and number of descents in the most ancient copies of it; whereof one will be found in the appendix of pieces, *num.* 4. by an author of the twelfth age, ending at king *William*; tht other is in *Radulfus de* (*a*) *Diceto*, dean of *London* in the same age.

3°. IT appears also that the (*b*) *Scots* preserved, with the same simplicity, the stories of *Gathelus*,

(*a*) Decem scriptor. Angl. col. 627;
(*b*) Fordun, l. 1. c. 10, 11, &c.

or *Gaidelglas*, and of *Milesius*, whom they call *Micelius* and *Miledespain*, in the native shape in which they had been first conceived by the *Irish* bards, and delivered to the *Scots* before they were refined. That *Gathelus*, son of *Niulus*, having fled to *Egypt*, married *Scota*, *Pharaoh*'s daughter, and that in *Moses*'s time: that on occasion of the plagues sent on *Egypt*, *Gathelus* left it, with his wife *Scota*, and followers; and after a long pilgrimage arrived in *Spain*, and there settled a kingdom of *Scots*, so called from this *Scota*; and from him descended *Micelius*, or *Milesius*, in the thirteenth degree, his successor in the kingdom of *Scots* in *Spain*. This *Gathelus*, before he died, sent the first colony to *Ireland*, under his son *Hyber*; and from him the island took its name.

This was the story of *Gathelus* or *Gaidelglas*, and *Scota*, such as we find it, not only in *Boece*, but in *Fordun*.

Now 'tis to be observed, (as we are informed by one of (*a*) *Fordun*'s continuators, who gives us an account of his travels, in order to collect materials for his chronicles) that *Fordun*, besides his consulting the *Scotish* seanachies upon the antiquities of the *Scots* in the earliest times, went over on purpose to *Ireland*, to consult also the seanachies or antiquaries of that island, looked upon as (*b*)

(*a*) Supra, p. 206. ex præf. Chron. de Cupro.
(*b*) In oraculis Hyberniæ. *Ibid.*

oracles

oracles in those matters; and 'tis remarked in particular by that writer, that *Fordun* not only conversed with the historians of all parts where he travelled, but inspected their annals, and conferred with them upon history and antiquities. This was in the fourteenth age, not long after the letter already mentioned, of king *Donald Oneyl* to pope *John* XXII. in which that prince gives, from the seanachies of those times, so different an account, both of the antiquity of the *Milesian* settlement, and of the number of kings of that race, from what the modern *Irish* writers relate of the one and the other. Now *Fordun* having compared the *Scotish* accounts of these remote antiquities, with those of the seanachies of *Ireland*, must have found them, in all appearance, conformable to some of the *Irish* accounts; (for by what we have observed from king *Donald*'s letter, they were not all of a piece) this renders *Fordun*'s authority more considerable in those remote antiquities; which, as it will appear in the sequel of this essay, was one of the chief objects of *Fordun*'s travels, in order to raise the *Scotish* antiquities as high as king *Edward* I. in his letter to pope *Boniface* VIII. had raised those of the *Britains*.

But to return to the story of *Gathelus*, or *Gaidelglas*: that the account that *Fordun* gives of that story, was conformable to what the *Scots* at first had received from the *Irish* seanachies, appears for

for the reaſon already alledged, to wit, that the *Scots* having become a diſtinct nation from the *Iriſh*, had no intereſt to rectify the errors of thoſe antiquities, and therefore preſerved the accounts of them, without examining whether likely or not, but contented themſelves to hand them down to poſterity, ſuch as they found them. But the ſeanachies of *Ireland* becoming more learned in after-ages, and diſcovering the palpable inconſiſtency of theſe firſt draughts of their antiquities with the holy ſcripture, and all true hiſtory, thought with reaſon that they had as good a right to correct and reform them, as the old bards their predeceſſors had at firſt to invent them. Having then obſerved, that there was no poſſibility of making *Moſes* and *Gaidelglas* contemporary, *Moſes* being in the ſeventeenth degree deſcended from *Noah*, and *Gaidel*, (according to the alteration made in the genealogy) only in the ſeventh degree; and there being, (as *Flaherty* obſerves) about ſix hundred years betwixt *Gaidel* and *Moſes*, they were forced to abandon the *Epoch* of *Moſes*'s time: but being, it ſeems, unwilling to loſe this *Scota*, daughter of *Pharaoh*, and her marriage with *Niul* or *Gaidel*, which their own ancient bards, as well as thoſe of the *Scots*, had maintained, they reſolved to have a new *Scota*, daughter alſo to another *Pharaoh*, king of *Egypt*, to be married to one of their leading-men, and give her name to the nation.

NONE was so fit for this match as *Milesius*, whom they intended to make the patriarch of the *Milesian* colony in *Ireland*, and stock of a long race of kings in that island. But *Milesius* was king of the *Scots* in *Spain*, where, according to the old form of the genealogy, his predecessors had reigned for about thirteen generations, down from the times of *Gaidelglas*; he is therefore conveyed away back from *Spain*, first to *Scythia*, where he is made to serve under king *Refloir*; and thence to *Egypt*, where he married the second *Scota*, daughter to another *Pharaoh*, and carried her with him to *Spain*.

4°. ACCORDING to the *Scotish* (*a*) tradition, this *Milesius* sent indeed to *Ireland*, a second colony from *Spain*, with his sons *Heremon*, *Partholom* or *Bartholm*, and *Hybert*: these two last it seems remained in *Ireland*. But as for *Heremon*, he returned back to *Spain*, and succeeded his father *Milesius* in the kingdom of *Scots* in *Spain*, where his posterity continued down the race of *Scotish* kings for twenty generations, till the time of one *Eondulf*, son of *Edanglas*, or *Etheon*. This *Eondulf*, or *Fondulf*, sent a third colony to *Ireland*, under the command of his son (*b*) *Simon Breac*, who carried with him the famous fatal stone, and placed it as the seat of the kingdom at *Themor* or

(*a*) Fordun, l. 1. c. 21.
(*b*) Ibid. l. 1. c. 26.

Teambra;

Teambra; and thus founded the monarchy of the *Scots* in *Ireland*, about the time of *Manasses* king of *Juda*; that is, about six hundred years before the birth of Christ. From this *Simon Breac*, say the *Scots*, are descended all the monarchs of *Ireland*, and in after-ages those of *Scotland*. And this was the account of the beginning of the *Irish* monarchy, as the *Scots* had it from them in ancient times; and so, in all appearance, it was the first draught of it, invented by the bards.

BUT the succeeding *Irish* antiquaries were, it seems, by no means satisfied with this first plan of the *Milesian Scotish* monarchy in *Ireland*, which placed their settlement and beginning of their monarchy no sooner than about six hundred years before the incarnation: and being resolved to give it a much higher date, they pitched, for the founder of it, on *Heremon* son to *Milesius*, about twenty generations before *Simon Breac*; and therefore, whereas the *Scotish* antiquaries had told us, that *Heremon*, after visiting *Ireland*, had immediately returned back, and succeeded *Milesius* his father as king of the *Scots* in *Spain*, and there his posterity reigned after him down till *Simon Breac*: the posterior seanachies of *Ireland* would not have *Heremon* to return to *Spain*, but to remain in *Ireland*, and there set up the *Irish* monarchy, some say two thousand years before the incarnation, others thirteen hundred; and *Flaherty* at last hath criticized away about one half of the time, and settled the

Epoch

Epoch of the foundation of the *Milesian* kings in *Ireland* by *Heremon* about a thousand years only before the birth of Christ.

AND as for *Simon Breac*, whom the *Scots*, on the credit of or tradition of the *Irish* bards, (their only vouchers for all these high antiquities) had brought from *Spain*, with the fatal chair, to become the first founder of that monarchy: the later *Irish* seanachies will have him never to have been in *Spain*, nor out of *Ireland*, and appoint him the thirty-eighth king of the *Milesian Scots* in *Ireland*, from *Heremon*; and at last perhaps to hinder any ever after to give him the honourable title of first founder of that monarchy, the succeeding antiquaries (*a*) of *Ireland*, by that soveraign power they have, as well as their predecessors, to make and unmake monarchs, and dispose in their rythms, as well of their fortunes, as of their beings, have doomed *Simon*, as the fancy took them, some of them, to be hanged on a gibbet; others to be torn to pieces.

I am afraid, that those among the *Irish*, who still set up for these remote antiquities, will be dissatisfied with the placing on a level the *Scotish* traditions concerning these antiquities, with those of the *Irish*: for what is *John Fordun*, a private churchman, who wrote only in the four-

(*a*) Ogyg. p. 249. — Keating.

teenth

teenth age, when compared to *Cormac Culenan*, a king and bishop, author of the *Psaltar Cashel*; who wrote in the tenth age?

But, in the first place, *John Fordun*, as hath been elsewhere observed, hath this advantage over the *Psaltar Cashel*, that his chronicle is in print, and the publick in condition to examine and judge of it; whereas *Psaltar Cashel* is kept still in the dark, with the rest of the *Irish* seanachies works: so that hitherto no judgment can be made of it. 2°. It is to be considered, that neither the *Psaltar Cashel*, nor *John Fordun*, can be alledged as records sufficient to vouch or attest transactions passed about two thousand years before their times, such as the stories of *Milesius*, *Heremon*, and *Simon Breac*; but the authority, both of the one and the other, can be valued only in so far as it is supposed that they copied from more ancient writers. Now if *Psaltar Cashel* quotes, as we are told, the book with the white cover, that of the immigrations and some *Irish* poems for its authorities: *John Fordun* quotes for his *Chronica & alia Chronica*, *Grossum Caput*, *Legenda Brandani*, *Legenda Congalli*, &c. and why may not these last be of as great authority as the first?

3°. The main question here, is of the stories of *Heremon*, son to *Milesius*, and of *Simon Breac*, which of the two was the founder of the *Milesian* monarchy in *Ireland*.

It is, in the first place, agreed on both sides, that the *Scots* in *Britain* had originally their accounts of these high antiquities from the *Irish*: now if at the time, when they first received these stories from the *Irish*, it had been the common tradition of the bards that *Heremon* remained in *Ireland*, and was the first founder of the monarchy, there can no reasonable motive be assigned why the *Scots*, having that tradition from the ancient *Irish*, should have altered it, and held so positively, that *Heremon* returned back to *Spain*, and there succeeded his father *Milesius*; and that the *Scotish* monarchy in *Ireland* did not begin till about seven hundred years after *Heremon*; that *Simon Breac*, son of *Eondulf* king of the *Scots* in *Spain*, came to *Ireland*, and began the monarchy there. Whereas it is evident, that the *Irish*, and they alone, had interest to alter that tradition, and set up *Heremon* for the first king, and founder of the *Milesian* kingdom in *Ireland*, in order to attribute to their monarchy about seven hundred years of antiquity, beyond what the first inventors of the story had thought of, and to create the number of thirty-nine or forty new kings of *Ireland* before *Simon Breac*, whom the *Scots*, according to the accounts they had from the most ancient *Irish* seanachies, held for the first king of *Ireland* of the *Milesian Irish* race.

Besides

Besides that, *Fordun* assures us, that he had this account from ancient chronicles, as I said before, whom he quotes frequently for every particular story of these high antiquities; as he does also verses or rythms. We have a short old (*a*) chronicle in *Latin* rythm, written about the time of king *Alexander* II. or III. above one hundred years before *Fordun*, which gives the same account of *Simon Breac*'s coming from *Spain* to *Ireland*, with the fatal stone, or marble chair, and of his being the first founder of the *Milesian Scots* monarchy in *Ireland*, about one thousand and two years after the *Egyptians* were drowned in the *Red Sea* in *Moses*'s time; that is, about six hundred years only before the incarnation.

But what seems to confirm still more the *Scotish* account, (if the more ancient writers may be depended upon) and that the *Scotish* tradition concerning the time of the first coming of the *Milesian Scots* from *Spain* to *Ireland*, in order to settle, was the ancient tradition of the *Irish* themselves: what seems to prove this beyond dispute is, that *Nennius*, a writer of the ninth age, and by consequence more ancient than *Psaltar Cashel*, or any writer that

(*a*) Post obitum regis Pharaonis mille duobus annis ut recolo, &c. *Chron. Rythm. Scotor. in append. num.* 6. *cap.* 4.

the

the *Irish* have yet produced, (*a*) tells us in the first place, that he had his information from the *most learned among the* Scots, *peritissimi Scotorum* (which if the *Irish*, as they use to do, interpret *the most learned of the* Irish, the proof will be the stronger.) *Nennius* then tells us from these vouchers, that the *Scots*, descended of *Scota, Pharoah's* daughter, came to *Ireland* from *Spain* one thousand and two years after the *Egyptians* were drowned in the *Red Sea*, that is, only about five or six hundred years before the incarnation; and by consequence, their monarchy in *Ireland* cannot be more ancient.

THIS then was the constant belief both of *Scots* and *Irish* in those days, that is, before the tenth age, when *Psaltar Cashel* is said to have been written: and this account of *Nennius* agreeing entirely with the accounts given by the *Scots* in *Britain* of these high antiquities, and absolutely contrary to those of the modern *Irish*; shews that the *Scots* in *Britain* have carefully preserved the first draughts of these high antiquities, made by the ancient bards or seanachies; and that the *Irish* seanachies and writers have alter'd them since the ninth or tenth age, in order to raise higher the

(*a*) .... Siquis voluerit scire quanto tempore fuit inhabitabilis & deserta Hybernia, sic mihi peritissimi Scotorum nunciaverunt ... p. 101. ..... Et postea venerunt [*Scoti*] ad Hyberniam post mille duobus annis post mersionem Ægyptiorum in mari rubro, &c. *Nennius edit. Rog. Gale, c. 9. p. 100.*

beginning of the *Irish* monarchy, and to multiply their kings, by adding about forty ancient kings to their number.

And by this it appears, that the modern *Irish* abettors of their high antiquities are obnoxious to the very ſame reproach that they make to the modern writers of *Scotland*, of having placed the beginning of the monarchy of the *Scots* in *Britain* about ſeven hundred years before the true *Æra* of that monarchy, and of having added to the number of their kings in *Britain*, from *Fergus* I. till *Fergus* II.'s forty kings that had been unknown to more ancient writers. For by what we have ſaid, not only from the accounts of the high *Iriſh* antiquities preſerved by the *Scots*, but from thoſe of the beſt skilled among the ancient *Iriſh* in the ninth age; and by conſequence more ancient than any writer the *Iriſh* have as yet publiſhed in favour of them: from all this it appears, that the *Iriſh* in later ages have ſet up a long race of *Mileſian Scotiſh* kings in *Ireland*, amounting to the number of about forty, from *Heremon* till *Simon Breac*, all of them unknown to their more ancient and beſt skilled antiquaries, as we learn from *Nennius*, and pretended to have reigned above ſeven hundred years before the *Mileſian* monarchy was ſet up in *Ireland*. So we may juſtly conclude, that however faulty or fabulous the modern *Scotiſh* writers have been in anticipating the ſettlement of the *Scots* in *Britain*, and multiplying the number of their

kings,

kings, they did not deſerve to be reproached and inſulted, at leaſt by thoſe of the modern *Iriſh* writers, who abet with no leſs confidence a ſcheme of remote antiquities, that ſeems no leſs incredible and groundleſs than thoſe of the modern *Scotiſh* writers.

However by all that hath been ſaid in this article, it appears, that the remote antiquities of *Ireland* were not all invented or arranged at once, but grew up, with progreſs of time, to the height and order that we find them digeſted in *Flaherty*, and in their other modern writers; the firſt bards having brought them forth in a confuſed and ſhapeleſs maſs, ſuch as we find them in *Nennius*, and other ancient (*a*) writers; they were afterwards digeſted into a more regular form, with conſiderable alterations and additions: and in fine, by the care and induſtry of more poliſhed writers in after-ages, they were brought, by degrees, into a more tolerable conſiſtency, to render them credible, and cover their original deformity and palpable contradictions to all true ancient hiſtory, that would clearly appear, if they were expoſed to the eyes of the publick in their native original dreſs; towards hiding of which, nothing is of greater uſe than never to publiſh their pretended ancient original poems and bardiſh rythms whole and entire,

(*a*) See the preface to St. *Cadroe*'s life, and that of St. *Abban*, in *Colgan*'s lives of the ſaints.

but to content themselves, as they have hitherto done, to refer to them in general, or to quote here and there a few passages or extracts as taken from them, but keep the entire originals still from the sight of the publick, so as the reader, however skilled, can never be able to make any fixed judgment of the age, or veracity of these pretended original histories or annals: but this deserves to be considered apart.

ART. VII. *That the* Irish *shunning to publish their pretended ancient original histories or chronicles, such as they are, without addition or retrenchment, gives a just ground to suspect the credit of them, and of the remote antiquities built upon them.*

WE are now no more in those ages of ignorance and credulity, where detail'd accounts of transactions passed in the darkest and most remote antiquity, tho' supported only by confident assertions, that they were taken from unknown ancient writers or records, went easily down. Men have begun, long since, to measure their belief of remote antiquities, by the credit that the vouchers, on which they are grounded, have obtained, when, after being made publick, they have passed the examination of the learned: and all trifling and shifting to expose pretended ancient writers, whole and entire to such a tryal, is much the same as to abandon them, and give them up, since it visibly shews a diffidence that they cannot abide the test,

HENCE

HENCE a new objection against the credit of the pretended ancient writers of *Ireland*, and by consequence against their remote antiquities, is drawn from this, that the abettors of these high antiquities persevere to keep these pretended ancient monuments and documents of these antiquities from the eyes of the publick (whilst they load it with so many other writings, pretended to be taken from them) by which they give some occasion to suspect that they are afraid, that if these writings of their bards, or poets, *&c.* were made publick, whole and entire such as they are, they would be so far from finding any credit with unbiassed persons, versed in ancient history, that on the contrary they would lose that small credit, which the confident assertions of their abettors procure them, in hopes of their coming out at last to make good what they assert of them.

AND indeed it appears a very odd thing, as we have already observed; that tho' there is scarce a people in *Europe*, that pretends to have any knowledge or light of the ancient state of their country, within many ages of the times of which the *Irish* pretend to give us chronological, genealogical, and detailed accounts of theirs; from ancient documents or monuments of history, which they assure us are still in being; yet the *Irish* are the only people of all the nations in *Europe*, who have never as yet published so much as one entire copy of any one of these much boasted of old MSS. of their civil history and antiquities, written by any author that lived before these last three hundred years; whilst at the same time they have published in this and the last age above 20 volumes of dissertations on pretended abstracts of these ancient MSS. And whilst all other nations have published all they could find of theirs, and continue daily to publish all they can discover, good or bad, of ancient monuments or documents of the history of their country: and by thus exposing those remains of their ancient history to the judgment of the learned world; and comparing them with the certain monuments of the ancient received histories of the *Roman* empire, of those of their own and neighbouring nations, they come to discern the genuine pieces from the spurious, and daily correct the errors and mistakes which the ignorance and credulity of former ages had mix'd with their history: and by that means gain to it credit among the learned of other nations, and to themselves the reputation of sincere lovers of truth. It is upon this principle, and with this view that we have so many volumes of the *English* history publish'd, under the title of *Scriptores Angliæ*; of the *French*, by the title of *Scriptores Francici*, or *Galliæ*; the *Scriptores Germaniæ*, and other northern nations, *Scriptores Italici*, &c. And as to the *Scotish* history, tho' most of their historical ancient monuments are perish'd, by the occasions that we shall afterwards relate; what as yet re-

main

main are publiſhed; ſuch as the chronicles of *Maylroſs*, two editions of that of *Fordun*, the ſhort chronicle of *Edinburgh*: ſo that the *Iriſh* being the only nation of *Europe* that have publiſh'd none of their original ancient hiſtories, give the publick ground to ſuſpect that they themſelves diſtruſt their authority.

But whatever there may be of thoſe pretended ancient hiſtories or annals of *Ireland*, or *Iriſh* affairs, preceding the time of king *Leogaire*, in the fifth age; which Sir *James* (*a*) *Ware* tells us are *fabulous, or ſtrangely mix'd with fabulous narrations*: and therefore he thought fit, in his account of the kings of *Ireland*, to drop them, and begin the ſeries of the kings of *Ireland* no higher than from this *Leogaire*: at leaſt, as for that part of the general hiſtory of *Ireland* that concerns the tranſactions ſince the time of St. *Patrick*, as I doubt not but the writers of it may, according to their more or leſs antiquity, fidelity, and judiciouſneſs, be relied on, as well as the hiſtorians of like qualifications in other countries: ſo I cannot help renewing here the wiſhes which I made in the beginning of this chapter, that they would publiſh their more certain chronicles and annals; it being, as it appears to me, a very great overſight in them, and may prove very hurtful to the true hiſtory of the *Iriſh* nation; that this only certain part of it

(*a*) War. Antiq. Hybern. c. 4. p. 20.

is left so long in obscurity, exposed to all the accidents to which histories, never yet published, are liable: so that there being but a few copies, and sometimes one single copy of them, they are frequently all at once irrecoverably lost: it is a great oversight, that among so many able and well qualified men that country produceth, skilled in the *Irish* tongue, none of them hath hitherto published their original histories, with faithful translations, into *Latin*, that being the only sure means to preserve them to posterity, and to give credit to the citations drawn from them.

SUCH among others, that seem most worthy of being published, are said to be the chronicle of *Tigernach*, which Sir *James Ware* possessed, and is now in the duke of *Chandos*'s library, which is a very ancient MS. but seems not so entire as one that is often quoted by *Flaherty*; the annals of *Innisfall*, those of *Ulster* (*Ultonienses*) so often mentioned in all the *Irish* writers; the synchronisms of *Flannus* and others, giving an account of their history, from St. *Patrick* down to the invasion of the *English* in the twelfth age, as they tell us. It were, no doubt, much for the honour and advantage of the *Irish* nation that these were made publick, thereby to hinder them from being lost, by some such accidents as they (*a*) inform us so many others of their historians perished in former ages.

(*a*) Colgan. præf. vit. MSS. Hyber.

I have

I have insisted so much the more upon this subject, that I am persuaded that nothing could contribute more to the honour of the *Irish* nation in this critical age, than that some of their learned men would impartially consider these difficulties and objections, and such others as may be made against their remote antiquities; and either render publick such vouchers of them as may bear the test of these times; or according to the example of so many other countries, who had in former ages set up for such other high schemes of antiquity, drop them, and remove from their country the reproach of too great credulity: and instead of insisting on these uncertain accounts of so remote and dark ages, publish in a body of history, as other polite nations have done, and daily continue to do, the chronicles, and annals abovementioned, and others that still remain, which may serve for a solid bottom to a true history of *Ireland*, since the fifth age, that would do honour to the nation.

CHAP. II.

Chap. II.

That supposing even the certainty or probability of the ancient settlement and monarchy of the Milesians *in* Ireland, *or in general that of the* Irish *remote antiquities, yet it does not follow, that these* Milesians *were properly* Scots; *but that on the contrary it seems certain, that the* Scots *were not settled in* Ireland *till about the time of the incarnation, or rather after it.*

BY all that we have said in the precedent chapter, I hope it sufficiently appears, that the remote antiquities of *Ireland*, that is, the coming in of the *Milesian* colony to *Ireland* under *Heremon*, and their long succession of kings after him, during the space of twelve or thirteen hundred years before the incarnation, with the rest of the ancient facts they relate, are destitute of all those grounds and historical proofs proper to gain them credit with impartial competent judges of ancient and remote transactions of this nature; and by consequence, that no certain proof can be drawn from them, of the *Milesians*, as they call them, being settled in *Ireland* about twelve

twelve or thirteen ages, or indeed of their being ſettled there at all before the incarnation of Chriſt.

But now I add further, that giving and not granting, that thoſe remote antiquities, concerning the ancient ſettlement, monarchy, and ſucceſſion of the *Mileſian* race in general, were probable, (however uncertain they really are) the queſtion which I here examine would not for that be determined, but ſtill remain dubious, to wit, whether the people *properly called* Scots were ſettled in *Ireland* before the incarnation. I ſay the people *properly called* Scots, by whom I mean the predeceſſors of thoſe *Scots* whoſe name appears in hiſtory for the firſt time (as we ſhall ſhew) in the third or fourth age of chriſtianity; who coming to *Britain* generally from *Ireland*, and joining with the *Caledonians* or *Picts*, made war againſt the *Romans* and provincials in *Britain* in the fourth and fifth age; in a word, I mean thoſe *Scots* of whom the *Scots* in *Britain* are deſcended and took their name.

For it might poſſibly have happened, that the *Mileſian* race had ſettled in *Ireland*, as the modern *Iriſh* tells us, twelve or thirteen ages before the incarnation; and that there had been a ſucceſſion of kings of that race, from *Heremon* downwards, (as no doubt there were moſt ancient inhabitants, and many kings too in *Ireland*, of old, as elſewhere;) and yet that none of all theſe have been

properly

properly *Scots*, nor the *Scots* as yet ſettled in *Ireland*, but that they came only into it long afterwards, about or after the birth of Chriſt; and that in a body of men accuſtomed to war, ſo as to have rendered themſelves maſters of moſt part of the country, (as we ſee ſo many other nations invaded other countries in the third, fourth, and following ages after the incarnation) to have ſubdued the ancient inhabitants, overturned their government, and ſet up a new one; ſo that the chief leaders of this new people became the firſt kings of the *Scotiſh* race in *Ireland*, and their deſcendants ſucceeded and reigned after them, whilſt their chief commanders under them became the governing party, and brought moſt part of the ancient inhabitants, by degres, under ſubjection. Thus the *Francs* invaded the *Gauls*; the *Goths* and *Swevès* poſſeſſed themſelves of *Spain*; the *Vandals* became maſters of *Africk*, the *Saxons* of the ſouth of *Britain*.

THAT the *Scots* were not the ancient inhabitants of *Ireland* ſettled there about twelve or thirteen ages before the birth of Chriſt, but were a foreign new people, who after, or about the times of the incarnation, came in upon the ancient inhabitants of *Ireland*, and rendered themſelves, by degrees, maſters of them, in the ſame manner as the *Francs*, the *Goths*, the *Vandals*, and other foreign people came in upon, and ſubdued ſeveral provinces of the *Roman* empire, and by degrees incor-

incorporated themſelves with them: that this was the caſe of the firſt ſettlement of the *Scots* in *Ireland*, is what I conceive may be ſhewn by ſuch arguments, as conſidering the darkneſs we are in, for want of ancient hiſtorians, will ſuffice to render it at leaſt highly probable, if not abſolutely certain.

THERE are in general only two kind of proofs or arguments, by which the coming in of a new people in paſt ages upon the ancient inhabitants of a country, and the revolution happening upon it, can be made out. The one is the teſtimony of contemporary, or ancient writers: the other is drawn from the effects that naturally follow upon ſuch an invaſion and revolution.

As to the firſt kind of arguments, it ſuppoſes neceſſarily, that there are extant contemporary, or ancient writers, near the times of ſuch a revolution: ſuch teſtimonies we have from *Gildas*, *Beda*, and other ancient hiſtorians, domeſtick and foreign, of the *Saxons* invading the ſouth of *Britain*: ſuch alſo we have from the *Roman* writers, from *Gregory* of *Tours*, and other ancient monuments, of the *Francs* invading the *Gauls* in the fifth age.

WERE there extant any ancient received writers, foreign or domeſtick, near the times of the incarnation, that contained either the hiſtory of *Ireland*,

Ireland, or at least gave us accounts of the state and inhabitants of it, and revolutions that happened in it in these early times; we might then expect to find, as I doubt not but we should, such direct proofs of the *Scots* coming into *Ireland*, as we have of the coming in of the *Francs* to the *Gauls*. But by what we have said in the preceding chapter, it appears, there is not extant any certain *domestick* history of *Ireland* in those early times, nor for any thing that hath yet appeared, till at least eight or nine ages, (if even then) after the incarnation, nor any certain account of the transactions of *Ireland*, nor any certain proof that they had even the use of letters in *Ireland*, till the fifth age, when they received christianity.

THE most ancient pieces we have now extant, believed to be written in *Ireland*, are the confession or apology of St. *Patrick* their apostle, and his letter to *Coroticus*; both published first by *Waræus*, from several very ancient MSS. and again by *Bollandus*; and they are quoted by the most ancient writers of the saint's life; as they are also by *Usher*, *Colgan*; and are generally esteemed by the learned as genuine: among others by the judicious historian M. *de Tillemont*, in his church-history, where he prefers them to all that hath been written of St. *Patrick*, and makes them the foundation of the history of that saint. All this renders indeed those pieces very valuable, and they fur-

furniſh us with ſome light on the ſtate of *Ireland* in the fifth age, when they were written; but all they contain, is ſome account of that ſaint's life, and labours in planting the goſpel in *Ireland*, and of the people to whom he preached: but nothing of the hiſtory of *Ireland* in former ages.

As to foreign writers, none of them before the ſeventh or eighth age after the incarnation, gives us any diſtinct account of what paſſed in *Ireland*; and the little they have of it, proves rather that the *Scots* were not there in ancient times, ſince they are never mentioned till the third or fourth age among the inhabitants of it, as we ſhall preſently ſhew.

FROM all this it clearly follows, that the firſt kind of proof, drawn from the teſtimonies of ancient writers, domeſtick or foreign, ought not to be expected towards fixing the time of the firſt ſettlement of the *Scots* in *Ireland*, or the finding out whether the *Scots* were the ancient inhabitants of it, or not.

BUT there is a ſecond kind of proof or argument, drawn from the uſual effects with which ſuch a revolution, as the coming in of a new and foreign people upon ancient inhabitants, would be naturally followed; and this kind of proof, as it is the only one by which a fact of this kind, in a country

country ſo deſtitute of all ancient hiſtorians as *Ireland*, can be cleared; ſo I conceive that it can be made out by proofs of this nature, ſufficient to ſatisfy all impartial judges, that the *Scots* were not the ancient inhabitants of *Ireland*, and in poſſeſſion of it twelve or thirteen ages, or indeed before the incarnation at all; but were a new foreign people, who about, or rather after, the birth of Chriſt, came to *Ireland* as conquerors, and rendered themſelves maſters of it, in the ſame manner as the *Francs* came in afterwards on the *Gauls*, and as other foreign nations invaded and ſubdued other provinces.

To apply this proof to the *Scots* in *Ireland*, we need only obſerve the marks and characters which the earlieſt or ſureſt writers, or other ancient monuments furniſh us with, of the *Scots* at their firſt appearance in hiſtory, and in the times immediately following their being firſt mentioned in *Ireland* and *Britain*; and compare theſe marks with the firſt appearances and beginnings of other conquering nations, in the ſeveral countries which they invaded, and in which they ſettled; and in particular with the *Francs* ſettling amongſt the *Gauls*, becauſe we have a more diſtinct account of them: and we ſhall ſee the ſame marks and characters of the *Scots* being not the ancient inhabitants of *Ireland*, but a new and foreign people come into it about the firſt ages of chriſtianity,

anity, as appear in the *Francs*, in the beginning of their ſettlement among the *Gauls*.

1°. Tho' we had no diſtinct account from undoubted hiſtory and records, that the ſettlement of the *Francs* in *Gaul* was in the fourth or fifth age, yet it would be ſufficiently evident, that their ſettlement was no ſooner, by this, that we never meet, in any ancient hiſtory or record, with any people, ſettled amongſt the *Gauls* before the fourth or fifth age, called by the name of *Francs*; and that ſince the fifth and ſixth age, all writers make mention of the *Francs* as inhabitants of *Gaul*. In like manner, tho' we have no ancient hiſtory that gives us a diſtinct account of the *Scots* coming into *Ireland*, and ſettling there only in the firſt ages of chriſtianity; yet it appears an undoubted proof, that the ſettlement of the *Scots* in *Ireland* can be placed no earlier than the time of the incarnation, or after it; that the name of *Scots* was never heard of in *Ireland*, or indeed at all, till the third or fourth age after Chriſt; and that they are ever afterwards mentioned as inhabitants of *Ireland*, or of the north of *Britain*.

All ancient writers, before the third or fourth age, of whatever country, never called the inhabitants of *Ireland* but *Hyberni*, *Hyberionæ*, &c. and what is moſt remarkable, *Ptolomy* the geographer, in the firſt or ſecond age, tho' he names about twenty different people inhabitants of *Ireland*, never mentions the *Scots* among them, nor indeed at all. And as for the country of *Ireland*, I never find it called by any writer, before the seventh age, but *Hybernia*, *Ierne*, *Iris*, *Britannia minor*; and the name of *Scots* is never once heard of, or mentioned by any writer before the third age, as bishop *Usher* grants. I might add, that we do not find the name of *Scots* in any writer now extant, before *Ammian Marcellin* in the fourth age, tho', I doubt not, but the name is more ancient, and may have been mentioned in writers that are now lost.

But as to the passages of the pretended *Bengorion* and *Egesippus*, quoted by *Usher*, both *Usher* himself, and all good criticks, agree that they are passages of authors much posterior to the times in which those writers lived. And as to the passage, *Scoticæ gentes*, &c. cited by the same *Usher*, from St. *Jerome*, as being taken from *Porphyrius*, (tho' even allowing it, it would not reach beyond the end of the third age) this passage is not of *Porphyrius*, but St. *Jerome*'s own, in his letter to *Ctesiphont*, written only after the year 412. That this passage is not *Porphyrius*'s, but St. *Jerome*'s own; the epithet he gives there to *Britannia*, of *fertilis provincia tyrannorum*, seems to demonstrate. For when *Porphyrius*, about *A. D.* 267, wrote the book against the christian religion, to which St. *Jerome* alludes in that passage, there had scarce till then appeared from *Britain* any considerable tyrant, or usurper against the empire; whereas, betwixt that year 267 and 412, when St. *Jerome* wrote that letter to *Ctesiphont*, there had risen in *Britain* no less than seven tyrants or usurpers; to wit, *Carausius*, *Allectus*, *Maximus*, *Marcus*, *Gratian*, *Constantin*, and *Gerontius*; these four last one after another, a few years before St. *Jerome* wrote, which made him call *Britannia* deservedly fertile of tyrants or usurpers: so it appears, that this passage is St. *Jerome*'s own, and not of *Porphyrius*, and of consequence written after *A.D.* 412.

THE first time then that we find the *Scots* mentioned in any ancient author yet known, is in *Ammian Marcellin*, towards the latter end of the fourth age. All former writers that we can find, who mention *Ireland*, or its inhabitants, never call them but *Hyberni*, and the country *Hybernia*, *Iris*, &c. and never once mention the *Scoti* among its inhabitants: such are *Cæsar*, *Diodor* the *Sicilian*, *Strabo*, *Mela*, *Ptolomy*, *Tacitus*, *Pliny*, *Solinus*. All these and other writers, who speak of *Ireland*, some of them give a short description of it, and the names of its inhabitants; but none of them ever mentions the *Scots*. And this universal silence of all writers, before the fourth age, that spoke of *Ireland*, seems a sufficient proof alone, that the *Scots* were not of a much older settlement there; especially when it's considered, that all those that speak of *Ireland* after the fourth age, never fail to mention the *Scots* as inhabitants of it: such are next to *Ammian*, *Claudian*, St. *Jerome*, *Orosius*, *Gildas*, and others in the fifth and sixth ages.

2°. THE *Francs*, before their first settlement amongst the *Gauls*, appear in history as a people unsettled, roving up and down, and seeking fixed habitations, for about two hundred years before *Clovis*, who gave the first form to their monarchy, and gave them a fixed establishment amongst the *Gauls*: so also the first account that *Ammian* gives of the *Scots*, is as of an unsettled people at least in *Britain* (a): *Scoti per diversa vagantes.*

3°. UPON the settlement of the *Francs* among the *Gauls*, two people appear thenceforth in history as the mixed inhabitants of the same country, the *Galli* and the *Franci*: the first as the ancient; the second as new inhabitants, not heard of before. In like manner in *Ireland*, in the fourth and fifth age, two sorts of people appear as the mixed inhabitants of that island, the *Hyberni* and the *Scoti*: the first as the ancient inhabitants known in all ages before; the second, to wit, the *Scoti*, appear on a sudden as a new people, never heard of in *Ireland* till then.

4°. THOUGH the *Galli* and *Franci* appear as mixed inhabitants of *Gaul*, yet in the first ages after the settlement of the *Franci*, they are distin-

(a) Ammian. lib. 27.

guished

guiſhed from the *Galli* by their qualities as well as by their name. The *Franci*, as being maſters, or conquerors, or the military men, appear as the nobility and gentry; whereas the *Galli*, or Gauls, the ancient inhabitants, appear as the *Coloni*, or Commons, as being ſubject to the former: of all which, the learned *M. Du* (*a*) *Cange*, who makes this obſervation, gives us many proofs from ancient records. So after the ſettlement of the *Scots* in *Ireland*, though the *Scoti* and *Hyberni* appear in the fifth age as common inhabitants of that Iſland, yet they appear diſtinguiſhed by their qualities as well as by their names. The *Scoti*, as being the conquerors, maſters and military men, appear as the nobility or gentry, in the confeſſion or apology of St. *Patrick*, (written by him (*b*) in the fifth age, and ſo the ancienteſt piece we have written in *Ireland*) *Filii* (*c*) *Scotorum & filiæ Regulorum*; which he repeats over again in his letter to *Coroticus*, joining, in both places, the *Scotti* and *Reguli* as being ſynonimous equivalent terms; and again, *Una benedicta Scota nobilis*, &c. adding generally to the name *Scottus*, that of *Reguli*, or *Nobilis*: whereas he never calls the native *Iriſh* in thoſe pieces, but *Hyberionæ*, or *Hybernigenæ*, as being the commons and ordinary people.

(*a*) Du Cange Gloſſar. to 2. col. 522, &c. ad vocem *Franc.*

(*b*) Ub. ſupr. pag.

(*c*) Confeſſio S. Patricii apud Bolland. ad 17. mart. n. 18. & epiſt. ad Coroticum n. 6.

M. de Tillemont (*a*), in his Life of St. *Patrick*, takes notice of this distinction, after *F. Bollandus* (*b*).

5°. The Inhabitants of *Gaul*, before the *Francs* settled among them, lived most part quietly under the empire, except when forced to take arms against the many barbarous nations that over-run them, or when they were obliged to take part in the schisms or divisions of the empire; and we do not read, that in those times the *Gauls*, of themselves, took up arms out of ambition to invade or conquer their neighbour countries: but no sooner had the new nation of the *Francs* settled among them, but we find them every year in a warlike posture, ready to invade the neighbouring provinces, and enlarge their dominions.

In like manner we have no certain account, that the old inhabitants of *Ireland* used, in ancient times, to come over and invade the *Britains*, before the coming in of the *Scots* to *Ireland*; and it appears, by what *Tacitus* (*c*) writes from his father-in-law *Agricola*'s relation of them in *Domitian*'s time, that they were little accustomed to the use of arms, and so far from making inroads on the *Britains* of the north, or *Caledonians*, that the *Irish* were much inferior to them in military valor; since *Tacitus* tells us, that *Agricola* had often asserted to him, that with one legion, and a few auxiliary troops, *Ireland* might have been con-

(*a*) Tillemont, hist. ecclef. to 16. p. 453.
(*b*) Boland. ubi supra.
(*c*) Tacit. Vit. Agric. f. 233. n. 24.

quered

quered and possessed: whereas we see, in the same book of *Tacitus*, that the *Caledonians* were able to dispute their ground with a powerful army of the *Romans*, supported by auxiliaries, and commanded by so able a general as *Agricola*. So that in all appearance, in those ancient times, the *Irish* were accustomed to no foreign wars, nor had any ambition to make invasions or conquests without themselves. *Eumenius* seems indeed to suppose, that the *Britains* had wars with the *Irish*, as well as with the *Picts*; but he doth not tell us, whether the *Britains* made inroads on the *Irish* in their own country, or the *Irish* came over to invade the *Britains*.

BUT at the very first appearance of the name of *Scots* in history, we find them in arms, come over in warlike expeditions to *Britain*, joined with the *Picts*, invading the *Roman* empire, over-running the provincials, and giving work enough to the *Roman* legions; inspiring the same warlike temper into the old *Irish*, till, by degrees, the strength of the *Scots* came over and settled in *North-Britain*, where they continued ever after in the same warlike temper; and being by degrees united into one people with the *Picts* of the *Caledonian* blood, gain ground upon the *Saxons*, maintain their country against the *Danes*, who had vanquish'd the *Saxons*, and for many ages (except when divided among themselves) defend their country and liberty, againſt the united force of their powerful neighbours.

6°. THE country of the *Gauls* retained ſtill the old name of *Gallia*, and it alone, for a conſiderable time after the *Francs* had ſettled, and were generally maſters of it: and it was only afterwards, and by degrees, that the kingdom of the *Francs*, amongſt the *Gauls*, was called by the new name of *Francia*, from theſe new inhabitants. St. *Gregory the Great*, about the end of the ſixth age, is believed to be the firſt that gives to *Gaul*, or rather the kingdom of the *Francs* amongſt the *Gauls*, this new name of *Francia*: but after him, *Gaul*, at leaſt the kingdom of the *Francs* there, is indifferently called *Gallia* or *Francia*, from the new and old inhabitants. In like manner, (and this appears to me a deciſive argument for what I am here proving) *Ireland* retained ſtill the old name of *Hybernia*, or *Ierne*, in all writers, long after the *Scots* were ſettled there, as we ſee by *Oroſius*, *Claudian*, and other writers of the fifth and ſixth age; who, whilſt they call the inhabitants indifferently *Scotti* or *Hyberni*, never call the country but *Hybernia*, *Ierne*, &c. And it was only by degrees that it got the new name of *Scotia*, from the new inhabitants the *Scots*, but ſtill retained the old name of *Hybernia*.

St. *LAURENCE*, archbiſhop of *Canterbury*, in the beginning of the ſeventh age, is the firſt that

4 I find

I find who gives to *Ireland* the name of *Scotia*, in his letter mentioned by *Bede* (*a*) to the bishops and clergy of that kingdom. After him *Isidore*, in the same age, and *Adamnan* in St. *Columba*'s life; and from thenceforth it is called, for some ages, indifferently *Hybernia* or *Scotia*, as *Synonymous* names from the old and new inhabitants; till at last it quite lost the name of *Scotia*, which followed the *Scots* into *Britain*, and was by degrees wholly appropriated to the kingdom of the *Scots*, in the north of that island.

Now I would willingly ask, wherefore *Ireland* should have taken, in the sixth or seventh age, the new name of *Scotia*, never heard of before, unless it was from a new people of that name settled among them? since we see, in all histories and countries, that the ordinary occasion or cause of all other countries taking a new name, was from new inhabitants settling in them. Thus the *Gauls* took the name of *Francia*; a part of *South Gaul*, that of *Gothia*; other parts those of *Burgundia*, *Normannia*, &c. *South Britain*, those of *Saxonia* and *Anglia*; a part of *Italy*, *Longobardia*, and the northern parts of *Britain*, the name of *Scotia*: all of them from new inhabitants bearing those names. In fine, the *Irish* writers make use of this as an argument to prove (*b*) that the *Scots* in

(*a*) Bed. lib. 2. c. 4.

(*b*) Usser. Britan. Eccles. Antiquit. p. 380, 381, 382, &c.

in *Britain* were of much later ſtanding there than the modern *Scotiſh* hiſtorians will have them; that the name of *Scotia* is not given to *Scotland*, or the north of *Britain*, but in later ages.

AND now to conclude. By all I have ſaid in this chapter, I hope it ſufficiently appears that the *Scots*, properly ſo called, are not originally the ſame race of people with the firſt and ancient inhabitants of *Ireland*, but a diſtinct people that came into *Ireland* only after the time of the incarnation; ſince they bear ſo viſibly, in the fourth age, as much the ſame character of new inhabitants of *Ireland*, as the *Francs*, or any other of the many conquering nations of theſe ages, bear the character of new inhabitants in the ſeveral countries which they invaded, and poſſeſſed themſelves of.

As to the objections that may be made againſt what is here proved, that the *Scots* were a new and foreign people that came into *Ireland* only ſince the incarnation, and were not the ancient inhabitants of that iſland; theſe objections may be reduced to two heads, to wit, 1°. Thoſe drawn from the pretended ancient MSS. monuments of the hiſtory of *Ireland*; ſuch as are ſaid to be the book of *Tara*, *Pſaltar Caſhel*, their poets, bards, and other domeſtick writers. 2°. Thoſe taken from *Britiſh* or other foreign writers, which (*a*) has been mentioned already, as being no leſs favour-

(*a*) Supra, ſect. 1. c. 2. p. 184.

able

able to the high antiquities of the *Scots* in *Britain*, than to those of the *Milesians* in *Ireland.*

As to the first, to wit, the pretended ancient *Irish* histories, we have treated of them at full length in the former chapter; and by exposing the difficulties and objections made against them, have shewn how little they are to be relied upon, or rather how groundless they are in all that they relate of what past in *Ireland*, especially before the time of the incarnation.

I easily foresee, that one of the greatest objections that can be made against what hath been proved in this chapter, by those writers that are still attached to the remote antiquities of *Ireland*, will be drawn from their genealogies; which, as they are set down by *Keating*, *O Flaherty*, Dr. *Kenedy*, &c. are carried up from king *Loegaire*, in St. *Patrick*'s time, to *Heremon*, son to *Milesius*; and thence up to *Noah* and *Adam.*

But I desire, in the first place, that it be considered, that the pretended ancient genealogies of *Ireland* were not grounded and proved, as those of modern times, by any publick or private acts or documents: for as to the committee of nine, and the other pretended regulations upon these matters, attributed to some of their ancient kings and parliaments, or assemblies of *Tara*, all these must still remain as dubious, and as likely to have been the fabrick of more modern ages, as the genealo-

gies

gies themſelves, and the reſt of the detailed accounts of their other remote antiquities, till ſuch credible documents of them appear, as have never yet been publiſhed. And in particular, that their genealogies were not invented till they had the knowledge of the holy ſcriptures, (after the goſpel was preached in *Ireland*) appears by their carrying them up to *Noah* and *Adam*.

2°. THAT all the credit of theſe genealogies depended wholly upon that of the bards or ſeanachies, whoſe character we have ſeen: now when once theſe genealogies paſſed the memory of the preſent age, or a part of the former, that is, five or ſix generations, they could neither be proved true, nor diſproved, or convinced of forgery; for theſe genealogies conſiſting barely of ſingle names, joined together by the word *Mac*, without any proof, the drawing them up required no more skill than to collect names already in uſe, or invent new ones, ſufficient in number to carry up the genealogy of the perſon, whom they intended to gratify, from his father or grandfather, or ſuch of his predeceſſors whoſe names were as yet recent in the memory of men, till former ages, when no body could contradict; and ſo upwards, till they grafted the name at laſt on ſome branch of the genealogies already compoſed, (in caſe any ſuch were) which led up to *Mileſius*; whence, by former bards, the degrees were carried up to

Noah

Noah. There was in our own time a *Scotish* gentleman, of an ancient family, (*Urquhart* of *Cromarty*) who took a fancy to draw up his pedigree, from age to age, up to *Noah* and *Adam*, and caused it to be printed by the title of *Pantochronocanon*; (*a*) or, *Pedigree of the name of* Urquhart *of* Cromarty, *from the creation of the world, until the present year of Christ* 1652. I have seen the book, with many others, useful to this work, by the favour of the honourable *Archibald Campbel*, in his curious collection of rare books.

Now it could not fail, but the first bards or seanachies that invented the *Irish* genealogies, being ignorant of letters, and more yet of chronology, would naturally exceed in the number of degrees or descents, having no certain rule by which they could govern themselves; and so it happened: when afterwards there arose among them bards or seanachies that had some knowledge of history or chronology, they found themselves obliged to make considerable retrenchments of the number and names of their genealogies, and so by degrees reduced them; till at last M. *O Flaherty*, one of the most learned of their modern writers, comparing them with the scripture-genealogies, makes a new reformation of them, and cuts off a number of them to make them agree with the

(*a*) *London*, printed for *Rich. Baddely*, within the *Middle-Temple*, A.D. 1652.

longest

longest genealogy set down by St. *Luke*, as we have elsewhere observed (*a*).

As to the second kind of objections, that is, those taken from the *British* historians, the only objections worth the taking notice of, are those that may be drawn from *Bede*, or *Nennius*; and first as to *Bede*, (*b*) he supposes indeed that the *Picts* found the *Scots* in *Ireland*, when they, the *Picts*, first came into *Britain*, which was certainly, as hath been shewn (*c*) elsewhere, long before the time of the incarnation. But 1°. it is to be observed, that *Bede* in that same place seems equally to suppose, that the *Scots* came before *Julius Cæsar*'s time, or at least before the *Romans* were well established, from *Ireland* to *Britain*; so that none of these learned criticks, and especially the *Irish*, who reject the early settlement of the *Scots* in *Britain*, notwithstanding of the authority of *Bede*, can press his authority for the early settlement of the *Scots* in *Ireland*, from his mentioning of the *Scots* in that Island, when the *Picts* came in. 2°. It appears by *Bede*'s never mentioning the *Caledonians*, but calling the northern inhabitants of *Britain* by the name of *Picts*, at their first entry to the island, that he took his accounts of the ancient inhabitants of the *North* of *Britain*, and of *Ireland*, rather from the relation of

(*a*) Supra pag. 486.
(*b*) Bed. l. 1. c. 1.
(*c*) Supra Book I. chap. 3. art. 1.

those

those of his own time, than from ancient monuments of history; hence he calls the most ancient inhabitants by the same names that they bore in his own time. Thus with him, the first inhabitants of the *Northern* parts of *Britain* are called *Picti*; so likewise the inhabitants of *Ireland*, called sometimes *Scoti* in *Bede*'s time, are called *Scoti* by him at the first entry of the *Picts* to *Britain*.

3°. It may have happened, that the stories of the *Irish* seanachies, concerning the early coming in of the *Scots* to *Ireland* before the time of the incarnation, were already begun to be broached, and perhaps spread and believed by several among the *Irish* and *Scots*, in *Bede*'s time, that is, in the eighth age; so no wonder if *Bede*, who took his accounts of *Ireland* from the *Irish*, or from the *Scots* with whom he conversed, believed upon their telling him so, that the *Scots* were already inhabitants of *Ireland* and *Scotland* before *Julius Cæsar*'s time, or rather, before the *Romans* were fully established in *Britain*.

What may have probably given occasion to the first broaching those stories of the early settlement of the *Scots* in *Ireland* by the bards, and to their gaining credit among the *Irish* and *Scots*, was, that the *Scots* coming into *Ireland* in a body of men accustomed to war, and rendring themselves, by degrees, masters of the ancient inhabitants, as the *Francs* did of a part of the *Gauls*; the *Scots* became soon the governing party in *Ireland*

land, and by the third or fourth age were become the leading men, and possessed of the sovereignty and chief places of power, and by consequence had the dispensation of all favours and rewards; and that alone was a strong temptation to such men as were the bards, accustomed to flatter and cry up all that came to be in power, and able to reward them, to ascribe to the leading men among the *Scots*, ancient genealogies and far fetched pedigrees, or to graft them on the genealogies of the ancient inhabitants, in case any such were already contrived: and this was the more easy to succeed, and obtain credit in such ignorant times, that after four or five ages of settlement in *Ireland*, and twelve or fifteen generations, the time of the coming in of the *Scots* was begun to be forgotten, and they to be looked upon as ancient inhabitants: besides that, the *Scots* were, by that time, so intermixed as one body of people with the ancient natives, that what belonged to these last, was more easily and imperceptibly attributed to the *Scots*. There are but too many examples of fabulous stories and inventions creeping into history, and gaining, in less time, an almost universal credit in countries and ages much more polished than *Ireland* was in those times.

WHAT we have said here may also, in a great measure, serve to answer another specious objection against the *Scots* first coming into *Ireland*, only about, or after the times of the incarnation:

this

this objection is drawn from what hath been elsewhere (*a*) observed, of the order in which (*b*) *Bede* seems to place or rank the first settlement or coming in of the ancient inhabitants of *Britain*: first the *Britains*, next the *Picts*, in the third place the *Scots*; and after mentioning of the *Scots*, he speaks of the *Romans* coming in; and last of all of the *Saxons*. By this it would appear, that in *Bede*'s opinion the *Scots* came in to *Britain* before the *Romans*; and that by consequence, they must have been settled in *Ireland* some time before, since it is supposed that the *Scots* came at first into *Britain*, immediately from that island.

THIS indeed would appear to have been *Bede*'s opinion; and it proves very well, that the *Scots* were esteemed, in *Bede*'s time, to have been ancient inhabitants of *Britain*, and not lately come into it, in the fifth or sixth ages, as some *English* writers pretend: for there's no appearance, that *Bede* could have attributed so ancient a settlement to a people, who had been but about two hundred years in the island; since besides that by the fifth age, they had the use of letters, and by consequence their accounts of themselves might be more certain, the bare tradition, from father to son, of their coming into *Britain* in the fifth or sixth age, would be as yet so fresh in the memory of men of the seventh and beginning of the

(*a*) Supra, p. 195.
(*b*) Bed. l. 1. c. 1.

 eighth

eighth age, (when *Bede* wrote his hiſtory) that it ſeems not poſſible, that he could have been miſinformed, or ſo groſly miſtaken, as to ſuppoſe they came in above ſeven hundred years before.

BUT we muſt reaſon very differently upon ſuppoſition of the *Scots* coming in from *Ireland* to *Britain*, four or five hundred years before *Bede* wrote his hiſtory; that is, about the beginning of the third age of chriſtianity, (which we ſhall have occaſion elſewhere to examine) and that they came in by degrees, and in times, when the uſe of letters was not yet received, either in the northern parts of *Britain*, or in *Ireland*; where, by conſequence, all the knowledge of paſt tranſactions depended on the credit of their bards. In this ſuppoſition, the queſtion being about an antiquity of ſettlement or poſſeſſion, (which all nations, the more they are ignorant, endeavour to carry the higher, and to over-reach their neighbours) it was no hard matter for their bards to have advanced two or three ages, the firſt coming in of the *Scots* to *Britain*, and to have introduced among them, before *Bede* wrote his hiſtory, the opinion of their being come over to *Britain* before the time that the *Romans* entered it.

THIS ſeems ſo much the more likely, that the bards in *Ireland* having begun before *Bede*'s time, to raiſe the ſettlement of the *Scots* in that iſland to a much higher antiquity than it was in effect,

the

the bards among the *Scots* in *Britain*, being men of the ſame genius, could ſcarce fail to imitate thoſe of *Ireland*, and to carry up the firſt ſettlement of the *Scots* in *Britain* to more ancient times; and the later end of the ſixth age, or beginning of the ſeventh, was a proper time for that, when the kingdom of the *Scots* in *Britain*, eſpecially during king *Aidan*'s reign, had begun to make a more conſiderable figure in the iſland.

AND it would appear, that this advancing the ſettlement of the *Scots* in *Britain* was ſo much the more eaſy to be done, that they came not over at firſt in great bodies of men, but in ſmall numbers, inſenſibly, and by degrees; firſt to the neareſt iſlands, and thence, as their number increaſed, to the weſtern coaſts of the main-land of *Britain*, which the *Caledonians* or *Picts* yielded with leſs difficulty to them, in order to have them for auxiliaries in their wars with the *Romans* and provincial *Britains*.

THUS the time of the firſt coming of the *Scots* to *Britain*, not being remarkable by any conſiderable event or revolution, it was the ſooner forgotten: ſo that after nine or ten generations had paſſed in ſo dark ages, when there was no learning in thoſe parts, nor any records kept of paſt tranſactions, it was certainly much more eaſy for the bards of thoſe times to raiſe the firſt ſettlement of the *Scots* in *Britain* to a much higher antiquity, than it was in effect for posterior writers of the fifteenth or sixteenth age, in times of light and learning, to multiply their kings of the *Scotish* line, and to impose upon the nation, so as to have it received, and generally believed, a new scheme of antiquities, detailed into particular facts, with a new genealogy, and a new series of ancient kings; as we have already proved that it happened.

AND if an emulation, not to be behind in the antiquity of monarchy with the kings of *England*, particularly with king *Edward* I. who valued himself upon an ancient succession of kings in the *British* race, down from *Brutus*, *Locrinus*, &c. contributed not a little, as it will afterwards appear, to raise in the *Scots*, in the beginning of the fourteenth age, the first notions of ancient kings of the *Scotish* line, before the times of the incarnation; it is very likely, that the like emulation with the *Picts*, or a view not to be inferior to them in so honourable a privilege, as that of an ancient establishment, or ancient possession, gave occasion to the *Scotish* bards, about the seventh age, to advance the antiquity of the settlement of the *Scots* in *Britain* beyond the time of the incarnation. That this emulation, or vying with the *Picts* contributed to it, is the more likely, that, as we have elsewhere (*a*) observed, the *Scots*

(*a*) Supra, p. 125, 126, &c.

at laſt, after they came to be maſters of the *Pictiſh* kingdom, carried this emulation ſo far, as to pretend to have been eſtabliſhed in *Britain* as early as, or even before the *Picts* themſelves.

Now ſuppoſing that the ſettlement of the *Scots*, both in *Ireland* and in *Britain*, had been thus advanced by the bards of each country to more ancient times before *Bede* wrote his hiſtory in the eighth age, there is no doubt but what he relates, of the *Scots* coming to *Britain* before the *Romans* entered it, was upon the information of ſome of the natives that gave credit to thoſe new ſchemes of the bards.

I know ſome of the learned among the *Engliſh* and *Iriſh* writers, give a different interpretation to this paſſage of the firſt chapter of *Bede*'s hiſtory, and pretend that the *Scots* coming into *Britain* before the *Romans* doth not follow from it; and ſo it is no wiſe contrary to what I have endeavoured to prove in this chapter, to wit, that the ſettlement of the *Scots* in *Ireland* was not before the time of the incarnation. But I cannot help thinking that the interpretation, that theſe learned writers put upon *Bede*'s paſſage, ſeems forced; and have therefore choſen rather to endeavour to find out, by probable conjectures, the true occaſion of *Bede*'s advancing this paradox, than to elude the difficulty by an evaſion.

As for the paſſages of *Nennius* the *Britiſh* writer, which ſeem to favour the remote antiquities of *Ireland*, and which we have elſewhere ſet (*a*) down, it is evident by *Nennius*, that theſe remote antiquities were already begun to be hatched by the bards before his time; but as yet only in a confuſed maſs, very different from the more regular order into which they were afterwards digeſted by more skilful hands. Nor were the inventions of the bards in *Nennius*'s time, that is, in the ninth age, raiſed as yet to that height of antiquity by many hundred years, to which the fertile genius of the ſeanachies have, in poſterior ages, advanced them.

FOR, according to the reckoning of *Nennius*, who informs us that he had his accounts from the moſt learned of the *Scots* or *Iriſh*, (*a peritiſſimis Scotorum*) the firſt coming in of the *Scots* to *Ireland* was only about ſix hundred years before the incarnation; whereas the later ſeanachies have raiſed their ſettlement, and beginning of their monarchy in *Ireland*, ſome of them two thouſand years, others thirteen hundred before the incarnation: ſo that *Nennius*, far from adding any force to the ſtory of theſe remote antiquities, ſerves rather to derogate from their credit, by ſhewing the variations and novelty of their ſchemes of an

(*a*) Supra, p. 193.

ancient

ancient ſettlement and monarchy in the *Mileſian* race; as it hath been elſewhere (*a*) obſerved.

HAVING now ſhewn that the *Scots* are not the ancient inhabitants of *Ireland*, but a foreign people come in upon the ancient inhabitants, only about or ſince the time of the incarnation; before we enter upon the examination of the preciſe time of their firſt ſettlement in the north of *Britain*, it remains to enquire of what origine they were, and whence they came at firſt into *Ireland*.

CHAP. III.

Of the origine of the Scots; *of their name, and of the time of their ſettlement in* Ireland.

THE obſcurity in which the origine and remote antiquities of all the northern nations are involved, ariſes from their wanting all domeſtick monuments of ancient hiſtory, and for the moſt part even the uſe of letters, till they were poliſhed, either by being ſubjected to the *Roman* empire or by the light of chriſtianity. This we have ſhewn in particular, was, in all appearance, the caſe of *Ireland*, till about the time the goſpel

(*a*) Supra, p. 496, 497.

was preached there in the fifth age: so till that time we can expect no certain accounts of the revolutions that happened among the *Irish*, no more than of other barbarous nations without the *Roman* empire, or which did not border upon, or interfere with it. And far from finding any account of the *Scots* in the first ages of christianity, their name is not so much as once to be met with in history, or in any of the ancient descriptions of the world left us by *Strabo*, *Mela*, *Ptolomy*, *Pliny*, or any other of the ancient geographers; nor is the name of *Scots* ever so much as once mentioned till the third or fourth age, as hath been (*a*) already shewn.

So in this enquiry into their origine, or the time, of their coming into *Ireland*, the only light we must walk by, is what may be borrowed by probable conjectures, grounded upon such accounts as the *Roman* writers give us of the state of the several barbarous nations in the neighbourhood of *Ireland* in the first ages of christianity.

And first, as to the name of *Scots*; tho' it be no where to be met with, as it is now written and pronounced, before the third or fourth age, yet it can scarce be questioned, but originally it is the same as that of the *Scyths*; there being a visible resemblance betwixt the names of *Scythæ* and *Scoti*, and only some difference in the pronunciation,

(*a*) Supra, p. 513, 514, &c.

very

very usual in the names of ancient nations, according to the different accent or pronunciation of the several people that spoke or wrote of them. Thus as *Gethi Gethicus*, are the same as *Gothi Gothicus*; so also from *Scythæ Scythicus*, come *Scoti Scoticus*. These are (*a*) *Walsingham*, an *English* writer's words; and before him (*b*) *Radulfus de Diceto*, dean of *London*, makes the same observation. *Nennius* (*c*), in the ninth age, uses promiscuously the names of *Scythæ* and *Scoti* for the same people; and *Gildas* (*d*), in the sixth age, calls *Scythica vallis*, the passage through which the *Scots* used to invade the provincial *Britains*. The *Germans* to this day call both *Scyths* and *Scots* by the same name *Scutten*.

But what is most remarkable, the *Britains* in their ancient tongue, (as (*e*) *Camden* observes) call both the nations of *Scyths* and *Scots* by the same name *Y-scot*. I say this denomination of the *Britains* is most remarkable of all, because the *Britains*, on the first appearance of that new people in *Britain*, giving them the name of *Y-scot* or *Scot*, whether from their being originally *Scyths*, or rather from their resembling the *Scyths* by their habit, arms, and customs, gave a natural occasion

(*a*) Walsingham Ypodigma Neustriæ, p. 552.
(*b*) Rad. de Diceto inter X. scriptores Angl. col. 627.
(*c*) Nennius, cap. 10.
(*d*) Gildas, c. 15.
(*e*) Camden Scoti.

to

to the *Romans*, than in possession of the south of *Britain*, to *Latinize* the name of these new enemies of the empire, and call them *Scoti:* and thus the origine of the name is not from the *Scots* themselves, or the *Irish*, (in whose ancient language it was never in use, nor is it among our *Scotish Highlanders* to this day, at least among the vulgar) but a foreign denomination given them by the *Britains*, and from them by the *Romans*, and those that spoke or wrote in the *Latin* tongue.

THIS occasion and rise of the name of *Scots*, furnishes a very probable conjecture of the country of their origine, whence they came at first to *Ireland*. In order to make this discovery, we are, in the first place, to find a people lying towards *Ireland*, called by the name of *Scyths*, or using their customs, habit, and arms. 2°. We are to find such a people in a motion and circumstances proper for a transmigration to *Ireland*, in the first ages of christianity. And we are furnished by the *Roman* writers with people under all these circumstances in *Scandia*, to the north of *Ireland*, and in *Cantabria* to the south of it; both the most proper places to invade *Ireland*, and a people in both these countries under these circumstances, which used to put them on seeking out new habitations, and that precisely in the first ages of christianity.

And first as to *Scandia*, or the ancient *Cherſoneſus Cymbrica*, now including the kingdoms of *Norway*, *Denmark*, &c. it hath been already obſerved, ſpeaking of the *Picts*, that all theſe countries, to the extremity of the northern continent, were called by the (*a*) ancients *Scythia*, and the inhabitants called *Scyths*. And they are called by (*b*) *Jornandes*, *Officina Gentium*, the workhouſe of nations; becauſe of the great multitudes that have, like an inundation, ſpread themſelves from thence into moſt of the countries of *Europe*.

It is alſo to be obſerved, that thoſe northern nations, (among whom I comprehend not only thoſe of *Scandia*, but all without the furtheſt limits of the empire, and beyond what is now called *Flanders*) were all (*c*) ſubject to frequent changes of dwellings; 1°. Becauſe of their extraordinary multiplying, which put them under a neceſſity of changing their habitations, and dilating themſelves, as their number increaſed; and their houſes or cottages being only for a day's ſervice, made them eaſily abandon their homes. 2°. Becauſe there being no other law among them, than that of the ſtrongeſt, they were often conſtrained to abandon their habitations to a greater

(*a*) Diodor. Sic. l. 6. c 7. Strabo, p. 507. Plin. l. 6. c 13.
(*b*) Jornand. l. 1. c. 4.
(*c*) Strabo, p. 291, & 305.

force;

force; and being bounded by the sea, they were forced to embark to seek new dwellings.

Now by all the best accounts that we have of these early times, there's none more likely for such a transmigration of a colony of these northern nations to *Ireland*, or to the north of *Britain*, than the interval from the reigns of *Augustus* and *Tiberius*, till the third or fourth age, in which the name of *Scots* is first heard of.

These northern nations, till *Julius Cæsar* conquered *Gaul*, had a fair field on the continent, to discharge their superfluous brood, the *Gauls* and *Germany* lying open to them. But from *Julius Cæsar*'s time, down till the third age, *Gaul* being conquered, and the *Roman* empire being generally in its full vigour, their legions quartered all over, and upon the borders of the empire towards the north, and hemmed in the northern nations on that side; and the *Barbars* of *Germany*, being also kept in awe by the *Romans*, were forced to canton within their own territories, and so left no room for the more northern nations beyond them, to come in and settle among them.

Besides that, during the later end of the reign of *Augustus*, and the beginning of that of *Tiberius*, these northern nations were confined into more narrow bounds than ever before, and further pressed back: the *Roman* arms under *Drusus* and

and *Germanicus*, as *Strabo* (*a*), *Tacitus* (*b*), and *Dio* (*c*), relate, having penetrated among the *Cherusci* to the *Elb*, near the confines of the *Chersonesus Cymbrica* and the *Baltick* sea.

THOSE nations of the north being thus penned up by the *Romans* on this side, and having no discharge among the nations behind them, over-burthened with their own yearly increasing multitudes; it was very natural, that the most warlike and resolute among them, impatient of being thus confined and inclosed, should resolve to put to sea, to purchase new habitations: nor had they a more natural course to chuse, than to the opposite coasts of the north of *Britain*; or, if repulsed by these warlike inhabitants the *Caledonians*, to sail from thence to *Ireland*, where they were more likely to succeed among a people unaccustomed to foreign wars. Nor could their coming to *Ireland* be more seasonably placed, than during these first ages of christianity, when the *Roman* empire was at the height of its power and extent. Besides that, the placing their invasion of *Ireland* in these first ages, agrees perfectly with their first appearance in *Britain*, in the third or fourth age, by the name of *Scots*: there being some time required for their rendering themselves masters of *Ireland*, before they could be in a condition to send out

(*a*) Strabo, p. 291.
(*b*) Tacit. lib. 1.
(*c*) Dio, lib. 5

bodies

bodies of men, able, in conjunction with the *Caledonians* or *Picts*, to attack the *Roman* empire in *Britain*, as we see by *Ammian* they did, towards the middle of the fourth century. And thus far as to the probability of the *Scots* coming into *Ireland* at first from *Scandia* and the north.

BUT after all, since the *Irish* tradition will absolutely have the inhabitants of that country come from *Spain*, it does not appear very hard to satisfy them in that: for, 1°. This tradition may regard other colonies coming to *Ireland*, whereof some may probably enough have come from *Spain* to *Ireland* before the *Scots* settled there. 2°. We may allow that the *Scots* themselves came originally from *Spain*, and yet not depart from what we have settled, about their coming in to *Ireland* only about the beginning of christianity, and from their having their name originally from the *Scythians*.

FOR we find, under the reign of *Augustus*, by *Florus* (*a*) and *Orosius* (*b*), that the *Romans* met with extreme difficulty in reducing the *Cantabrians*, and *Asturians*, with other unconquered nations of *Galicia*, in the northern extremities of *Spain*, that look towards *Ireland*; and that the inhabitants of those parts, who were a very warlike people,

(*a*) Florus, l. 4. c. 12.
(*b*) Orosius, l. 6. c. 24.

and

and never as yet ſubdued, choſe rather, for the moſt part, to retire to the hills and rocks, and to the moſt deſert and remote places, than to loſe their liberty and ſubmit to the *Roman* yoke.

It is true, that *Florus* and *Oroſius*, who give an account of this *Cantabrian* war, do not expreſly inform us, that any colony of the *Galicians* left *Spain* on this occaſion, to ſeek a foreign habitation; but what they relate of their averſion to ſubmit to, and live under the *Romans*, of the extremities they choſe to be reduced to, rather than to part with their liberty, makes it very credible, that the moſt valiant of them would rather have abandoned their habitations, and ſeek out new ones, than ſubmit themſelves to the *Romans*. Moreover, the paſſage from thoſe parts of *Spain* to *Ireland* was very eaſy, they wanted not ſhipping, nor could they be unacquainted with *Ireland*; and that the conqueſt of it was not a difficult matter, the natives being ſo little accuſtomed to foreign enemies.

Now the people who inhabited thoſe northern provinces of *Spain*, were of old deſcended of the *Celtes* and *Scyths*: for we meet, in thoſe parts of *Spain*, both with the *Scythian* and *Celtick* promontories; and a part of the inhabitants were called *Celtiberi*. And whatever there may be of their origine from the *Scyths*, being hitherto an unconquered people, the retaining the manners and

arms

arms of the ancient *Scyths* and *Celtes*, might give occasion enough to the *Britains* to give them, when they first appeared in the island, the name of *Scyth* or *Y-scot*. And their common name in *Spain*, which no doubt they would bring with them, being *Gallæci*, or as some write it, *Callaici*, might have given occasion to their calling themselves, in their own language, *Gael* and *Gaelick*, as they pronounce it. *Pomponius Mela* (a), an author of these times, telling us that all those northern parts of *Spain*, from the *Celtick* promontory, to the river *Durius*, were inhabited by the *Celtes*; and that the *Artabri*, a people of these parts, were a *Celtick* nation, seems to prove, that though those people were also called *Scyths*, they were all nevertheless originally descended of the *Celtes*, and by consequence spoke the *Celtick* language, or a dialect of it; and the language of the ancient inhabitants of *Ireland* being also, as we observed before, another dialect of the *Celtick*, the new and old inhabitants of *Ireland* were sooner and more easily cemented together by degrees into one people, without any lasting difference in their languages.

To conclude, whencesoever the *Scots* came originally to *Ireland*, and from thence to the north of *Britain*, whether from *Scandia*, and other extremities of the north, or from *Spain*, I think what is here

(a) Pomp. Mela, l. 3. c. 1.

said,

faid may fuffice to fhew, with great probability, that they had their name from that of *Scyths*; whether from the *Scots* being originally of that people, or rather from their refembling the *Scyths*, on their firft appearance, in their habit, armour, and cuftoms; and that the placing their firft coming in to *Ireland* no fooner than about, or after, the times of chriftianity, is conformable to the fureft accounts that we have, in the earlieft times, from the beft hiftorians, concerning the ftate of thefe countries, from whence it is moft likely, that the *Scots* originally came out at firft to *Ireland*, as well as to the firft appearance they make in hiftory in the fourth age, by the name of *Scots* in *Britain*.

DISSERTATION II.

Of the writers of the Scotifh *hiftory, of the time of the firft fettlement of the* Scots, *and of the beginning of their monarchy in* Britain.

HAVING fhewn in the firft differtation, how little ground there is for all that the *Irifh* writers have delivered, about the ancient fettlement of the *Scots* in *Ireland* about twelve or thirteen ages before chriftianity; and made it appear, by all the fureft lights we can find in ancient hiftory, concerning the ftate of *Ireland*, that the firft coming in of the *Scots* to it was, in all likelihood, either about, or even pofterior to the times of the incarnation: it follows necessarily, in the same degree of certainty, that the antiquity of the settlement of the *Scots* in *Britain*, and that of their monarchy in the *Scotish* line, must be proportionably abated. By what hath been said in the account that we have already given of the *Picts*, it hath, I hope, appeared that neither the royal family, nor the inhabitants of *Scotland*, stand in need of the remote antiquities of the *Scots* in *Britain*, to prove their antiquity beyond that of any kingdom of *Europe*: and by the discussion we have made at length, of the accounts given us by *Boece*, *Buchanan*, and their followers, of their forty kings of *Scotland*, preceding *Fergus*, the son of *Erc*, commonly called *Fergus* II. it hath, I conceive, been made evident, that the history of these forty kings can be of no service, at least, among impartial judges, to the antiquity of the *Scotish* monarchy; and, as it is set forth by these historians, hath very much prejudiced the rights of it. This supposed, I hope that the lovers of truth, among the learned of our countrymen, will not find fault, after due examination, with the freedom that I have taken, in settling the beginning of our monarchy in the *Scotish* line, to depart from the schemes of our historians in modern ages; and that I take, among other vouchers, for my guides, the few remains that we have of our more ancient writers.

And therefore, in order to put what I am to treat of in a better light, it seems necessary, before

fore I enter upon the examination of the *Epoch* of the settlement of the *Scots*, and beginning of their monarchy in *Britain*, to give previously a short and distinct account of the writers of the history of *Scotland*.

So this second dissertation shall contain three chapters. In the first, I shall treat of the writers of our history. In the second, I shall examine the *Æra* of the first settlement of the *Scots* in *Britain*, and of the beginning of the monarchy in the *Scotish* line. In the third, for a general answer to all objections against what is here established, I shall endeavour to give an account of the different steps and degrees by which the remote antiquities of the *Scots* grew up, by length of time, in the several hands through which they passed into the plan of history, in which they are delivered by the modern writers.

CHAP. I.

Of the writers of the Scotish *history*.

I Shall reduce all that concerns the writers of the *Scotish* history to these three heads; 1°. Of the writers of our history in general. 2°. Of the many disasters befallen in past ages to the records and monuments of our history. 3°. Of the monuments of our history which yet remain.

ART. I. *Of the writers of the* Scotish *history in general.*

IT cannot be reasonably doubted, but that the *Scots*, as well as other nations, had anciently writers of their history long before *Fordun*; and even *Stillingfleet* (*a*) does not doubt of that. To say nothing here of *Gildas*, who, according to the most ancient account we have of his life (*b*), was born at *Alcluyd*, or *Dunbarton*, in the north of *Britain*; the most ancient pieces of history, written in *Britain*, that are extant, are of authors living in *Scotland*, and who wrote before the *Saxon* historian *Bede*. Such are *Cumineus* and *Adamnanus*, both abbots of *Ycolmkill*; who, besides other historical treatises, wrote the life of St. *Columba*, apostle of the northern *Picts*: these works are still extant, and received by all the learned; and in them are several passages, relating both to the *Pictish* and *Scotish* history, and to their civil and religious customs, the names of some of their ancient kings, and some account of their actions, above eleven hundred years ago. Nor can it be doubted, with any tolerable ground, but these same authors, or some of their successors, or other religious men in that ancient monastery of

(*a*) Stillingfl. Antiq. Brit. præf. p. xvii.

(*b*) The life of *Gildas* was written by a Monk of *Ruise* in *Little Brittany*, and published by *P. Mabillon Sæc. Benedictin*, tom. I.

Ycolmkill,

Ycolmkill, (where the kings of *Scotland* used anciently to be crowned before the union of the *Pictish* and *Scotish* kingdoms, and where they all had their burial-place till the eleventh age) it cannot be doubted, but some of the religious men of that monarchy, would record the succession, lives, deaths, and chief actions of the kings, and the more remarkable transactions of the kingdom.

THE same thing may be said of the ancient religious houses of *Abirnethy*, *Dunkeld*, *Kilrimund* or St. *Andrew*'s, *Brichen*, and others. Would all these houses, where, no doubt, there were men capable to write, against the custom of all other such places, in all countries, since they had the use of letters, in contradiction to the natural inclination of mankind, leave their posterity in ignorance? Were not their religious and civil interests so interwoven with the knowledge of past, and the preservation of present transactions, that they must be supposed to have been, against common sense, unmindful of the first, not to have recorded the last? In short, such negligence and supineness among men otherwise studious and knowing, would suppose either a formed design of entailing ignorance on posterity, or the extinction of all sense of humanity. Nor needs more be said, since there cannot be the least doubt, but that the *Scots* and *Picts* had anciently writers of history, as well as other nations.

An author of the twelfth age, contemporary to *Andrew* bishop of *Catness*, (who died (*a*) *A. D.* 1185) who is quoted by *Camden* (*b*), and is still extant: this ancient writer, in a description of *Albany*, the ancient name of *Scotland*, makes mention of our ancient histories in these words; *Legimus in historiis & chronicis antiquorum Britonum, & in gestis & annalibus antiquis Scottorum & Pictorum*, &c. (*c*) There were then extant chronicles and annals, containing the actions of the *Scots* and *Picts*, and these too of so long a standing, that they were esteemed ancient by an author of the twelfth age.

Art. II. *Of the many disasters befallen the monuments of the* Scots *history in past ages.*

As to the want there is at present, and in these later ages, of ancient histories, and other works of ancient writers among the *Scots*, this will not seem a considerable objection against their having had such in former times, to any who will consider the many disasters that have happened to ancient histories, MSS. and monuments, of all kinds, in our country: but it will rather seem a wonder, that we have any remains of them at all, after so general and redoubled misfortunes that have hap-

(*a*) Chr. Mayl. ad hunc an.
(*b*) Camden in Scotia.
(*c*) Append. num. 1.

pened to them; 1°. By casual accidents, more frequent in *Scotland* than in most other countries of old. 2°. By a set purpose, as our historians relate, of a powerful enemy, master of the kingdom, and a formed resolution to abolish or carry off all ancient monuments, records, or documents of past transactions, especially as to our civil antiquities. 3°. By the zeal of *John Knox*, and others of his spirit, among our first reformers, equally animated, and resolved to destroy all ecclesiastical monuments.

§. 1. *Of casual accidents.*

And in the first place, how great a loss of records of history and ancient monuments ensued, on the frequent invasions and ravages made by the *Danes*, in the famous monastery of *Ycolmkill*, during the ninth and tenth ages? (*a*) Historians reckon up no less than six different devastations of it in the tenth age: insomuch that St. *Margaret*, in the 11th, found it quite ruined, and rebuilt it a new; as (*b*) *Oder. Vitalis*, a contemporary historian, relates. What further destruction and loss of ancient records, over all the kingdom, happened by the wars with the *Picts*, before they had

(*a*) Chron. Inf. Hyensis ex Colg. Triade Thaumat, p. 498.

(*b*) Inter cætera bona, quæ nobilis illa hera gereret, Huense monasterium quod ... tempestate præliorum & longa vetustate dirutam fuerat, fidelis regina reædificavit. *Oderic. Vital. inter Scriptores Normanniæ*, p. 701, 702.

had totally submitted, by the ravages of the same *Danes*, especially in times when the houses, as was ordinary in those days, and long after, were generally all of wood: which is the reason we find often in our history conflagrations, not of houses only, but of whole towns, and sometimes many towns burnt in one year; as (*a*) *A. D.* 1244, no less than eight of the royal burghs, without any foreign invasion, were burnt to ashes; and many others, both towns, churches, and abbeys, at other times and occasions, especially on this side of the *Forth*, by the frequent invasions of the *English*.

§. 2. *Destruction of our historical monuments by king* Edward I. *of* England.

As to the second occasion of the loss of our histories, and other ancient records and monuments, it was not by accident or casual, as at other times, but, as our other writers relate, a formed design to abolish, if possible, for ever all memory of past transactions among the *Scots*. We have already mentioned how, after the untimely death of king *Alexander* III. of *Scotland*, in the debate among the competitors, especially betwixt *John Baliol* and *Robert Bruce*, concerning the right of succession to the crown, king *Edward* I. known among the *Scots* by the surname of *Longshanks*, having got himself chosen umpire betwixt the two

(*a*) Fordun, l. 14. c. 19.

con-

contending parties; and having in that quality obtained the custody of the kingdom, and thus becoming master of all the castles and strengths thereof, in order to put in possession of it which ever of the two should be found to be next heir by law and custom, under pretext of examining the order and right of succession, according to the use and precedents in former reigns in *Scotland*, to which he soon added a new pretence of searching in the *Scotish* histories and records, for proofs of his pretended superiority over *Scotland*, he caused a search to be made over all the churches, monasteries, libraries, and archives of the kingdom, and all the histories and ancient chronicles, to be gathered up; and getting them once in his possession, together with all the publick records, he caused some of them to be carried up to *England*, and burned and destroyed the rest.

KING *Edward*'s aim and intention in this was palpable enough, to wit, that the *Scots* being quite destitute of all certainty of past transactions, and deprived of all proofs and evidences of their just rights and privileges, as well as of the knowledge of all the brave actions of their ancestors, he might more easily enslave them, and impose what he pleased upon them without their being in a condition to produce either history or record, to defend themselves, or dispute his pretensions. And we have too visible proofs of this destruction of our histories and records, and in consequence, of

the

the ignorance in which the *Scots* were, of the ancient ſtate and hiſtory of the kingdom: we have, I ſay, too full proofs of this, in the debate and proceſs about our independency, *A.D.* 1301, before pope *Boniface* VIII. and in the *Scotiſh* nobility's letter to pope *John* XXII. *A.D.* 1320.

It appears, by the *Engliſh* writers and publick records, that king *Edward*'s animoſity againſt all the titles or marks of honour, or antiquity of the monarchy of *Scotland*, carried him to take away or deſtroy all that could preſerve the memory of its being a kingdom, ſuch as the crown and the *Regalia* (*a*), the famous ſtone (*b*) chair in which our kings uſed to be enthroned; and even the abby of *Scoon* itſelf, where they were wont to be crowned. This ſame animoſity he tranſmitted to his ſon *Edward* II. during whoſe reign we meet with repeated remarks (*c*) of his preſſing ſolicitations to the pope to have that abbey deſtroyed, or removed elſewhere.

But of this ſearching for, deſtroying or carrying off our records or hiſtories, we have ample proofs, not only in *Boece* and our other modern hiſtorians, but in writers and records, both *Scotiſh*

(*a*) Math. Weſtmonaſt. 428. n. 17, 18.

(*b*) Walſingham.

(*c*) Rymer's Fœder. tom. II. p. 1000, 1003, 1031, 1043.

and

and *English*, much more ancient; and some of these very times.

We have the fullest account of it in the preface to the chronicle of *Couper*, which I have set down already, written about three hundred years ago, in these words; *At ipse* (*R.* Edwardus) *statim occasione, ut prætendebat, cognoscendi quis eorum* (Bayliol *an* Bruce) *per vetustorum grammatum indagationem, pleniorem in regno* (Scotiæ) *vindicare poterat facultatem, rimatis regni cunctis librariis, & ad manus ejus receptis authenticis & antiquatis historiarum chronicis, aliquantas secum & ad Angliam abstulit, reliquas vero flammis incinerandas despicabiliter commisit.*

All the continuators of *Fordun*'s history, in the fifteenth age, take notice of these searches made every where, by king *Edward*'s order, for the ancient annals and chronicles of *Scotland*; among others, the continuation of *Fordun*, attributed to bishop *Elphinston* in the *Bodleian* library, gives much the same account of this enquiry as the rest; and that king *Edward* was not content to make search through *Scotland* alone, but in all places where any *Scotish* history might be found; (*b*) *Exquiruntur interim gesta & chronica tam in regno Scotiæ, Angliæ, Hyberniæ, quam Franciæ;... non tantum de jure & consuetudine eorum*

(*a*) Supra, p. 205, 206.

(*b*) Scotichron. (Elphinston) MSS. bibl. Bodl. I 8. c. 11.

(competitorum)

(competitorum) *propter decisionem quæstionis inter Robertum de Broys & Joannem de Balliolo, verum etiam magis ad investigandum & inquirendum de jure regis Angliæ super subjectione regni Scotiæ.* By this we see the endeavours king *Edward* made to get into his hands all chronicles and histories of *Scotland*; not only those within the kingdom, but those also that might be in *England*, *Ireland*, and that part of *France* where he was master.

For a further proof of the histories of *Scotland* in being at the time of this search, made by *Edward* for them, and carried to him, to be inspected for deciding the right of the competitors; (a) *Knygbton*, an *English* writer, informs us expresly, that king *Edward caused a search to be made for all the chronicles in the monasteries, and in all places of the kingdom of* Scotland, *and caused them to be brought up to him and examined, concerning the order of succession in the preceding times, for the space of 15 reigns, or successions backwards,* which reached back to the reign of king *Keneth* III. in the tenth age. No doubt these chronicles contained the history of the *Scotish* kings, from the beginning; but there was no

(a) Statimque rex (Edwardo) pro certiori fide habenda fecit quærere & examinare omnes chronicas in abbatiis cunctis locis regni (Scotiæ) per datam quindecim regum Scotiæ *Knygbton inter X. scriptores Angliæ. col.* 2469. *n.* 63.

occasion,

occasion, in the present debate betwixt the competitors, concerning the right of hereditary succession, of going farther back than to this *Keneth* III. he being the author of the law for establishing more fixedly the succession to the immediate heir, of what age soever; as all our historians (*a*) agree: the account of the succession of the kings, who preceded *Keneth* III. could not be so serviceable to the decision of the present case.

But we have an ample testimony of king *Edward*'s carrying off, or destroying our records, histories, and all the ancient monuments of the kingdom, from a publick document of these very times, presented *A. D.* 1301 to pope *Boniface* VIII. in the name of the three states of the kingdom of *Scotland*, whereof I shall have occasion to give a fuller account. At present I shall only remark what they say of the want they were in of their ancient records and histories, by the havock made of them by king *Edward*; by which the *Scots* were deprived of many helps these records and titles would have furnished them in the defence of their rights and privileges: (*b*) *De iis autem omnibus & aliis regni Scotiæ defensionibus, libertatibus & juribus existentia monumenta publica in thesauraria regni Scotiæ, idem rex Angliæ* (Edwardus)

(*a*) Fordun, l. 4. c. 29.

(*b*) Instructiones prelat. baron & conf. Scotiæ contra R. Edw. ap. Scotichron. l. 8. c. 52. edit. Th. Hearne, p. 855, & 876.

wardus) *cum regni Scotiæ habuit custodiam ex eadem thesauraria abstulit, & vi & metu secum in Anglia cum multis aliis bullis, cartis & munimentis regni Scotiæ, cum quibus confirmabantur regni Scotiæ privilegia memorata & libertates*, &c.

ANOTHER, no less authentick document, we have, dated the 12th of *August* 1291, printed by *Prinn* (a) among his collections from the rolls. It is a precept of king *Edward*'s to the keepers of *Edinburgh* castle, to deliver up all the charters, instruments, rolls and writs whatsoever, that might concern the rights of the competitors, or his own pretended title to the superiority of *Scotland*, to be carried off, and placed where he should appoint; and these to be put into the hands of five persons, two *Scots*, and three *English*; and these last to act by themselves, if the two first happened to be hindered. All which was accordingly executed; and all either lost or destroyed, or carried up to *London*; whereof the remains of our records, partly printed by M. *Rymer*, partly to be met with as yet in the tower of *London*, and archives of *Westminster*, make too evident a proof. Among others, there's in the *Cotton* library, (*Nero* *C.* III.) an inventory of the instruments touching the kingdom of *Scotland*, kept in the archives of *Westminster*; whereof one hath for title, *Tres sce-*

(a) Prinn's collect. tom. II. p. 545.

dula

dulæ facientes mentionem de bullis chartis & aliis inventis in thesauro regis Scotiæ apud Edinburgh.

AND as to *Edward*'s carrying up to *England* what was not destroyed of our histories; 1°. The chronicle of *Maylres*, continued till near these times, as both the subject and character of the writing manifests, and abruptly broken off a few years before king *Edward*'s invasion, may be reckoned, for one proof, sufficient enough. It is still preserved in the *Cotton* library in the original MS. 2°. In the same library there are other two MSS. which contain extracts of four different chronicles of *Scotland*; the first is (*Claudius D.* VII.) and contains a collection of many extracts of different histories, whereof the fourth bears the title of *Nomina regum Scottorum qui regnaverunt post Pictos*; and this extract is written before *John Fordun*'s history. This series of our kings is taken from two of our ancient chronicles compared together. The author marks their differences thus, *In alio libro sic*, &c. The other MS. is *Vitellius A.* 20, under the title of, *Historia Angliæ a Bruto ad A. D.* 1348. In the end of this collection, the author gives a chronological series of our kings that reigned since the *Picts*, with a short account of their lives, from two other *Scotish* chronicles, distinct from the former. So we see these two *English* writers had in *England* no less than four distinct books, or chronicles of *Scotland*; all much older than *Fordun*. I might also reckon, among the

the remains of our chronicles carried up to *England*, that chronicle of *Edinburgh*, publiſhed in *Anglia Sacra:* for it cannot be doubted, but the latter part of that chronicle was written by a canon of *Holy-Rood-Houſe*. In ſhort, almoſt all that remains to us, of monuments of our civil hiſtory, antecedent to king *Edward*'s I's invaſion, have been found in *England*; ſome of which will be in particular mentioned hereafter, and inſerted in the appendix.

AND how many more of this kind have been carried up, of which we have no account? As to theſe two extracts of our *Scotiſh* chronicles in the *Cotton* library, made by *Engliſh* writers, the intention of theſe collectors being only to extract the ſeries of the kings of *Scotland*, from the union of the *Pictiſh* and *Scotiſh* kingdoms in one monarchy, as the title bears, they begin their extracts no farther up; tho', it is very likely, that theſe *Scotiſh* chronicles, whence they are taken, contained a compleat hiſtory, or ſeries of our kings, from the beginning of the monarchy.

HOWEVER that be, theſe chronicles are now no where, that we can hear of, to be found entire; nor have we any compleat chronicle or hiſtory of our kings, from the beginnning, more ancient than that of *John Fordun*.

AFTER

AFTER all, it must be considered, that king *Edward* was a declared enemy of the *Scotish* nation; and was, besides, animated against them by their unrelenting endeavours to shake off his yoke. Their frequent rising in arms to recover their liberty, after he had thought them totally subdued, enraged him against them, and made him resolve to destroy all marks of a kingdom, or a free nation, and all that could renew the memory of their ancient glory and independency. But we do not find that he designedly either burnt their churches or religious houses; or that, with the civil histories and records, he either carried off, or destroyed the writs, records, registers, or libraries of their churches. The destruction of these was reserved for other hands, and those too of natives of *Scotland*.

§. 3. *Destruction of historical, and of other ancient monuments, at the* Scotish *reformation.*

THE third loss, or destruction of ancient records, histories, and all sorts of MSS in *Scotland*, and chiefly those relating to ecclesiastical matters, was occasioned by the zeal of our first reformers in the sixteenth age. It is with reluctancy that I revive the memory of that tragedy; but I cannot but give here an account of it, in order chiefly to answer the objection drawn from the few remains that are now to be found in *Scotland*, of records, ancient hiſtories, and MSS. of any kind, if compared with the plenty they have ſtill of them in *England*, notwithſtanding the reformation equally made in that kingdom; from whence it is inferred, by ſome that are not enough acquainted with the tranſactions at the reformation in both kingdoms, that the ſcarcity which we have ever ſince in *Scotland* of MSS. muſt proceed from there having been but few of them even before the reformation, otherwiſe why might there not have remained after it as many ancient MSS. in *Scotland*, in proportion, as in *England?*

To anſwer this objection, drawn from the few remains of MSS. we have ſince the reformation, it is ſufficient to expoſe the plain matter of fact, from proteſtant writers, who lived at or near that time; and, in the firſt place, to obſerve the vaſt difference there was as to records and MSS. betwixt the method by which the reformation was carried on in *England*, and that in which it was hurried on in *Scotland*.

1°. In *England* the reformation was begun and carried on by authority of the ſovereign, and had the outward countenance of legal proceedings. In *Scotland* the ringleaders of the reformation, far from any countenance of the ſovereign, or laws, were in open rebellion againſt the queen, then their ſovereign, and acted in defiance of all the then ſtanding laws.

2°. In

2°. IN *England* the cathedral churches, with all their buildings, records and libraries, were left untouched, at least in the first heat of the reformation. In *Scotland* the buildings, records, archives, and libraries of the cathedrals, were no more spared, than those of the abbeys and monasteries.

3°. IN *England* the suppressing or defacing of abbeys and monasteries was not permitted to the multitude or rabble, but (*a*) deputies on purpose appointed by authority, with express order to preserve all things of value, to register, and make an account of them; and in particular, care was taken to preserve all evidences, MSS. and records.

AND under the reign of king *Henry* VIII. upon the dissolution of the abbeys and monasteries, so great care was taken for the preservation of all ancient monuments of history, that *A.D.* 1543, (*b*) by a special writ of that king, commission was given to *John Leland*, a learned and zealous antiquary, *to peruse and search all the libraries of the monasteries and colleges throughout the whole realm that were then dissolved and broken up, that as much as might be, all ancient monuments of the land... might be preserved.* And notwithstanding

(*a*) Burnet's Hist. Ref. tom. 1. Collect. p. 152.

(*b*) Strype's Memorials of the Reformation, vol. I. p. 385.

all these precautions, *Leland* tells us that many of these monuments were destroyed.

How much more in *Scotland*, where no such precaution was used, nor was it practicable, the government being at the time unhinged; and the executioners of this reformation of churches, as it was called, being the gentlemen of the congregation and an inconsiderate multitude, with arms in their hands against their sovereign, led on by the fiery exhortations of their new preachers, with a blind zeal to burn and destroy all monuments of religion, as superstitious and idolatrous; and particularly animated against all MSS. and records, relating to religion, in order to abolish the memory of what they termed idolatry; and especially to burn all books that had red letters, as belonging to the popish worship, by which means such MS. histories that came in their way, were sacrificed without distinction, all of them having the titles in *miniature*, or red letters, as well as books of liturgy or laws: and even in the burning the books of the old liturgy, we made considerable historical losses; for 'tis to be observed, that frequently in old missals, breviaries, and such others, where there were, at the beginning or end, blank leaves; the churchmen, or religious men of these times, used to fill them up for their own use, with extracts or copies of parts of the history or chronology of the country. I have seen some of this kind; but the most valuable I have met with,

was

was at *Drummond-Castle*, the ſeat of the noble family of *Perth*; where, among the remains of an ancient library belonging to it, I found in an ancient breviary, on vellum, written about the end of the fourteenth age, an exact chronology, beginning *A. D.* 1067, at the marriage of *Malcolm* III. and *S. Margaret*, and from thence down till about *A. D.* 1390, (when it appears to have been written) containing the principal tranſactions of the kingdom, each with its proper date of the year, and often of the day and month. In the ſame library there is, among other MSS. a valuable ſacramentary, or miſſal, in a *Saxon* or *Iriſh* character, that appears to be about ſeven hundred years old, in the ſame character as the MS. ſacramentary, entitled, *Miſſa S. Columbani*, in the advocates library at *Edinburgh*.

And I doubt not, but if I had been able to travel, and been allowed freedom to go through the kingdom into the ancient ſeats of others of our nobility and gentry, I might have met with others of that kind. For what were ſaved of the monuments of hiſtory, ſuch as ſome of the copies of the *Scotichronicon*, and a few others, owed their preſervation to the care of ſome noblemen or gentlemen, into whoſe hands they happened to fall, when all was going to wreck.

4°. In *England* the reformation, as to religious places, was carried on gradually by certain ſteps, and thoſe authorized by publick acts of parliament or commiſſions: all which were as many warnings to thoſe concerned, to prepare againſt the ſtorm. In *Scotland* nothing contributed more to the general loſs of records, MSS. and monuments of hiſtory, than that ſudden and unforeſeen invaſion, plundering, and burning of religious houſes: like a hurricane, or violent ſtorm, that drove all before it, before any body, but the contrivers, was aware; and what is moſt to be lamented, this ſtorm fell more violently and more ſuddenly on theſe religious places which were the chief repoſitories of ancient records and MSS. and which being more remote from the invaſions of *England*, had been, till then, preſerved more entire. To inſtance in a few examples.

IN St. *Andrew's*, as being the metropolitan church, were kept the chief eccleſiaſtical records of the kingdom; and being the moſt ancient ſeat, and in great veneration even in the time of the *Pictiſh* kings, the moſt ancient records or hiſtories, both of the *Picts* and *Scots*, were more ſafely preſerved there than any where elſe, being moſt remote from the ordinary ſeat of war. And now of all thoſe ancient monuments, we hear not of any other remaining, but one or two chartularies. The reaſon is obvious, *John Knox* himſelf (*a*), who carried on the work, tells us the reformation at

(*a*) Knox's Hiſt. p. 150.

St.

St. *Andrew's*, that is, the ransacking some churches, and razing others, was carried on, all on a sudden, with expedition, upon an exhortation which he himself made to the people, on our Saviour's driving the buyers and sellers out of the temple, whereby he so (*a*) inflamed the rabble, that they went instantly to work, and made spoil of the churches, burnt the archives, and razed the monasteries of the *Black* and *Grey Friers*.

SCOON was the place appointed for the coronation of our kings, where, till the time of king *James* I. all the great councils or parliaments used frequently to be held; and, by consequence, where the accounts of all publick transactions were most likely to be preserved: yet we have nothing left of all these ancient records; and no wonder, for on the 28th of *June* 1559, as (*b*) *Spotswood* and (*c*) *John Knox* relate, the royal palace, and chiefly the church and abbey, were totally consumed to ashes by the furious reformers of *Dundee* and *Perth*: notwithstanding that *Knox*, as he says, and others of the chief reformers, being content that the church was reformed, that is, spoiled and plundered, endeavoured to stop the fury of the mobb from burning the palace and church; but in vain. The people, once possessed by his declamations, that all such places were to be

(*a*) Spotwood's Hist. p. 123, 124.
(*b*) Ibid. p. 125.
(*c*) Knox's Hist. p. 155.

made sacrifices of, were not to be stopt in the heat of their fury.

THE *Black Friers*, or *Dominicans* of *Perth*, *Domus fratrum prædicatorum de Perth*, was famous for being the ordinary place of meeting of all our national councils, which by an order settled above five hundred years ago, were to be yearly kept by all the bishops and clergy of the kingdom; and whereof we have on record an account of many such councils held anciently in *Scotland*, both in that church, and in others. I shall subjoin to this §. an index of the dates of such of these councils, as I have met with on record; but, except the copy of the canons preserved in a chartulary of *Aberdeen*, I could never as yet hear of the acts or canons of any of them before the year 1549. The reason is plain, these acts and canons, besides the authentick copies deposited in St. *Andrew's*, and other churches, were of course kept in the archives of this convent of the *Dominicans* of *Perth*, to be represented at each council: now this convent and church suffered the same calamity as that of St. *Andrew's*, or rather a greater, with no less expedition and suddenness. Upon the 11th of *May* 1559, the reformers being assembled in arms against their sovereign at *Perth*, after a vehement declamation of *John-Knox* against churches and convents, as monuments of idolatry, and inforcing the commandment of God for destroying all such places, the rabble rose and destroyed

ſtroyed not only this convent and church of the *Black Friers*, but thoſe of the *Grey Friers*, and of the charter-houſe, or *Carthuſians*, (a building, ſays (*a*) *Knox*, of wonderous coſt and greatneſs) all theſe were ſo deſtroyed, that in two days time the walls only remained of all theſe ſtately edifices. It is *Knox* himſelf who hounded out, or led on the furious mobb in this wretched expedition, that hath thought fit to record it, with many other ſuch noble exploits, more becoming the *Goths* or *Vandals*, than an apoſtolical man, as he pretended to be. This made *Johnſton*, a zealous proteſtant writer, but a lover of his country, ſpeaking of the miſchiefs that *Knox* occaſioned to the kingdom, charaсterize him as a man (*b*) *famous for the burning of churches, and for the renewing*, in his native country, *the barbarous devaſtation of the* Vandals, *&c.*

These were a part of the exploits of our reformers, againſt all ancient religious monuments of their native country, performed in the firſt year of their ſetting up, and may be chiefly attributed to the rabble, inflamed by the violent de-

(*a*) Knox's Hiſt. p. 136, 137.

(*b*) Verum enimvero Johannes Knoxius templorum incendiis, & Wandalica vaſtitate notiſſimus, qui priſcæ pietatis monumenta, obtentu religionis diruit, companas & plumbea eccleſiarum tecta ſacrilega rapacitate invaſit, inteſtinis diſſidiis accendendis acerrimam facem prætulit. *Rob. Johnſton hiſt. rerum Britan. Amſtelod.* 1655. *p.* 2. *n.* 40.

clamations

clamations of their new preachers. But, as if the fate of the new reformation had depended on abolishing all memory of antiquity in the kingdom, the exploits of the second year were more fatal to all remains of ancient monuments, records, or history, than all that had hitherto happened.

THE leading men of the reformation met together in their usual manner, without the commission or authority of their sovereign; and, among other acts, *passed one*, says archbishop (*a*) *Spotswood*, *for demolishing cloisters and abbey churches, such as were not yet pulled down; the execution whereof was committed* to the most violent men of the party; *for the west, to the earls of* Arran, Glencarn, &c. *for the north, to the lord* James Priour *of St.* Andrew's; *and for the in-countries, to some barons who were held the most zealous.*

THEREUPON, adds the same writer, *ensued a pitiful vastation of churches, and church-buildings, throughout all parts of the kingdom; for every one made bold to put their hands; the meaner sort imitating the example of the greater. No difference was made, but all churches either defaced or pulled to the ground. The holy vessels, and whatsoever else they could make gain of, as timber, lead, and bells, were put to sale: the very sepulchres of the dead were not spared*; and, among others,

(*a*) Spotswood, p. 174, 175.

those

those of all our kings and queens since king *Malcolm* III. at *Dumferlin*, and elsewhere; as at *Scoon*, *Arbroth*, *Melros*, the charter-house of *Perth*, &c. insomuch, that of all our kings and queens, there is not so much as one monument left entire within *Scotland*.

THE registers of the churches and bibliothecks, or libraries, were cast into the fire, says *Spotswood*, and these were so entirely destroyed, that if in *Scotland* there had happened a debate, such as lately in *England*, (into which I do not enter) about the consecrations or ordinations of bishops and priests, either before or about the time of the reformation: I do not believe, that of all our ancient bishops and priests, ordained within the country, there could have been found the register or act of consecration or ordination of any one of them. So careful were our first reformers to sweep clean away all that could renew the memory of the religion in which they had been baptized, and all that belonged to it. Of which it were easy to give surprizing instances: but this is a sufficient one, of the difference betwixt the violent manner in which the reformation, as to all old MSS. or records, was carried on in *Scotland*, and the moderate course, which was followed, in *England*; in which, during this late debate concerning ordination of bishops, so many publick acts and registers of churches have been produced.

Now

Now as no body, that hath the leaſt tincture of eccleſiaſtical diſcipline, can doubt, but that in all the cathedral churches of *Scotland*, in former times, beſides the archives, where the proper records of each church were preſerved, there were regiſters of all ordinations of prieſts and inferior miniſters, and of all other eccleſiaſtical acts belonging to that dioceſe: that at St. *Andrew's*, the metropolitan church, beſides the archives where all the records and rights of the church, ſuch as bulls of popes, charters of the kings; all eccleſiaſtical acts, ſuch as thoſe of national councils, of *Dioceſan* ſynods, of proceſſes in the eccleſiaſtical court, *&c.* were preſerved; there were alſo regiſters where all the conſecrations of biſhops within the province, or within the kingdom; all ordinations, diſpenſations, *&c.* were in courſe recorded: and though ſince the time of the reformation, all theſe original records are no leſs entirely and univerſally diſappeared, than if they never had been: (excepting ſome of the chartularies) yet no perſon of underſtanding would conclude, from the preſent want, that there never had been any ſuch original records, or regiſters in *Scotland*.

In like manner it were very unreaſonable, after all the diſaſters which have happened to our MSS. of all kinds, to conclude, from the few remains there are of our ancient hiſtories and chronicles, that

there

there were not anciently as many of that kind proportionably in *Scotland*, as in other countries; for it was not barely ecclesiastical monuments that suffered in the times of our reformation; for since abbeys, convents, and churches, where our chronicles and other historical monuments used to be written and preserved, were burnt or destroyed, and that generally on a sudden, and without forewarning, so as that nothing could be removed or secured; it cannot be easily conceived how many valuable records or monuments of all kinds perished in their ruins.

FOR in a word, says (*a*) *Spotswood*, *all was ruined*; *and what had escaped the first tumult*, *did now undergo the common calamity*, *which was so much the worse*; *that the violences committed at this time were coloured with the warrant of* an apparent *publick authority*. Thus archbishop *Spotswood*, and more to this purpose, where he lays the blame chiefly on *Knox*, and others of the first preachers of the reformation; and on their misapplying scripture texts to excite the people to react, in their native country, the part that the *Goths* and *Vandals* had acted on the *Roman* empire.

BUT what is farther to be regreted, and deserves to be particularly taken notice of, in this

(*a*) Spotswood, p. 175.

promiscuous burning of religious houses, with the registers and libraries of churches, is that besides those historical and other records that might have been known, and valued by the churchmen, or religious, who were the inhabitants and possessors of these churches or convents, it frequently happened that in the libraries of the churches and monasteries of ancient establishment, there were old chronicles, records, acts and canons of councils, and other valuable monuments, civil and ecclesiastical, of which the actual possessors of these churches or convents, (especially in those days when there was no knowledge of critical learning, and as little taste of antiquity) either took no notice, or were not skilled enongh to know the true value of them. Nor was this ignorance and neglect of ancient monuments, peculiar to many churchmen and religious men in *Scotland*, in the ages preceding the reformation; but too common in all other countries in those days, and even in after-times.

Thus we have seen in the last age, when the true taste of antiquity, of critical learning, and of discernment of genuine ancient MSS. revived, how many valuable monuments of history, of councils, of fathers, of ecclesiastical writers, and other pieces of all kinds; some of them whose names and titles had never been known or heard of, out of the houses where they had been at first composed; others that were believed to have been loſt, how many ſuch valuable monuments have been diſcovered; and, if I may ſay ſo, dug up from the bottom of old libraries, in monaſteries and churches, where they had lain buried, ſometimes unknown to their poſſeſſors: and this particularly by the labours, skill and diligence of ſuch men, as *Dacherius*, *Caniſius*, *Mabillon*, *Baluze*, *Labbe*, *Martene*, and many others abroad, who have enriched, and daily continue to enrich the republick of letters with ſo many volumes of collections of ancient monuments of all kinds, and among theſe, ſo many ancient chronicles and annals, which had never been known out of the houſes where they were found, and had infallibly periſhed with them, without ever being heard of, had they met with the fate of the churches and abbeys of *Scotland*.

AND not to go out of *Britain*, whence have we in *England*, the *Decem* and the *Quindecem Scriptores*, the *Anglica*, *Normanica*, &c. publiſhed by *Camden*, the collection of councils in two volumes by *Spelman*, thoſe in *Anglia Sacra* in other two, and other ſuch ancient monuments; but from the remains of the libraries of the churches and monaſteries? Several of which had never been known or heard of, even as to their names and titles, no more than thoſe in *Scotland*, had not *Leland* made his literary voyages and ſearches, and had the *Engliſh* monaſteries and churches met with ſuch thorow reformers as thoſe in *Scotland*.

HAD

HAD our ancient churches, abbeys and convents, with their libraries, ſtood till theſe times that the taſte and value of the genuine monuments of antiquity is renewed in our country, as elſewhere; what might not, for example, have been found at *Abernethy*, the moſt ancient church in *Scotland*, and which had ſubſiſted from the firſt converſion of the *Picts* in the fifth and ſixth age, which had a proper chronicle (*a*) of its own, (mentioned in the *Scotichronicon*, but periſhed now with the reſt) and where the *Keledees* remained till the later end of the thirteenth age; in *Kilrimund*, or St. *Andrew*'s, in *Dunkeld*, in the priory of the *Lochleven*: all which were already famous in the *Pictiſh* times: what remains might not have been found in all theſe of the *Pictiſh* hiſtorical monuments; and of the *Scotiſh* in the ſame, as well as in *Scoon*, *Dunfermlin*, St. *Colmſinch*, *Reſtennot*, &c. And if the zeal of our reformers muſt needs ruin theſe ſtately edifices, (according to *John Knox*'s famous maxim, *That the ſureſt means to hinder the rooks to come back, was to burn their neſts*) at leaſt had the libraries and MSS. been preſerved; or had there been deputed, before they were deſtroyed, antiquaries, ſuch as *Leland* in *England*, that knew the true value of ancient pieces, to inſpect and make catalogues of them, to preſerve and

(*a*) Scotichron. Paſlæten. lib. 4. c. 12. in Biblioth. Regia Londin.

put in ſafety the more precious, *&c.* Had we had in the heat of this new kind of reforming the church, when ſo many valuable pieces of antiquity, that had eſcaped the fire, were ſold for almoſt nothing to the book-binders, grocers, *&c.* Had we had in thoſe days men of the fine taſte and temper of Sir *Robert Cotton*, and others in *England*, who preſerved ſo many of thoſe perſecuted remains and monuments of their forefathers piety and glory: nay, had we then had men of ſuch a publick ſpirit, as ſome in our own time, I doubt not but we might in that caſe have had collections of *Scotiſh* ancient monuments, no leſs valuable for *Scotland*, than thoſe of the *Cotton* library and others are for *England*, eſpecially of eccleſiaſtical matters; after which, it appears that king *Edward* I. in his ſearches had not deſignedly enquired: ſo they remained much more entire, till the time of the reformation, than what concerned the civil hiſtory.

And now 'tis eaſy to perceive the vaſt diſparity there was as to the loſs or preſervation of records, and all ſort of MSS. betwixt the manner in which the reformation was carried on in *England*, and that in which it was hurried on in *Scotland*; and that whatever plenty there might have been in former times in *Scotland*, of hiſtorical, eccleſiaſtical, or other monuments of antiquity, it is rather a wonder that any at all ſhould have remained, than that there ſhould be ſo very few in compariſon of what have been preſerved in *England.*

And after this account of the fate of our ancient monuments of this kind, eſpecially thoſe of eccleſiaſtical matters, I think I need not inſiſt upon refuting the groundleſs ſtory of their having been tranſported abroad by the ancient churchmen, or religious men, at the time of the reformation; for, excepting a part of the records of *Glaſgo*, with the two chartularies, ſaved by the archbiſhop *James Beaton*, it was never as yet heard that any of our countrymen have met with any thing conſiderable of that kind in any foreign country: though within theſe laſt hundred years, and upwards, ſince the truth of our antiquities, as ſet down by *Boece*, hath been violently conteſted, and many other warm diſputes betwixt the *Scots* and the *Iriſh*, ſeveral of the moſt learned of our countrymen have uſed all poſſible diligence in ſearching every where abroad, after all remains of our hiſtory or antiquities. Such were *Thomas Dempſtar*, ſo famous for his conteſts and debates with the *Iriſh*; *George Conne*, a *Roman* prelate; *David Chambers*, and others, all of them in great credit at *Rome*, and elſewhere abroad. We have had others that have ſearched through *Flanders* and *Germany*; and of late the learned Dr. *John Jameſone*, who lived many years in *Rome*, and had acceſs to all their libraries, and ſearched with zeal every where both in *Italy* and *France*, yet

yet never could hear of any conſiderable monument concerning *Scotland*, except, what every body knows, of the above-mentioned charters or writs of the church of *Glaſgo* at *Paris*; and a hiſtory of the *Abbots* of *Kinlos* in *Murray*, written by *Fererius Pedemontanus*, the continuator of *Boece*'s hiſtory. Others of late have made farther ſearches abroad in the ſame view: ſo that there appears no other ground for that ſtory, of the tranſportation of ancient *Scotiſh* hiſtories, or other monuments, but the care and zeal of the aforeſaid archbiſhop of *Glaſgo*, to ſave what he could of thoſe of his church from the common fate of all the reſt. It had been indeed to be wiſhed, that his example had been followed by other prelates, churchmen, or religious men of thoſe times; but by all that hath yet been diſcovered, there is little or no appearance that he had any conſiderable imitators: beſides that, it muſt be conſidered, that this violent burning and deſtroying all churches, with their records and monuments, came on ſo ſuddenly, as we have obſerved, and was carried on with ſo great impetuoſity, that thoſe among the churchmen or religious men, who remained firm in the old religion, had difficulty to provide for their own ſafety, and were not in a condition to ſave any thing elſe.

After this melancholy relation of the deſtruction of hiſtorical, and of all kind of ancient monuments at our reformation, which fell heavieſt

 on

on thoſe that concerned the church, it remains now to give ſome ſhort account of ſuch ancient pieces that eſcaped the zeal of thoſe times. And, in the firſt place, ſome of the *Scotichronicons*, and other hiſtorical pieces, were ſaved by ſome curious men, lovers of the honour of their country, into whoſe hands they happened to fall when all was going to wreck. It was alſo by the ſame means that ſome of the chartularies of four of the cathedral churches, (beſides the two of *Glaſgo* ſaved by the archbiſhop *James Beaton*) were preſerved; to wit, thoſe of St. *Andrew's*, of *Murray*, of *Aberdeen*, and of *Brechin*. But the chartularies of the other eight cathedrals, together with the original writs or charters, records and regiſters of all of them, periſhed in the manner that (*a*) *Spotſwood* hath related.

BUT it appears, that no kind of monuments had ſo good a luck to eſcape, as many of the chartularies of the abbeys: and there were particular motives for ſaving of them, preferably to any other monuments of eccleſiaſtical antiquities. For almoſt the only pieces, I may ſay in general all that they contain, are the authentick copies of the temporal lands, poſſeſſions and juriſdictions that anciently belonged to theſe religious houſes, or churches, whoſe chartularies they are; ſuch as the bulls, charters or writs of their foundations,

(*a*) Supra pag. 486.

dona-

donations, confirmations, *&c.* by the popes, kings, bishops, nobility, *&c.*

Now 'tis to be observed, that the first preachers of our *Scotish* reformation had carried to that height their invectives against the old churchmen, and religious men of those times, and against the riches and possessions of churches and convents, (towards which, to speak the truth, the abuses of those times furnished them too great a handle) that they condemned all the ancient foundations and donations of lands and revenues, made to churches or convents, as sinful; and as being given towards superstitious uses, and therefore to be reformed away. On the other hand, in their declamations against the avarice of churchmen, in performing their functions, to render them more odious to the people, they themselves in the beginning spoke the language of men who aimed at no worldly settlement, but purely at the glory of God and salvation of souls; and as they gave themselves out for men extraordinarily raised up to re-establish the doctrine of the apostles and apostolical men, so the people were at first made to believe that these new preachers would equally imitate the apostles and their disciples, in looking no farther than their daily bread, and depending entirely on providence for their subsistance; this gained over to them numbers of people: and this cant lasted till the assembly held in *August* 1560, called by that party a parliament, in which the first acts were made against the old religion, and in favour of the reformation. And from thenceforth the preachers changed their note, and they began immediately to cry for stipends, and in proportion, as their credit was established, to lay claim to the old church-lands and possessions, as sacred things given irrevocably to God, and which could not be lawfully disponed, but for settling of the ministers, or to charitable uses, at their disposal (*a*). But in this they were over-ruled by more powerful pretenders.

For many of the nobility and gentry over the kingdom, that had embraced the reformation, had heard and received, with no less pleasure, the instructions of the first preachers of it, concerning the abuse and misapplication of so much riches, and so many temporal lands and baronies disponed to abbeys and churches for uses, they had been informed, were superstitious; and being thus easily persuaded that all these foundations and donations of churches and convents were null, and of no effect from the beginning; and by consequence, that they reverted in course to the sovereign, to the nobility, or to the heirs of the first founders and donors; upon this, some of those among them that had been the most zealous promoters of the

(*a*) See *Knox's* Hist. edit. in fol. p. 319, 320, 325, 326, 339, 349, &c. and the acts of the first general assembly, *December* 1560; and the following assemblies.

work

work of the reformation, were among the first to get into the possession of the temporals of the abbeys and churches, partly as having been, by a mistaken zeal, lavished away by their predecessors to bad uses; partly by obtaining a gift, and generally, for greater security, a confirmation of them from the sovereign, to whom they supposed they were by right returned, as to the chief founder: and queen *Mary*, to be able to enjoy some freedom, peace, and quietness amidst the disaffected and divided parties, she found in the kingdom at her return from *France*, was liberal enough to them all, in her concessions and grants of church-lands.

NOW the original writs or charters of the foundations and donations of the lands of the abbeys and churches, having been for the most part destroyed over the kingdom, together with the religious houses and churches themselves, as we have seen; and the only remaining authentick copies or duplicates of all these writs being contained in the chartularies of those abbeys or churches, those chartularies came to be in esteem, were carefully sought among the spoils of those religious houses, and saved chiefly by those that had obtained the possession of their temporality, as containing a kind of progress of writs, or as being so many authentick land-books, in which an exact indication and enumeration of all that had belonged to these abbeys and churches was to be found. And thus so many of them are still remaining; for there being generally several copies of the chartularies of each abbey, some of them escaped the common fate, and were easily to be found in those days.

There are still remaining a sufficient number of them, which, if put together, and printed, would make at least one large volume of a *Monasticon Scoticanum*, and be of great use towards the illustration of the ancient families of the nobility and gentry of that kingdom, especially during the twelfth, thirteenth, and fourteenth age; and that is now the chief, or only use of them; for they serve very little towards giving light into the affairs of the church, most part of all that they contain being writs of foundations, donations, and other rights of the temporal lands of the churches and abbeys. However, they being very curious and useful towards giving light into ancient families, in order to preserve them, many of them have been of late acquired by the honourable and learned gentlemen of the faculty of advocates at *Edinburgh*, who, out of zeal for their country, have spared no expence to buy up, at any rate, and preserve from perishing, those and many other precious remains of the history and antiquities of *Scotland*, and placed them in their library, consisting of a great collection of printed books; all which, for the improvement of learning in their country, they have generously ordered to be open to all learned and curious men.

But

But no private family hath ſhewn greater zeal for retrieving the hiſtorical and other ancient monuments of their country, than that of *Panmure*; which, beſides an ancient *Scotichronicon*, is in poſſeſſion of the original chartularies of St. *Andrew's*, and of *Brechin*, and of copies of almoſt all the other chartularies remaining, with a rare collection of many original writs of the abbeys and other valuable monuments: all which the preſent chief of that noble family was pleaſed to communicate to me, with ſingular marks of kindneſs, during the time I ſtaid at *Edinburgh*.

Had there been, in the days of the reformation, (when ſo many precious monuments of our antiquities were daily periſhing, or put to ſale for waſte paper or parchment) men of ſuch a publick ſpirit as theſe, and as zealous for the honour of our country, in that caſe, inſtead of this long and lamentable enumeration of the loſs of ancient monuments, that our country made in thoſe times of confuſion, I ſhould have had the pleaſure to have had to ſet down here a detailed account or catalogue of the many valuable MSS. of our civil and eccleſiaſtical hiſtory ſtill preſerved; and, among others, of the acts and canons of our national councils: whereof we have now remaining only the dates of a few of them: which, as I promiſed before, I ſhall here ſubjoin, both as a farther proof of the loſs that our antiquities have ſuſtained

ſuſtained from blind zealots, and to confirm what I have here advanced, that the few remains we have now of ancient monuments is no argument that we had not, before the reformation, as many in proportion as our neighbours; and in order alſo, towards the furniſhing materials for an eccleſiaſtical hiſtory of *Scotland*, to excite the learned among our countrymen to make farther enquiry for any thing of this kind, that may ſtill remain undiſcovered, and unknown in private hands, as that precious collection of canons in the chartulary of *Aberdeen*, in the advocates library, had done for ſo many years, till they diſcovered and bought it up. For the canons and regulations of national or provincial councils, are ſo eſſential an ingredient into the eccleſiaſtical hiſtory of any country, that without ſome account of them, it muſt needs appear almoſt a skeleton.

A Chrono-

A Chronological Index of ſuch of the National Councils of the Church of Scotland, *as I have found mentioned in History and Records.*

I. THE firſt of this kind that I find recorded in hiſtory, was under the reign of king *Keneth Mac Alpin*, about the year of our Lord 850: among theſe laws, which (*a*) *Fordun* calls *Leges Macalpinæ*, as they are ſet down by (*b*) *Boece*, there are ſome ſtatutes concerning eccleſiaſtical matters, which were no doubt made in an aſſembly with the concurrence of the biſhops, as it was the univerſal diſcipline of the church in thoſe times, that no eccleſiaſtical laws could be enacted without epiſcopal authority and concurrence. And tho' we have now no farther accounts of theſe laws, than what the two above-mentioned writers and *Winton* contain, it cannot be reaſonably doubted of, but that this victorious king would not fail, upon the union of the *Pictiſh* and *Scotiſh* kingdoms, after the confuſions of war were over, to make new laws for his united kingdoms, proper to heal all inteſtine diſcords. It is moſt likely, that theſe laws were

(*a*) Fordun, lib. 4. c. 8. p. 293. edit. Hearn.
(*b*) Boeth. Hiſt. fol. 208. 1ſt edit.

made

made at *Scoon*, where king *Keneth* had settled the chief seat of his united kingdoms.

II. We have a more certain account of another council or assembly, holden also at *Scoon*, (*a*) *the sixth year of the reign of our king* Constantin, *son of* Eth, (A. D. 906) in which this *king* Constantin, *and* Kellach *the bishop*, *with the* Scots, *solemnly vowed to observe the laws and discipline of faith, the rights of the churches, and of the gospel, on a little hill, called from thence* Collis credulitatis (*Knoc-creidimh*, I suppose, in the vulgar language) *near the royal city of* Scoon. 'Tis like it was the same place so famous afterwards by the name of the *Mute-Hill of Scoon*; in *Latin*, *Omnis terra*. *Vid. Skein's Glossary*.

III. During the reign of *Malcolm Keanmore*, about *A. D.* 1073, or 1074, several national councils were held in *Scotland* by the pious zeal of his royal consort St. *Margaret*, as *Turgot*, (who, 'tis like, assisted himself at these councils) relates in her life, for the re-establishing ecclesiastical disci-

(*a*) In vi. anno (regni sui) Constantinus rex [*filius Edii*] & Kellachus episcopus leges disciplinasque fidei, atque jura ecclesiarum, evangeliorumque pariter cum Scottis in colle credulitatis prope regali civitate Scoan (sic) devoverunt custodiri; ab hoc die collis hoc [*nomen*] meruit, *i. e.* collis credulitatis. *V. Append. n.* 3.

(*b*) Vita S. Margaretæ reginæ in actis sanctor. Boland. ad 10 Jun.

pline, and the reformation of manners. Some extracts of the canons of these councils are set down by *Turgot*. But the whole acts and canons at length were no doubt deposited either at *Dunfermlin*, founded in this reign, or at St. *Andrew's*.

IV. *A. D.* 1126, under the reign of king *David* I. a council holden at *Roxburgh* by the cardinal-legate *John* of *Crema*. *Decem Scriptores Angliæ*, *col.* 252.

V. *A. D.* 1138, in the same reign, another national council of the bishops of *Scotland*, holden by the legate *Alberic* at *Carlisle*, where, in those days, king *David* kept ordinarily his court. *Decem Scriptores Angl. col.* 264.

VI. *A. D.* 1177, a national council at *Edinburgh*, holden by the cardinal legate *Winian*, with the bishops of *Scotland*, in which many ancient canons were renewed, and new ones enacted. *Chron. Maylr. hoc anno & Fordun edit. Hearne*, *p.* 714.

VII. *A. D.* 1201, in *December*, a national council was holden at *Perth* by *John de Salerno*, cardinal-legate, in which many canons were made. *Chr. Maylr. Houeden. p.* 468, *&c.*

VIII. *A. D.* 1206, a national council, (called in the original writ *Synodus Generalis*) holden at *Perth* in *April*. *Ex charta penes Vicecomitem de Arbuthnot.*

IX. *A. D.*

IX. *A.D.* 1211, a national council holden at *Perth* by *William* bishop of St. *Andrew's*, *Walter* bishop of *Glasgo*, and the other bishops of *Scotland*. *Scotichron. Paslaten. in biblioth. Regia Londin. lib.* ix. *c.* 78.

X. *A.D.* 1221, *James* canon of St. *Victor* at *Paris*, penitentiary of the pope, and legate to *Scotland*, held a national council of all the prelates of *Scotland* at *Perth*, during four days in the month of *February*. *Scotichron. idem. lib.* ix. *c.* 37.

A.D. 1225, a mandate of pope *Honorius* III. the 19th of *May*, the ninth of his pontificate, to all the bishops of *Scotland*; by which, after having told them, that whereas he had been informed by some of them, that for want of a metropolitan, by whose authority they might regularly hold provincial councils, the canons were not duly observed, and many other abuses happened; therefore he enjoins them, that since they had not a metropolitan, they should convene, by his authority, to celebrate provincial councils, which, says the pope, ought not to be omitted. *Ex Chartular. vet. Moravien. fol.* 11. & *Chartular. Aberdon. fol.* 25. *in Biblioth. Jurid. Edinb.*

XI. In consequence of this mandate, and upon receiving it, the bishops held a (*a*) national or provincial

(*a*) Statuta generalia ecclesiæ Scoticanæ, can. 1. in Chartul. Aberd. supra.

vincial council of all the prelates of the kingdom, in which they regulated the form of holding it; and enacted, 1°. That, according to the (*a*) canons of the church, a provincial council should be holden every year, at which all the bishops, abbots, and priors, should assist, to regulate all ecclesiastical affairs. 2°. That at each (*b*) council a *conservator*, being one of the bishops, should be chosen by common consent to preside instead of a metropolitan; and who, in that quality, should punish all transgressors of the statutes of the councils, and by the authority of the same. 3°. That (*c*) at each council the bishops should preach by turns, beginning by the bishop of St. *Andrew's*, &c.

XII. In the chartulary of *Murray* we have an account of another national council, indicted to be holden (*d*) *in domo fratrum prædicatorum de Perth*, on *Wednesday* before the feast of St. *Luke*, in *October*, but without the date of the year; only it must have been some years after *A. D.* 1230, when the *Black Friers* first came into *Scotland*. However, in this act we have the form of the bishop conservator his indicting or convocating the yearly council, *authoritate conservatoria*, as the act bears, by a letter to each bishop, charging him to give his

(*a*) Ibid.
(*b*) Ibid. can. 2.
(*c*) Ibid.
(*d*) Chartul. vet. Moravien. fol. 93, in Bibl. Jurid. Ed.

presence

presence at such a place, (which was commonly the convent of the *Black Friers* of *Perth*) on such a day, with continuation of days; together with the abbots and priors, the proctors of chapters, colleges and convents of his diocese; there to treat of the reformation of the state of the church, *&c.*

I call all these councils *national*, because they were composed of the bishops, prelates, proctors of the chapters, and of all the clergy of the kingdom, though in the precise language of the canon law, these councils being held by the bishop conservator, instead of a metropolitan; and so by an archiepiscopal authority, according to the pope's mandate, they are called by the pope and by the bishops themselves *provincial* councils; and by our parliaments *general*, or *general-provincial* councils.

XIII. *A.D.* 1239, the cardinal-legate *Otho*, having at last obtained leave of king *Alexander* II. (who (*a*) two years before had absolutely refused to suffer any legate to enter his kingdom) came into *Scotland* about the end of *September*, held a national council at *Edinburgh* the 19th day of *October*, and departed in the beginning of *November*. *Scotichr. Paslat. lib.* ix. *c.* 54.

XIV. *A.D.* 1242, a national council held at *Perth*. *Scotichr. Paslat. lib.* ix. *c.* 59.

(*a*) Matth. Paris. p. 301.

XV. *A.D.*

XV. *A. D.* 1268, *Othobon*, cardinal-legate in *England*, cited the biſhops of *Scotland* to a council, which he was to hold in *England*; two of them went as deputies from the reſt, but refuſed to accept of the canons of his council; and being returned home, they, with all the reſt of the biſhops and clergy of *Scotland*, held a national council of their own, in their uſual manner, at *Perth*. *Scotichr. lib.* x. *c.* 25.

XVI. *A. D.* 1273, a national council at *Perth*. *Scotichr. lib.* x. *c.* 33.

XVII. *A. D.* 1275, a national council at *Perth*, in preſence of *Bagimond* the pope's nuncio, who came to collect the taxations of all benefices, and ſettled a roll of thoſe taxations that ſerved for a rule in following times, to which our acts of parliament (*a*) refer. *Scotichr. lib.* x. *c.* 35.

XVIII. *A. D.* 1280, a national council holden at the *Black Friers* of *Perth*, on *Monday* after St. *Bartholomew*'s day in *Auguſt*; mentioned in a ſentence of *Archbald* biſhop of *Murray* this year. *Chartular. vet. Eccl. Moravien. fol.* 46. *in bibl. Jurid. Edin.*

XIX. *A. D.* 1310, a national council holden at *Dundee*, in which, among other acts, king *Robert* I's

(*a*) Jam. III. parl. 6. c. 44. Jam. IV. parl. 4. c. 39.

right to the crown is asserted by all the bishops and clergy of *Scotland*. *Independency by M. Anderson, append. num.* 12.

XX. *A. D.* 1321, a national council holden at *Perth* in *July*, mentioned in the rolls of king *Robert* I. *n.* 85. *Ex Collect. Comitis de Panmure, p.* 65.

XXI. *A. D.* 1324, a national council holden in *March* at *Scoon*: it is called in the act, *Generale Concilium. Mentioned in a writ in the chartulary of Glasgo of this year.*

XXII. *A. D.* 1420, a national council holden the 16th of *July*, at the *Black Friers* of *Perth*, by *William* bishop of *Dunblain*, conservator; and in that quality president of the council. There is an act of this council, concerning the *quotes* of testament; but the act is more considerable, because it describes the form of the council, which is there called *Synodus Provincialis & Concilium generale Cleri Regni Scotiæ*, with the names of the bishops present in person, or by procurator, *&c.* Among other things it appears, that the decrees or statutes were sealed by all the bishops seals. *This act is in the original chartulary of Brechin penes Comitem de Panmure, fol.* 62.

XXIII. *A. D.* 1457, a national council at *Perth*, in which, among other acts, a declaration was made concerning the king's right of nomination to to benefices during vacancies of bishopricks, *&c. Records of parliament of king James* III. *fol.* 75.

XXIV. *A. D.* 1459, a national council holden in *July*, at *Perth*, by *Thomas* bishop of *Aberdeen*, conservator; and in that quality president of the council: in which the aforesaid declaration was renewed. *Records of parliament as above.*

XXV. *A. D.* 1487, I find, in a chartulary of *Arbroth*, a deputation made by the abbot and convent of that abbey, of procurators to assist at a general or national council, to be holden this year at St. *Andrew's*. *Chartular. maj. Aberbroth, fol.* 115. *in Bibl. Jurid. Edinb.*

XXVI. *A. D.* 1512, a national council holden at *Edinburgh*. *Mentioned by bishop Lesly in his history of Scotland, p.* 356.

XXVII. *A. D.* 1536, a national, or as it is called in the act, a general provincial council of *Scotland*, to be holden the 1st day of *March* next to come, 1536, in the *Black Friers* at *Edinburgh*, by the archbishop of St. *Andrew's*; ordered by act of parliament, in *Jan.* 1535. *Records of parliament of king James* V. *fol.* 8.

XXVIII. *A. D.* 1546, a national council holden at *Edinburgh*, by cardinal *Beaton*, archbishop of St. *Andrew's*, and primate, for the reformation of the lives and manners of churchmen. *Buchanan's Hist. lib.* 15.

XXIX. *A. D.* 1549, a national council begun at *Lithgo* in *August*, and transferred in *September* to *Edinburgh*, holden by *Jo. Hamilton*, archbishop of St. *Andrew's*, and primate for reformation of the ecclesiastical discipline.

XXX. *A. D.* 1552, a national council holden at *Edinburgh*, in *January*, by the same archbishop. It was in this council that the large catechism, printed at St. *Andrew's* in *August* following, by this archbishop's order, was approved. *Lesl. Hist. p.* 476.

XXXI. *A. D.* 1559, the last national council of *Scotland*, holden at *Edinburgh* in *March*, by the same archbishop, for reformation of ecclesiastical discipline. *Lesl. Hist. p.* 504, 505.

These are the dates of such of the national councils of *Scotland*, as I have hitherto had occasion to observe in records or history; and though their number may appear not inconsiderable to those who, by reason of the universal destruction of ecclesiastical acts and monuments within that kingdom, may have imagined that those canonical assemblies had been extremely rare in our country; yet we have assured proof, that these thirty-one councils which I have remarked, are almost nothing in comparison of the great number of such national assemblies that were holden in former ages: since it was (*a*) solemnly enacted, about five hundred years ago, by the whole bishops and clergy assembled in council, according to the example of their predecessors, that a national or provincial council should be holden *every year*, convocated by the bishop conservator for the time, at which all the clergy of the kingdom were to convene by themselves, or by deputies, under pain of being proceeded against for their absence, &c.

It is easy to judge by this, that if the acts and canons of all these councils, which, as we see, were yearly to be assembled, had been preserved entire, such as they were before the reformation,

(*a*) Auctoritate Dei omnipotentis & sacrorum canonum, ac sacro sanctæ Romanæ ecclesiæ, nos prelati ecclesiæ Scoticanæ concilium provinciale nostrorum prædecessorum more celebrantes, & laudibilem consuetudinem observantes, unanimi consensu statuimus & ordinamus ut SINGULIS ANNIS singuli episcopi & abbates ac prioratum priores in habitu solemni ad concilium celebrandum ad certum diem, per conservatorem concilii sibi competenter præfigendum, devotè conveniant, ut per triduum, si necesse fuerit, in eodem concilio valeant pro necessitatibus divinis & ecclesiasticis commorari, & invocata spiritus sancti gratia statum ecclesiasticum ibidem ad modum debitum & placentem Deo reformare. Si quis vero eorum canonica præpeditione fuerit impeditus, procuratorem vice sua sufficientem substituat. Non autem veniens personaliter, cum venire posset, & noluerit, auctoritate concilii & arbitrio puniatur. *Ex Statutis generalibus ecclesiæ Scoticanæ, cap.* 1. In Chartular. vet. Aberdon. in Biblioth. Jurid. Edinb.

we might have had this day not only two, such as *Spelman's*, but many volumes of national councils of *Scotland*; besides so many other valuable ecclesiastical acts and monuments of all kinds: which had been proper materials for a history of the ancient church of that kingdom, which being now deprived of such proper vouchers, can never come up to make a figure like to those of other nations.

But to conclude this melancholy subject, at least I hope that no reasonable man, after considering all that hath been said in this article, will henceforth, from the scarcityof civil and ecclesiastical monuments, under which the *Scots* at present labour, conclude that there must have been fewer of both kinds of those monuments in past ages in *Scotland*, in proportion to its extent, than in other civilized and christian countries.

Art. III. *An account of the monuments, writers, and records of the* Scotish *history that yet remain.*

I am now to give an account of the few historical pieces of our country, which, after all the disasters above-mentioned, still remain, especially of those that are more ancient and less known; and in this account I shall endeavour to follow the order of the time, in which these pieces seem to have been written, and the various *Epochs* of our history, which they respect.

BUT to avoid uſeleſs repetitions, the learned Dr. *William Nicholſon*, late biſhop of *Londonderry*, having publiſhed an exact and impartial account of the *Scotiſh* hiſtorians, eſpecially from *Fordun* downwards; and the late Dr. *Mackenzie* having alſo treated, at great length, of the *Scotiſh* writers in general, I ſhall not inſiſt upon a ſubject which theſe learned gentlemen have ſo lately handled; but endeavour only to ſupply what may not have come under their conſideration; and ſhall confine myſelf to give an account of ſome ſhort pieces relating to the *Scotiſh* hiſtory, which are leſs known, or have been leſs taken notice of by thoſe that have treated the ſubject before, and chiefly give a more particular account of thoſe pieces that may give more light into the point I am about to examine; to wit, the time of the ſettlement of the *Scots*, and of the beginning of their monarchy in *Britain*.

IN treating this ſubject, I ſhall reduce all that remains of the domeſtick monuments of hiſtory, that have come to my knowledge, to four heads, or claſſes. Firſt claſs; remains of the ancient *Scotiſh* hiſtory antecedent to the year 1291. Second claſs; records or monuments of our ancient hiſtory, written betwixt the year 1291, and the publiſhing *John Fordun*'s hiſtory about the year 1447. Third claſs; of *John Fordun*'s hiſtory, his continuators, followers, and other writers of our history, till the year 1526, in which *Boece*'s history came out. Fourth class; of the histories of *Hector Boece*, *Buchanan*, and their followers.

§. *Containing such remains as we have of our ancient history, written before the year 1291.*

It is not to be wondered at, that the remains we have of our ancient history, written before the year 1291, are very few and lame; since, besides the disasters which happened in king *Edward* I's time, our posteriour writers, with a view to make up that loss, having framed to themselves, as will afterwards appear, new schemes of our history, very different from our more ancient writers, it could not be expected that great care would be taken of the remains of these ancient chronicles, that did not agree with these new draughts of our history: so at best, such of our old chronicles, or other historical monuments, which had escaped the searches in king *Edward*'s time, lay in the obscurity of some corner of the libraries of our churches and monasteries, with many other valuable ancient monuments oft-times unknown to their possessors, till the zeal of our new reformers burnt down and destroyed the churches and abbeys, with their libraries, and all that they contained, which had been, till those times, preserved.

Some of these, which I am here to account for, are remains of that kind; and though they are

are all very short, yet being written before the year 1291, whilst our old annals were as yet subsisting, and so being extracted from, or conformable to them, they appear to be the surest guides that we can follow in order to have a true account of the ancient part of our history. The few that I have met with of them will be printed in the appendix to this essay, with some other short ancient pieces relating to *Scotland*; of all which I shall here give a short account, beginning at these pieces which have been more than once already mentioned.

I. The first piece is a kind of description of *Albany*, or of *Scotland*, on the north side of the *Friths* of *Cluyd* and *Forth*; it bears in the MS. this title: *De situ Albani quæ in se figuram hominis habet; quomodo fuit primitus in septem regionibus divisa; quibusque nominibus antiquitus sit vocata, & a quibus inhabitata.* This short treatise was written about the twelfth age, as appears by the author's assuring us, that he had a part of his information from *Andrew*, bishop of *Catness*, who, according to the chronicle of *Mailros*, died *A. D.* 1185.

I think that there is ground to believe, that the author of this description was *Giraldus Cambrensis*, for I remember to have observed somewhere in his works, that he promises to give a description of *Albany*, or *Scotland*; and *Andrew* bishop of *Catness* may have seen him in *England* in king *David* I's time, or in that of his grandchildren, king *Malcolm*,

Malcolm, or king *William*, for *Andrew* was already bishop, *A. D.* 1150. (as appears by a writ of the church of *Glasgo*) besides this, several passages of this description are to be found, word for word, in *Ralph Higden*'s *Polychronicon* (*a*), as being taken from a work of *Girald*'s, which it seems is now lost; and the terms in which the author speaks of bishop (*b*) *Andrew*, and some other expressions in this piece prove, that the author of it was no *Scotsman*. *Camden*, in his last editions of the description of *Scotland*, hath given an extract of this piece, having no doubt seen the MS. from whence I copied it, in the lord *Burghleigh*'s library. It is the same already (*c*) mentioned, which was bought up by order of M. *Colbert*, and is now, as I am informed, with the rest of the *Colbertin* MSS. in the king's library at *Paris*. The three following pieces are in the same MS. which also contains some other pieces relating to the history of *Britain*.

II. THE second piece is intitled, in the MS. *Chronica de origine antiquorum Pictorum*. I have already (*d*) given an account of it; and have only to add, that there is prefixed to it a kind of preface, composed in part of passages of some *British* writers, and of *Isidor* of *Seville*, which seems not to an-

(*a*) Polychron. edit. Reg. Gale, p. 185, 209.
(*b*) Andreas natione Scottus.
(*c*) Supra, p. 105.
(*d*) Ibid.

swer

over the title of the piece in this preface, giving little or no true light into the origin of the *Picts*; and it is so incorrectly written, that it is hard enough to make sense of some parts of it. What is truly valuable, is the body of the piece, being a chronicle, as it is called, or a catalogue of the seventy *Pictish* kings, from *Cruithne* to *Constantin*, with the rest of them, down to the union of the *Pictish* and *Scotish* kingdoms; and the last part of it, as it hath been already observed, is the exactest account of the succession of the *Pictish* kings that is extant.

III. THE third piece is an extract of an ancient history, or chronicle of eleven of the kings of *Scotland*, containing their succession, and a short account of their lives and chief actions from the subjection of the *Picts* by king *Keneth-Mac-Alpin*, till the reign of king *Keneth* III. son to *Malcolm* I. during the space of about one hundred and thirty years. The only copy I have seen of this short chronicle is taken from the same MS. as the former, whence also *Camden* hath quoted some passages. The history or chronicle, from whence it hath been extracted, appears evidently to have been originally written in the *Gælick* or *Irish* language; and the mention that it makes of the succession and deaths of some kings of *Ireland*; as also some particulars that it contains, (such as the confused manner in which it relates king *Gregory*'s reign) all this makes me doubt whether it

be

be not rather an extract of *Scotish* matters, from some *Irish* chronicle, than from a *Scotish* one. The *Latin* version, such as we have it in this only MS. is most barbarous, and every way imperfect, and written by an ignorant transcriber, that hath not known the *Latin* tongue; and by consequence is so incorrect, that in some places no sense can be made of it. However, the piece containing some particulars of the *Scotish* history, which are not to be met with in our common writers, and some remarkable passages, I shall give it, such as it is, entire in the appendix (*a*).

It was from this abstract that *Camden* had the famous passage, *In hujus* [Indulfi Regis] *tempore oppidum Eden evacuatum est, ac relictum est Scottis usque in hodiernum diem.* This passage was quoted from *Camden* first by bishop *Usher*, and after them by some other *English* and *Irish* writers, to endeavour to prove, that the *Saxons* were in possession of *Lothian* till king *Indulf*'s time, about the middle of the tenth age: but besides that, we have an account from *Giraldus* (*b*) *Cambrensis*, no friend to the *Scots*, and from other authors, (probably as ancient as this anonymous writer) of whom *Ranulfus Cestrensis* gives us extracts in his *Polychronicon*, that king *Keneth Mac-Alpin*, about one hundred years before this, was master of all the territories from the *Friths* to the *Twede*; that he had

(*a*) Append. num. 3.
(*b*) Polychron. edit. Galas, p. 194, 209, 210.

vanquiſhed the *Saxons* ſix times: this ſame anonymous piece informs us alſo, that king *Keneth* attacked the *Saxons* ſix times; that he poſſeſſed himſelf of *Maylros* and *Dunbar*; and relates other advantages that our kings, predeceſſors to *Indulf*, had over the *Saxons*: ſo the moſt that can be made of this paſſage is, that the town *Eden*, or *Edinburgh*, had been taken from the *Scots* after king *Keneth*'s time, and was rendered back to them in king *Indulf*'s time. And after all, we know nothing certain about the *Epoch*, nor of the authority of this extract.

I come now to give account of ſome other ancient pieces, which have immediate relation to the queſtion I am about to examine: they are written by *Scotiſh* authors, or rather extracted from our ancient *Scotiſh* annals before the year 1291, when, as our hiſtorians relate, moſt of theſe annals periſhed in king *Edward* I's time.

IV. The firſt, which is the fourth in the appendix, is intitled in the ſame MS. above-mentioned, *Cronica Regum Scottorum* cccxv. *annorum*. It contains the ſeries or names of our kings, with their lineal deſcent, and the years of their reigns, from king *Fergus* ſon of *Erc*, till king *William* in the twelfth age, in whoſe time it was written or extracted, as appears by its ending preciſely at the firſt year of his reign, and with his genealogy, which it carries up, as all the others of this kind do, do, to *Noah*. This genealogical ſeries is entirely conformable to that which is contained in all our *Scotiſh* writers already (*a*) mentioned, before the new genealogy given by *Boece* appeared. From *Malcolm Keanmore*, down to king *William*, this gives ſome particulars of the lives of our kings, and of their children; and it gives ground to conjecture, that the author of it was a monk of *Maylroſs*, or had ſome relation to that abbey. The date of CCCXV. *annorum*, at the end of the title of this ſmall chronicle, ſeems to reſpect either the number of years, from the beginning of king *Fergus Mac Erch*, to the union of the *Pictiſh* and *Scotiſh* monarchy; or from this union to the firſt year of king *William*'s reign.

V. THE fifth ancient piece in the appendix is another chronological ſeries of the kings of *Scots*, with their deſcent and years of their reigns, from *Fergus* the ſon of *Erc*. It ends the third year of king *Alexander* III. *A. D.* 1251. There is inſerted in it a catalogue of the *Pictiſh* kings. This ſeries is taken from one of the moſt ancient and moſt authentick hiſtorical monuments of *Scotland*, the regiſter of the priory of St. *Andrew*'s, fol. 46. It was ſent to me ſome years ago, with ſome other extracts of that regiſter or chartulary, by the late Sir *Robert Sybbald*, M. D. a moſt zealous perſon for collecting all ancient monuments of the

(*a*) Supra, p. 236, 237.

Scotish history that he could find. It is worth remarking, 1°. That Sir *Robert* sent me, along with it, this caution or advice; to wit, that it was of little or no use to prove the antiquity of the *Scotish* monarchy, meaning that it could not serve to prove the scheme of our monarchy, as set down by *H. Boece*, and our other later historians, of which Sir *Robert* was very full. 2°. It is no less to be remarked, that this catalogue itself, being registered among the records and charters of that ancient church, is a full proof of its being held authentick at the time it was written, that is, *A. D.* 1251, whilst our ancient annals and monuments of history were yet in being, and forty years before the searches made in king *Edward*'s time.

THE certainty of the succession of our kings, contained in this register, is confirmed by the account we have of them from *Winton*, and from *James Gray*, who both of them had their information from the same records of St. *Andrew*'s, as we shall have occasion to observe more at length afterwards. It was from the extracts of this register of St. *Andrew*'s, that the passages set down in Sir *James Dalrymple*'s collections were extracted; and with the extracts sent to me by Sir *Robert Sybbald*, the folio of the register was marked whence each extract was taken. As every great church had several of these chartularies or registers, this register of St. *Andrew*'s was different from

from another (*a*) valuable one already mentioned, in which these catalogues of our kings are not set down, as not belonging to the subject, which concerns only the temporal lands and rights of that church.

In this series, or catalogue of our kings, contained in this register of St. *Andrew*'s, from *Keneth Mac-Alpin* downward, there is a short account of the death and burial-place, and of some of the actions of our kings: and this last part of the series is entirely the same, word for word, with another chronological account of our kings from *Keneth Mac-Alpin*, contained in a MS. of the *Cotton* library, (*Vitellius A.* 20.) It is also conformable to another chronological account of the same kings, in verse, and printed at the end of *Melross*'s chronicle. Now this conformity of several ancient accounts of our kings, written by different hands, and preserved in different places, proves the account of them to be true, because they agree one with another.

VI. A sixth piece is a short *Latin* chronicle, in verse or rythm, subjoined to most of the copies of the *Scotichronicon*: there is an entire copy of it at the end of the *Scotichron. MS. Colleg. Scot. Paris.* without those interpolations which are in some other copies. This chronicle gives a very different

(*a*) Penes Com. de Panmure.

account

account both of the beginning of the *Scotish* monarchy, and of the succession of the first kings from the chronicle of *John Fordun*; and in every thing it differs from him, it agrees as to the names and number of kings with the fourth and fifth chronological series of our kings, which I have already mentioned. It consists of eleven chapters; and tho' at first it would appear to be one continued piece, it is really composed of at least two distinct parts, written in different ages, as the preface to it insinuates, and the tenor of the poem proves. The first part being written *veteri metro*, in ancient metre or verse, as the preface calls it; and the last parts in new verse of the same sort of metre; *& novo ad propositum respondente.*

THE first part, consisting of eight chapters, was written in *Alexander* II or III's time; for the author, after relating king *William*'s death, before he speaks of his son *Alexander* II, begins the ninth chapter with these words:

Hactenus haec dicta novi per chronica scripta
A modo quae novi scriptis describere vovi.

So all this part of the chronicle was composed whilst our old annals as yet subsisted; that is, before the year 1291.

THE last part was composed about the year 1448, by a new hand, in order to bring down the succession to the time of king *James* II. who then reigned.

In general, the first three chapters of this chronological poem contain a rude draught of the vulgar traditions of the *Scots*, in those times, concerning their remote antiquities; their coming from *Egypt* to *Spain*, from thence to *Ireland*, and so to *Albany*. The fourth chapter gives some account of the *Pictish* monarchy in *Albany*. The fifth mentions the beginning of the *Scotish* monarchy in *Albany*. The sixth, seventh, and eighth chapters give the series of the kings from *Fergus* son of *Erc*, till the death of king *William*, with the years of each reign. The ninth and tenth chapters contain the succession of our kings from king *William*'s death, till the reign of king *Robert the Bruce*. The eleventh chapter brings down the series from *Robert the Bruce*, till king *James* II. who, the author of this last addition says, was seventeen years of age when he composed it, which answers to the year 1448.

Besides these six ancient pieces which will be found in the appendix, there are some few other monuments of the *Scotish* history in posterior times, already published, which also were written before *A. D.* 1291; such as the chronicle of *Maylross*, which ends *A. D.* 1270. But the series of our kings, contained in it, reaches no higher up than the year 731, where *Bede* left off his history, ry, and where his chronicle begins; and even this series of our kings (which begins only at the death of king *Ewan* in the eighth age) is not of the first hand, in which the rest of the MS. of that chronicle in the *Cotton* library is written, as the learned editor hath remarked, but of a later hand, and inserted very negligently and incorrectly, especially as to the chronology. The first author of this chronicle is all *English*, and gives but short hints of *Scotish* matters till the time of king *Alexander* I. and king *David* I, except one leaf, which in the original MS. is of a hand about one hundred years more ancient than that of the chronicle itself. This leaf is abruptly inserted in the original MS. and interrupts the thread of the chronology, as may be seen, *p.* 158. *l.* 27. of the printed copy, where this leaf begins; ----*Malcolmus filius Dunecan suscepit regnum Scotiæ jure hæreditario*, &c. This old writ ends *p.* 159. *l.* 3. with the death of king *Malcolm* IV. *A. D.* 1165, when it was written.

THE chronicle itself contains a good series of *Scotish* affairs, from the time of the second foundation or restoration of *Maylros*, A. D. 1136, by *S. David*, *R.* I.

THE title of the chronicle in the printed edition, where it is said, *incboata per abbatem de Dundraynan*, is a wrong reading of the word *incboavit*, instead of *mutuavit abbas de Dundraynan* in the original, in a character of a later hand. Our country is obliged to the late Dr. *Gale* for the edition of this chronicle, which is in the first volume of the XV *Scriptores Angliæ*, and to him likewise for the first edition of *Fordun* in the second volume.

ANOTHER very short chronicle, written in king *Malcolm* IV. or king *William*'s time, is printed in the *Anglia Sacra*, and intitled *Chronicon S. Crucis de Edynburgh*; but it contains little of *Scotish* matters, till king *David* I's time.

ANOTHER piece of our history, written before the year 1291, is a poem in *Latin*, containing the elegies or epitaphs of our kings; being a short account of their lives and deaths, from *Keneth* the first monarch of all *Scotland* or *Albany*. It is inserted by a later hand in the MS. of *Maylros* chronicle in the *Cotton* library, and published alone by itself, at the end of the printed edition. This copy comes no farther down than the death of king *Malcolm* IV. But there's another copy of it in a MS. of the *Bodleian* library, that brings the succession down to the beginning of the reign of *Alexander* III. at which time it was written, as is clear from the last verses of it:

ALEXANDER III.

Nomen habet patris, utinam patris acta sequatur.
Filius Albanica qui modo sceptra tenet.

THESE

THESE are all the remains that I have as yet met with, of *Scotish* chronicles or history, written before the year 1291. I do not mention here the remains of our ecclesiastical monuments, these not belonging properly to this first essay; but an account of some of them hath been already occasionally (*a*) given in this essay.

§. 3. *Of records or monuments of our ancient history, written since the year* 1291, *and before the publishing of* Fordun's *chronicle.*

ALTHO' we had no other proofs of the loss of our histories and records in the year 1291, and of the ignorance of the ancient state of the *Scots* in *Britain*, which ensued upon that loss, it would but too evidently appear by the uncertainty in which our countrymen were at that time, and the contradictory accounts they give of the state of the north of *Britain* in ancient times: and those not barely private writers, but men of the best figure selected on purpose to defend the cause of the whole kingdom in one of the most solemn debates that we ever had, and that before the pope; in a word, the whole body of the nation, bishops, nobles, and commons, in their memorials and letters upon this occasion. There are yet remaining three publick pieces, presented to the pope in the

(*a*) Supra, p. 587, &c.

name of the *Scotish* nation; in which the sentiments that they had in that age of their antiquities, profane and sacred, do appear.

To understand the subject of those pieces, 'tis necessary to observe, that upon king *Edward* I's claiming the superiority of *Scotland*, and invading the kingdom; the *Scots* had recourse to the pope *Boniface* VIII. and sent to *Rome* three procurators; to wit, *William* (*a*) archdean of *Lothians*, *Baldred Bizet* and *W. Eglisham*, as their deputies, to represent their grievances, and seek remedy; carrying with them such proofs of their freedom, and independency, as they had yet remaining.

Upon which, the pope wrote to king *Edward* (27 *June*, 1199) monitory letters, by which, supposing *Scotland* to be a *Fief* of the see of *Rome*, and proving the liberty and independency of that kingdom by bulls and charters in king *Edward*'s father *Henry* III's time, and in his own: at the same time the pope summoned king *Edward* to send procurators to *Rome* in six months to defend his claim, declaring, all he should in the mean time enterprise against *Scotland* to the contrary, null, and of no effect.

King *Edward* let pass above a year and a half without any answer, and then being pressed, caused first his nobles (*b*) (12 *Feb.* 1301) to answer, that

(*a*) Fordun. Continuat. edit. Hearn. p. 795.
(*b*) Fordun. Continuat. edit. Hearn. p. 984. 806.

Scotland

Scotland was not a *Fief* of the apoſtolical ſee; but of *England*, and that they would not ſuffer their king to anſwer or ſend procurators to *Rome* upon this debate, *&c.* At laſt, *Edward* himſelf anſwered (7 *May*, (*a*) 1301) endeavouring to prove the ſubjection of the *Scots* to the *Engliſh*, by a long deduction, beginning from *Brutus*, *Albanactus*, &c.

THESE letters being communicated by the pope's orders to the *Scotiſh* agents ſtill at *Rome*, they ſent them to *Scotland*, to the council of the kingdom, who cauſed anſwers to be drawn up in haſte, (*cum feſtinatione*) and ſent them back to their agents at *Rome*, with inſtructions bearing this title; I. (*b*) *Inſtructiones prælatorum, baronum & conſulum Scotiæ miſſæ ad curiam Romanam contra Edwardum regem Angliæ.*

BESIDES this, *Baldred Biſet*, one of the chief of theſe agents, anſwered *Edward*'s reaſons apart by another memorial, with this title; II. (*c*) *Proceſſus ductus in curia Romana per procuratores regni Scotiæ & ſpecialiter per M. Baldredum Biſet juriſperitum & clericum notabilem contra figmenta regis Angliæ.*

(*a*) Ibid. p. 809.
(*b*) Fordun. edit. Hearn. p. 835.
(*c*) Fordun. Continuat. Hearn. p. 853.

Both these pieces may be seen at length in the *Scotichronicon* MS. and in the exact new editions of *Fordun* by M. *Hearne*; and both of them, on occasion of king *Edward's* running up to *Brutus*, and the other ancient *British* stories, give us an account of the notion the *Scots* had then of their own high antiquities, rather by tradition and hearsay, than by monuments of history; of which it appears, that before this time they had been generally deprived, and in the hurry and confusion matters were in, they had not leisure to consult such remains as they might have of them; for the continuator of *Fordun* (as I said) remarks, that they were drawn up in haste, *cum festinatione*, and the circumstances of the time required expedition.

III. The third piece remaining of these dark times, betwixt the year 1291, and the publishing of *Fordun's* history, concerning the remote antiquities of the *Scots*, is the famous *letter of the* Scotish *nobility to pope* John XXII. *dated the 6th of* August 1320, and often (*a*) published.

Now as to the substance of these three pieces written betwixt the year 1291, and the publishing

(*a*) In Dr. *Burnet's* collection of records, in the history of the *English* reformation, in M. *Anderson's* independency, and in M. *Hearne's* edition of *Fordun*, p. 787.

ing the history of *John Fordun*; in the first place it must be acknowledged, that the liberties and independency of the crown of *Scotland* from *England*, (which is the main scope of these memorials and letter of the *Scots*) are maintained with great vigour, and supported with better documents and grounds than could well have been expected in such times, and after the loss the *Scots* had suffered (as they justly complain) of their ancient monuments, and of the best proofs of their liberties.

As to the accounts they give of their remote antiquities, they are much the same in substance with those given in the *Chronicon Rythmicum*, already mentioned, which contains an abridgment of the traditions of the *Scots* on that subject, such as they were believed to be commonly in the thirteenth age. But those remote antiquities being only incident matters to the chief subject of the debate of the *Scots*, about their independency on *England*, they are only occasionally mentioned in the memorials and letter to the pope, not to be behind-hand with king *Edward*, who had valued himself on his having succeeded, by a long descent of kings, to *Brutus*, *Locrinus*, &c. and as having entered in their rights over the northern inhabitants of *Britain*. Besides that, the accounts that the *Scots* deliver in these pieces, were drawn up, as hath been remarked, in so great haste, that they had not leisure, in the hurry of war, to examine them maturely, or consult those that were most versed in the antiquities of the nation; but were obliged to set down such notions of them as their memory or popular tradition furnished them with, and at the same time to give them the most favourable turn they could, to the honour and advantage of their nation, beyond the *English*. In a word, those productions of the *Scots*, I mean as to their remote antiquities, ought to be considered, such as they truly were, as the pleadings of advocates, who commonly make no great difficulty to advance with great assurance all that makes for the advantage of their cause or clients, tho' they have but probable grounds, and sometimes but bare conjectures to go upon.

It must not then be wondered at, that we meet with in these productions of the *Scots*, and others of those times, many particulars concerning our remote antiquities, very different from what more ancient documents contain, and some notions quite new, and singular. Now it is to be observed, that though they were only broached in haste, in order to serve the present turn; yet some of these notions having been taken up by posterior writers, and made the foundations of new schemes of our history, its necessary to give some account of the more singular particulars that those pieces contain.

1°. The instructions of the states insinuate, *Scota* herself, *Pharaoh*'s daughter, came to *Scotland* (bringing

(bringing along with her ſome of the inhabitants of *Ireland* as ſhe paſſed) together with her ſon *Erc*; from whoſe name, and that of his father *Gathelus*, the firſt lands that the *Scots* poſſeſſed in *Britain*, were called *Argadia*, or rather *Ercgatheyl*. 2°. The letter of the nobility inſinuates, that tho *Scots* came from *Spain* ſtraight to *Britain*, without mentioning *Ireland*. 3°. Theſe pieces tell us, that from the firſt coming of the *Scots* to *Britain*, the old name of *Albania* was changed into that of *Scotia* (from *Scota*) which the *Scots*, ſay they, thenceforth kept up with an uninterrupted poſſeſſion of their independency, whilſt the ſouth of *Britain* changed many names and maſters. (To be ſure our highland ſeanachies were not conſulted in this account, of the aboliſhing the name of *Albany* in thoſe firſt times, ſince the *Highlanders* ſtill retain it to this day.) 4°. As to chriſtianity, the inſtructions inform us, that the *Scots* received it four hundred years, *Baldred*'s proceſs ſays five hundred years, before the *Engliſh*; which would come up to the year one hundred of Chriſt. And the nobility's letters ſeem to ſay, that the *Scots* embraced chriſtianity among the firſt, after Chriſt's reſurrection and aſcenſion.

5°. The inſtructions and proceſs affirm, that in conſequence of our chriſtianity, and afterwards by the famous donation of the emperor *Conſtantine*, *Scotland* became a *Fief* of the church of *Rome*; and they are at great pains to prove, by all the argu-

arguments they could think of, their immediate dependence on the see of *Rome* in temporals: but withal, they do not so much as insinuate, that ever any of our kings submitted his kingdom to the pope in temporals, as indeed there was never any such thing heard of in *Scotland*. The truth is, that the *Scots* at this time (*circ. A. D.* 1300) being divided among themselves, were grievously oppressed by king *Edward*, and but faintly assisted by the *French*; so expecting no relief from abroad, but from the pope and the censures of the church, they make use of all arguments that could move him to exert his power against king *Edward*: and therefore they plead merit at his hands, by their being a most ancient people among the first that embraced christianity; and more yet, by their being vassals to the pope, from which they inferred, that king *Edward's* claiming superiority over them was a sacrilegious invasion of the rights of the apostolical see, which was therefore more strictly obliged to protect them. In a word, they considered that the pope lying at such a distance from them, their having some dependence on him even in temporals, was incomparably better, and less burthensome, than to be vassals to king *Edward*, so heavy upon them, and so nigh at hand in the same island. Upon the whole, they say all that men in a stress will say to serve a turn, without examining matters so nicely. And for a proof that all this was merely the effect of their present pressures, when those were once over, and that king

Robert

Robert the Bruce's victorious arms had ſhaken off the *Engliſh* yoke, there is never a word more to be found of the kingdom's being a *Fief* of the church of *Rome* in the nobility's letter to pope *John* XXIII. (*A.D.* 1320) nor at any time after. But they think it enough to call themſelves the humble and devout ſons of the pope, and the kingdom the patrimony of St. *Andrew*, brother to St. *Peter*, and their ſpecial patron; being well aſſured that none of St. *Andrew*'s ſucceſſors would claim any vaſſalage on them.

6°. BUT the moſt remarkable thing to be met with in theſe memorials, and the moſt material to the ſubject, we are now about, is, that in them we find, for the firſt time in any piece I have yet met with, mention of ancient kings of *Scots* in *Britain* before the fifth or ſixth age: this became a bottom for poſterior writers to work upon. And thus far as to the ſecond claſs of the monuments of our ancient hiſtory.

IV. BUT before we come to the third claſs, we have as yet two writers to mention: the one is *Andrew Winton*, who, though he probably outlived *Fordun*, yet he wrote before *Fordun*'s chronicle was publiſhed, and certainly had never ſeen his work, and ſo belongs properly to this ſecond claſs of the monuments of the *Scotiſh* hiſtory, written after the year 1291, and before the publiſhing *Fordun*'s chronicle, which, though written in the reign of king *Robert* II. or III. was not publiſhed till that of king *James* II.

ANDREW WINTON was a canon regular of St. *Andrew*'s, and prior of *Loghlevin*; he wrote a chronicle, in *Scotish* metre, during the end of the reign of king *Robert* III. and beginning of that of king *James* I. There are in the register or chartulary of the priory of St. *Andrew*'s (*a*) several authentick acts, or publick instruments of *Andrew Winton*, as prior of *Loghlevin*, from the year 1395 till 1413. What precise year he died in, I do not find. His work is divided into nine books. The first five contain a kind of abstract of univeral history, intermixed with such lame accounts of the *Picts* and *Scots*, as the author had met with, till the reign of *Keneth Mac-Alpin* in the ninth age. From the sixth book forwards he is more full on the *Scotish* affairs; and in the three last books he gives almost a continued history of *Scotish* matters, from *Malcolm Keanmore* till the beginning of the reign of king *James* I. where his chronicle ends about the year 1408.

The character of this writer (as indeed of most writers of that age) is to set down with simplicity, and almost without any examination, whatever he found proper to his subject in former writers, or in the common traditions of the times in which he lived, about the matters of which he treats. By consequence, the chief thing we may

(*a*) Penes comitem de Panmure.

learn

learn from *Winton*, is what notions the *Scots* had of their origin, of the beginning of their monarchy, and of the other antiquities of *Scots* and *Picts* in the end of the fourteenth age, before the publishing *Fordun*'s chronicle.

As to the *Scotish* antiquities, *Winton*, in his first five books, gives us the genealogy of our kings in the different ages, from *Noe* till *Fergus* son of *Erc*, the same that all our ancient writers, before *Boece*, contain. He tells the story of *Gathelgas*, or *Gatheyl*'s marrying *Scota*, the daughter of *Pharaoh*, from whom the *Scots* were so called; his coming to *Spain*; that *Simon Breac*, about thirty three generations from *Gathelglas* or *Gatheyl*, and twenty two from *Milesdespain* or *Milesius*, came from *Spain* to *Ireland*, and began there the kingdom of the *Scots*, bringing with him the fatal stone. That the *Scots* came from *Ireland* to the north of *Britain* about four hundred and forty years before the incarnation.

But, what is very remarkable, he takes no particular notice of *Fergus* son of *Feradach*, called king *Fergus* I. by *Fordun* and his followers, but sets down his bare name, without any mark of distinction, among the other names in that genealogy of our kings. But as to *Fergus* the son of *Erc*, whom he calls *Fergus the Great*, *Winton* informs us, that it was he who carried over the famous stone from *Ireland* to the north of *Britain*, and who

became

became the first king of the *Scots* in this island; as it will farther appear when we come to examine that matter.

AMONG many other MSS. which I have seen of this chronicle of *Winton*, there is one belonging to the king's library, (now joined in with the *Cotton* library) at *London (Num. 16. D.* xx.) that appears to me the most entire and most valuable of them all. It is written upon strong paper, intermixed with vellum from place to place, and, by the form and character of it, seems to have been written towards the beginning of the fifteenth century, near the author's time. But what is most valuable in this copy is, that it appears to be the last review and edition (if I may speak so) that *Winton* made of his chronicle, containing several corrections, additions and alterations made in it upon better information.

(*a*) THE most material addition that this copy contains, is a compleat chronology, or series of the kings of *Scots*, from *Fergus* son of *Erch*, with the years of their reigns, down to *Eochad-Rinneval*, (*Mac Dongard - Mac Domnuil - Bric*, called by our modern writers *Eugen*. V.) This series is not in another very ancient MSS. of this chronicle in the *Cotton* (*b*) library, nor in any other that I have hi-

(*a*) Chron. Winton. Bibliothec. Regiæ Lond. Book IV. chap. 8.

(*b*) Bibl. Cotton Nero, D. XI.

therto

therto met with. It is taken from the records of St. *Andrew's*, whereof *Winton* was a canon, as appears by its conformity to the series in the (*a*) appendix, taken from a register or chartulary of that church, and to that of *James Gray*, both taken from the same records of that ancient church. This first part of that series in *Winton* being so rare, I shall give it in his own language with the rest of the pieces in the appendix (*b*). The following part of that series of our kings, which begins book VI. chap. 1. being intermixed with the rest of the history, and in all the other copies of that chronicle, I shall not follow it.

As to corrections or retrenchments that *Winton* hath made in this last review of his chronicle, one of the most remarkable is, that *Winton*, it seems, hath been advised, by persons more skilled in history, after the first editions of his chronicle appeared, to leave out, what he had advanced in the first draughts of it, that *Fergus-mac-Erch* (whom in all his draughts of it first, and last, he still makes the first king of *Scots*) began his reign about two hundred and forty years before *Cruythne*, the first king of the *Picts*, who, according to him, began only about two hundred years before the incarnation; whereas he had made the reign of *Fergus-mac-Erch*, first king of the *Scots*, to begin about four hundred and forty years before the birth of Christ. We may

(*a*) Append. numb. 5.
(*b*) Append. numb. 7.

elsewhere have occasion to observe the intricacy into which this drove him; for their being but ten or eleven generations, according to the old genealogy universally received, betwixt *Fergus-mac-Erch* and *Keneth-mac-Alpin*, who lived in the ninth century, the placing *Fergus-mac-Erch*'s reign four hundred years before the incarnation, was followed by this absurdity, that ten or twelve generations behoved to extend to twelve centuries. *Winton* himself had observed (*a*) this in the first draughts of his chronicle, and after useless efforts to get rid of it, he is forced at last to leave it to others, or rather to give it up, and to own that the *Picts* were already reigning in *Albany*, before *Fergus-mac-Erch*, first king of the *Scots*, began to reign. It seems that *Winton* was advised to omit all this in the last review and correction of his chronicle, where accordingly we meet no more with it.

As to *Pictish* matters, he brings down their settlement, and beginning of their monarchy, two hundred years later than that of the *Scots*, as it was usual with all the other *Scotish* writers to bring it as low as they could, in order to give the *Scots* a preference of antiquity before the *Picts*, as it hath been (*b*) observed. For which reason *Winton* tells us, that the *Picts* settled in *Britain*

(*a*) Wint. Chron. fol. 37, 43, &c. Bibl. Cott. Nero, D. XI.

(*b*) Supra, p. 125, 126, &c.

two hundred years only before the incarnation; that their kingdom lasted about one thousand and sixty years; and that they were subdued by *Keneth-mac-Alpin*, *A. D.* 843. He gives us the names of the *Pictish* kings from *Cruythne* their first king, much in the same manner as the extract of the register of St. *Andrew* contains them.

THE other writer, who belongs to this second class, is Mr. *James Gray*, a publick notary, and priest of the diocese of *Dunblain*. He was a person of character in his time, being successively secretary to the two first archbishops of St. *Andrew's* after *Patrick Graham*; to wit, to *William Schevez* and to prince *James* duke of *Ross*, brother to king *James* IV.

THERE is extant, in the hands of the learned M. *John Kerr*, professor of *Greek* in the royal college of the *Old-town* of *Aberdeen*, a collection of pieces made by this *James Gray* for his own use, and fitted to his calling, which M. *Kerr* was pleased to communicate to me. Among other curious pieces in this collection, there is a short chronicle, in which, after setting down a short account of the five first ages of the world, according to the common calculation of those times, there follows, with the title of *Cronica brevis*, in the first place, a genealogy of the kings of *Scotland*, from *Adam* down to king *James* IV. just the same that is given by all other writers that treat of it, before the new genealogy produced by *Hector Boece* appeared. This genealogy inserted by *James Gray*, as it differs entirely, as well as all the old ones, as we have seen, from that of *Boece*; so it agrees with all the old ones, except in mistakes and faults of copyists, whereof the chief are, that the transcriber, by mistake, takes sometimes the sirnames in the genealogy for a new name, and so multiplies, by consequence, the descents or the generations, by making one descent of the name, and another of the sirname, thus: instead of *Eakak* or *Eachach Munremore*, *cujus filius fuit Erch*, *cujus filius Fergus*, &c. he has read, *Eakak cujus filius fuit Munre*, *cujus filius fuit Erth more*, &c. At other times, by a contrary mistake, he joins two names or descents in one, thus: instead of *Forgo* or *Fergus*, *cujus filius fuit Maynus*, *cujus filius fuit*, &c. as it is in all other copies of that genealogy, he hath *Forgo Magnus* (reading g for y, and joining two names) *cujus filius fuit*, &c.

In the next place, *James Gray*, though he supposes (according to a tradition received among the *Scots*, as we have seen, from about the twelfth age) that they came to *Britain* four hundred and forty three years before the incarnation; and insinuates, as *Winton* doth, that they had kings from the beginning, or that their kingdom began with their first settlement in *Britain*, *Notandum quod Regnum Scotiæ incepit ante Incarnationem*, *A. D.* 443. which was an opinion received among the *Scots*, since the debates before pope *Boniface* VIII. against

againſt king *Edward* I. about their independency, as we have ſeen elſewhere; yet when *James Gray* comes to ſet down the ſeries of the kings of *Scotland*, he follows exactly the extracts of the ancient *Scotiſh* chronicles, ſuch as they were long before theſe debates with king *Edward* I. It being manifeſt, by the text of the chronicle, or abſtract of our chronicles, that *James Gray* had before him, that it was written during the reign of king *William*, and before the end of the twelfth age, from theſe words, where giving an account of the number of years that the *Scots* had reigned ſince the end of the *Pictiſh* kingdom, or its union with that of the *Scots*, he ſays, it was only three hundred and thirty ſeven years and five months. *Summa Scotorum poſt Pictos* 337 *ann.* & 5 *menſ.* Now whatever year be aſſigned to the end of the *Pictiſh* monarchy, whether 839, as *Fordun* reckons, or 842, as it ſeems more probable, the *Epoch* of the chronicle, that *James Gray* copied, will be towards the end of the twelfth age, *A. D.* 1176. or 1169. during the reign of king *William*. And this copy of *James Gray*, bating faults of tranſcribers, which are many, eſpecially in ſlipping over ſome few of the kings names, and in the numerical cyphers of the years of ſome reigns, agrees perfectly with the extract already mentioned of the old regiſter of St. *Andrew's*, in the ſeries of the kings of the *Scots* and *Picts*, and in the order in which they place them. Both of them begin with theſe words; *Fergus filius Erch primus regnavit in Scotia tribus annis ultra Dromalbain*, &c. *Dovenghart fil. Fergus quinque annis regnavit. Congal. fil. Dovenghart*, &c. and continue down the succession till king *Alpin*, of whom they both give the same account in the same words: *Alpin filius Heoghed annuine 3 annis regnavit. Hic occisus est in Galwathea postquam eam penitus destruxit & devastavit. Et hinc translatum est regnum Scotorum in regnum Pictorum.*

AFTER that, both the register and *James Gray* set down the catalogue or series of the *Pictish* kings, beginning both in the same words: *Cruthnie fil. Kynne clemens judex accepit monarchiam Pictorum & 50 an. regnavit*, &c. and both finish them in the same manner: *Drust* or *Durst*, *fil. Ferat 3 annis regnavit. Hic occisus est apud Forteviot: secundum alios apud Sconam a Scottis.* And then they both resume the series or catalogue of the *Scotish* kings, from *Keneth Mac-Alpin*, in the same words thus: *Kinath Mac-Alpin* XVI. *ann. regn. super Scottos. destructis Pictis & mortuus est in Forteviot & sepultus in Yona insula: ubi tres filii Erch scilicet Fergus, Loarn & Oengus sepulti fuerunt. Hic mira calliditate duxit Scotos de Argadia in terram Pictorum.* From this, *Kynath* or *Keneth*, the first king after the union, they both carry down the catalogue of the kings of *Scotland*; to wit, the register of St. *Andrew*'s, till the second or third year of king *Alexander* III. about which time it was written, and *James Gray* till *Malcolm Keanmore*; where perhaps the chronicle, whence he extracted it, ended.

And,

And, after giving a ſhort eccleſiaſtical kind of chronology, he reſumes that of the *Scotiſh* kings at *Malcolm Keanmore*, and carries it down to his own time.

By all this it appears, that either *James Gray* hath copied the regiſter of St. *Andrew*'s, or, which is more likely, that both he and the regiſter have followed the ſame original; that is, the records of St. *Andrew*'s: which *James Gray* had a fair opportunity of doing, during his abode ſeveral years in that city, as ſecretary to two archbiſhops; which gave him ready acceſs to all that had been preſerved of records in that ancient church. And thus the agreeing teſtimony of theſe two writers confirm each other; and aſſure us of the ſeries and ſucceſſion of the *Scotiſh* kings, ſuch as they were contained in their ancient annals and hiſtories before the year 1291.

I cannot finiſh this account of *James Gray* without taking notice that he is probably the ſame perſon mentioned at the end of the ſecond book of the MS. *Scotichronicon*, (one of the fulleſt of that kind) belonging to the honourable family of *Panmure*. The words of this MS. are; *Explicit liber ſecundus Scotichronicon 9 Januar. in Edinburg. oppido, A. D.* 1480. *per me magnum Macculloch*, (and in another hand) *&* *per me Jacobum Gray illuminatus*. If this was the ſame *James Gray*, author of the aforeſaid catalogue of our kings, as both this date and the name makes me think it was, then in that case it would appear, that either this catalogue of our kings must have been extracted by him before he saw *John Fordun*'s chronicle; or if after he saw it, which is more likely, we must suppose that he looked upon the records, whence he took his catalogue, as of greater authority than *Fordun*'s chronicle; since in the names, succession and chronology of our kings, he hath followed these records, preferably to *Fordun*. And thus far as to our writers of the second class.

§. 3. Of John Fordun; *of his continuators and followers, and other writers of our ancient history, till the year* 1526.

We have (a) already given an account of *John Fordun*, and of the occasion of his compiling the *Scotish* history; and we shall again have farther occasion elsewhere to treat of him. At present it suffices to remark, that he wrote in the reigns of *Robert* II. or III. but that it appears that his history was not published, or much known till afterwards; that *Walter Bowmaker*, abbot of *Inchcolm*, made additions to it, and a continuation of it, in the reign of king *James* II. This chronicle was followed on, or continued by several others; such as *Patrick Russel* a *Carthusian* monk, *Macculloch* canon of *Scoon*; and in general all our o-

(a) Supra, pag. 201.

ther

ther monastery books, (except that of *Maylross*) such as *Liber Paslatensis*, *Cuprensis*, *Sconensis*, &c. were nothing else but copies of *Fordun*, till the death of king *David* I. with some few interpolations of their own, and a continuation of his history down to the death of king *James* I. and these copies of *Fordun*, with the continuation, is what is called *Scotichronicon*. Of all which there were also several abridgments: whereof a large account may be found in Dr. *Nicholson*'s *Scotish* historical library; and in M. *Hearne*'s remarks and appendixes to his edition of *Fordun*: to which I refer for brevity.

II. To this third class of our writers ought to be referred, a MS. chronicle of *Scotland*, translated from *Latin* into *French* by one *Grem. Domate*, and dedicated to *John* duke of *Albany* in the year of our Lord 1519. This MS. belongs to the library of the abbey of St. *Geneoveve* in *Paris*. It is in folio, marked M 2. It is a very literal translation into *French* of *Fordun*, with the same continuator, which in the *Bodleian* library, *Cod. MS.* 3888, bears the title of bishop *Elphinston*'s history: but it would seem by this MS. that the original was written by order of the abbot of *Dunfermlin*; and probably the copy that *Domate* made use of, belonged to that abbey.

This translator hath made many mistakes in his translation, and the copy is very defective.

What

What seems most remarkable in it, is an appendix in eight leaves on vellum, containing a kind of abridgment of the *Scotish* history, with pictures of the kings, from *Galabel* or *Gaythel* and *Scota* downwards, in very coarse miniature: and here we have a first essay of the names of these ancient kings of *Scots* that are said to have preceded king *Fergus* son of *Erc*. Their names, according to this writer, are as follows:

1. *GALAHEL*, or *Gaythel*, and *Scota*. 2. *Hiber*. 3. *Himec*. 4. *Nonael*. 5. *Micelium* (*Milesius*.) 6. *Bartholon*. 7. Another *Micelio*. 8. *Simon Breac*. 9. *Ethac Rothsay*. 10. *Fergus*. 11. *Rether*. 12. *Maher*. 13. *Anonyme*. 14. *Jayr*. 15. *Eteorac*, in the time of *Dioclesian*. 16. *Phaleg*, in the time of *Carausius*. 17. *Eugenius*. 18. *Hurgust*, (who was king of the *Picts*, otherwise called *Eubotba*.) 19. *Fergus*, (this was *Fergus* II. son of *Erc*) and from him he continues the ordinary names of the kings, as in *Fordun*, with their pictures, till king *James* I; but as the number of kings he mentions before *Fergus* II. are far short of the forty-five, which *Fordun* says we had, so they are very different names and personages from those forty that *Boece* found about six years after *Domate*, in his famous MSS. of *Veremund*, &c. However, we may observe by this, that attempts were made to fill up this gap of the history before *Fergus* II. which *Fordun* and his continuators had left. All of them, tho' they tell us there were forty

forty-five kings before *Fergus* II. yet they neither give us any account of them, nor so much as their names, except of three, *Fergus* I. *Rether*, and *Eugenius*.

III. To this third class of our writers belongs also *John Major*'s history; it being a short abridgment of *Fordun*, or of some of his continuators, intermixed with an abstract of the *English* history, and with many reflexions and scholastick reasonings of his own. It gives us no farther account of the forty-five kings before *Fergus* II. than *Fordun*. It was printed very incorrectly at *Paris*, *A. D.* 1521, whilst the author was absent in *Scotland*. Among other errors of copyists, or of the print in *John Major*'s printed history, ought without doubt to be reckoned this passage, *L.* 2. *c.* 1. *Inter hunc Fergusium filium Erth & primum Fergusium filium Ferchardi quindecim Scotorum erant Reges, & ultra Septingentorum annorum tempus*, &c. for all the copies of *Fordun*, (whereof *Major* is only an abstract) have forty-five kings; and in *Major*'s own account, in the following seven hundred years from *Fergus* II. till *Edgar*, there are fifty-one kings, that is, above thrice fifteen: so this must be visibly a mistake of the cyphers 15 for 45, either in *Major*'s copy, or in that which he followed, which the publisher hath printed at length by mistake.

IV. To the same class ought to be reduced a short abridgment of the *Scotish* history, by the title

title of *Brevis Chronica*, annexed to *Winton*'s chronicle MS. in the lawyers library at *Edinburgh.* This ſhort chronicle begins with *Gathelus* and *Scota*, and brings down the hiſtory to the reign of king *Robert* II. Tho' the author lived after *Boece*, and even after his tranſlator *Bellenden*; yet as to our remote antiquities, and all that paſſed before *Fergus* II; he is to be claſſed among the followers of *Fordun*, of whom he is an exact abridger, till *Fergus* II's time, and hath no more than he of the firſt forty kings, not ſo much as their names, tho' he had before him *Boece*'s hiſtory tranſlated by *Bellenden*, and follows him from *Fergus* II. downwards, in the character of our kings; and from *Conſtantine* III. he generally quotes book and chapter of *Bellenden*'s tranſlation of *Boece*. This his deſignedly omitting all the ſtory, and even the names of the firſt forty kings of *Boece*, which he had before him, ſhews plainly, that *Boece*'s accounts of them, over and above what *Fordun* had left, was not at firſt reliſhed even by all our *Scotiſh* writers.

§. 4. *Or fourth claſs of* Scotiſh *writers; of* Boece, Buchananan, *and their followers.*

I have already treated at ſo great length of *Hector Boece*, *George Buchanan*, and their chief followers performances, that it would be ſuperfluous to inſiſt farther on them in this place. What more may be proper to ſay of them will come in more ſeaſonably elſewhere.

CHAP.

CHAP. II.

Of the true Epoch *of the first Settlement of the* Scots, *and beginning of their monarchy in* Britain.

AFTER the account I have given in the preceding chapter, of the writers of the *Scotish* history, and of the remains we have of monuments or records, concerning the most ancient part of it, I am now to treat, 1°. Of the time of the first settlement of the *Scots* in *Britain.* 2°. Of the first king of the *Scots* in *Britain.* 3°. Of the beginning of his reign, which is the *Epoch* of the monarchy of the *Scots* in this island. 4°. For a more full satisfaction, and a general answer to the objections against the system of the high antiquities of the *Scots,* which I have here set down, I shall conclude the essays, by an account of the different steps and degrees by which the high antiquities of the *Scots* seem to have grown up by length of time, in the several hands through which they passed, into the plan of history in which they were delivered by our modern writers.

ART.

Art. I. *Of the first settlement of the* Scots *in* Britain.

The opinion of the coming in of the *Scots*, and of their having been settled in *Ireland* many ages before the incarnation, having been received among the *Irish*, as we see by *Nennius*, before the ninth age, it is no wonder that the *Scots* in *Britain*, looking on themselves, as descended of the *Scots* in *Ireland*, and having among them bards of the same genius as those in *Ireland*, should have afterwards, by degrees, claimed to themselves a high antiquity.

But having already shewn the uncertainty of the grounds on which the *Irish* build their pretensions to remote antiquity in the *Scotish* line, and having proved that there is much more ground, from the best information that we can have of ancient times, to be persuaded that the settlement of the *Scots* even in *Ireland*, was only about the time of the incarnation, or even after it; from this it follows, that the settlement of the *Scots* in *Britain* must be yet of a later date, since it would seem natural that there should be some time allowed to the *Scots* in *Ireland*, to establish themselves there, and multiply so, as to be able to send out a colony to the northern parts of *Britain*.

But

But if we ſuppoſe what is credible enough, and wants not ground in antiquity, that the *Scots* did not ſettle at firſt in a full body and by force in *Britain*, but came in by degrees; that they firſt poſſeſſed ſome of the weſtern iſlands, and coming over in ſmall numbers, obtained habitations, with the allowance of the *Picts*, on the north-weſtern coaſts, where they lived at firſt united to the *Picts* in *Britain*, and joined with them in their expeditions againſt the *Romans*, or provincial *Britons*. In this ſuppoſition, the firſt coming in of the *Scots* to *Britain*, may have been not long after their ſettlement in *Ireland*. Beſides, that in in the ſuppoſition of the *Scots* coming originally from *Scandia*, (of which we have (*a*) treated elſewhere) whilſt the greateſt number of them paſſed forward to *Ireland*, ſome of them might have ſtopped at the weſtern iſlands, or coaſts of *Britain*, and there fixed their ſeats by conſent of the *Picts*, willing to have them auxiliaries in their wars againſt the *Romans* and *Britons*, as we obſerve they were, from the firſt time of the *Scots* ſettling in *Britain*. And a farther proof of the early ſettlement of the *Scots* in *Britain* is, that the firſt author that ſpeaks of them (*b*), mentions them in *Britain* about the year 360; as we ſhall ſhew.

(*a*) Supra, pag. 539.
(*b*) Ammian. l. 20.

(*a*) BEDE

(a) BEDE leaves it uncertain, whether the *Scots* settled at first among the *Picts by force or by favour*; [Scoti] *Duce Reuda de Hybernia egressi vel amicitia vel ferro sibimet inter eos (Pictos) sedes quas hactenus habent, vindicarunt. A quo, viz. duce, usque hodie Dalreudini vocantur.* *Bede* adds, that the *Scots*, on their coming to *Britain*, settled on the north side of the *Frith of Cluyd*, which was of old the boundary of the *Britons* and *Picts* on the west of *Britain*. *Bede* informs us here, that in his time the *Scots* in *Britain* were called as yet *Dalreudini*. *Nennius* (b) also in the ninth age calls the possessions of the *Scots* in *Britain*, *Regiones Dalrietæ*; and long after *Nennius*, the anonymous writer, printed in the appendix (c) to this essay, calls the kingdom of the *Scots* in *Britain*, before their union with the *Picts*, by the name of (d) *Regnum Dalrietæ*, or kingdom of *Dalrede*.

THE *Irish* (e) writers give ample accounts of the origine of the name *Dalriada*. These accounts may be seen set down at great length by Dr. *Kenedy* (f). They derive the name *Dalriada*,

(a) Bed. Hist. l. 1, c. 1.
(c) Append. num. 3.
(b) Nennius, c. 9.
(d) Iste [*Kenethus*] biennio antequam veniret Pictaviam *Dalrieta* regnum suscepit. *Append. n.* 3.
(e) Usser. Antiq. Brit. p. 320, 321.
(f) Ken. Geneal. p. 103, 104, &c.

not without probability from *Eocha Riada*, who, they say, was also called *Carbre Riada* (son of king *Conar*) the same with *Bede's Reuda*. He is called in the best copies of the old genealogy of the kings of *Scots*, *Eocha*, or *Eochad Riada* or *Riede*, (as may be seen in the genealogical table, *pag.* 235.) and, in the later and more incorrect copies, the name is written *Ethod Riede*; from whence is derived *Boece*'s twenty fifth king *Ethodius* I. who reigned, according to *Buchanan*, *A. D.* 163.

THE same *Irish* writers acknowledge, that the *Scots* came from *Ireland* to *Britain* under the conduct of this *Eocha Riada*, son of *Conar*, who, according to them, was king of *Ireland*, and died *A. D.* 219: so the coming over of his son *Eocha Riada* with the *Scots* into *Britain*, may have happened about the beginning of the third age. But it must have fallen out more early, if we could depend upon the tenor of the old genealogy of our kings, such as I have shewn (*a*) that all our writers do uniformly deliver before *Boece*'s new genealogy appeared. For, according to this old genealogy (*b*), *Eocha Riada Mac-Conar*, was, in the thirteenth degree before *Erc*, father to *Fergus*: so that though this *Fergus mac Erch* be placed in the end of the fifth or beginning of the sixth century, allowing thirty years to each generation

(*a*) Supra, p. 236, 237, &c.

(*b*) Vide the tables, p. 235.

the coming in of *Eoc ba Riada* with the *Scots* to *Britain*, would have happened in the beginning of the ſecond century; which would have been too early, ſuppoſing that the *Scots* came into *Ireland* only about the time of the incarnation; ſince ſome length of time muſt be allowed to the *Scots*, after their coming into *Ireland*, to ſettle themſelves and multiply in that iſland, before they could ſend out any colonies.

It were eaſy to ſolve this difficulty, by the method that ſome *Iriſh* writers make uſe of in like caſes. For when they find in their genealogies the number of generations too great to agree with any period of time for ſettling a chronology, they do not heſitate to reduce theſe exorbitant generations to the preciſe number that fits their purpoſe; making no difficulty to cut off as many generations, as they find expedient of theſe old genealogies composed by their ſenachies; notwithſtanding all the regulations of their parliaments of *Tarach*, of the committee of *Nine*, and all the ſtrict examinations that they pretend (*a*) were made of theſe productions of their ſeanachies, and the precautions for preſerving them. We have elſewhere (*b*) obſerved their reductions of this kind; and *O Flaherty* alone could furniſh many examples of it. And, not to depart from the preſent caſe,

(*a*) D. Kened. Geneal. Pref. p. 17, 18, &c.

(*b*) Supra, p. 485, 486, &c.

they

they tell us (*a*), that there are, according to their antiquaries, eleven descents or generations from *Eocha Riada* till *Fergus* the son of *Erc*, which, as they think, is two generations more than enough for that period of time: and accordingly Dr. *Kennedy* (*b*) is at great pains to make a reduction of them to a smaller number, and strikes off two of them.

BUT as all these genealogies, and other domestick accounts of the remote antiquities of the *Irish* and *Scots*, appear very uncertain, considering the little probability there is, that they had, before the fifth age, the use of letters, or any other sure means to preserve true accounts of past transactions; we must therefore endeavour to find some light into this dark subject, of the first coming in of the *Scots* to *Britain*, in the more certain accounts given us by the *Roman* writers.

(*c*) *AMMIAN MARCELLIN*, the first writer that mentions the *Scots*, gives us the following account, That *A. D.* 360, towards the latter end of the reign of the emperor *Constantius* in *Britain*, the *Scots* and the *Picts*, two fierce people,

(*a*) D. Ken. Gen. p. 115.

(*b*) Ibid. p. 116, 117, &c.

(*c*) In Britanniis Scotorum Pictorumque gentium ferarum excursu, rupta quiete, condicta limitibus loca vastata sunt, & implicabat formido vicinas provincias, praeteritarum cladium congerie fessas, &c. *Ammian. lib.* 20.

ple, having violated the peace, and broken into the fixed limits of the empire in that island, were ravaging the provinces of it, which filled with terror the provincials spent and wearied with their former invasions in times past. Upon this news, the *Cæsar Julian*, then residing in *Gaul*, began to give orders for repulsing of them, *&c.* which, nevertheless, as appears by the following part of *Ammian*'s history, was not effectually done till about the year 367 or 368, that the general *Theodosius* was sent over to *Britain* by *Valentinian* I.

It is to be remarked in this narrative of *Ammian*, that though this be the first time that the *Scots* are mentioned by him, or indeed by any certain writer of or before these times, yet it appears, by him, that the *Scots* were already looked upon not only as formidable enemies of the empire in *Britain*, but that this was not the first time that the *Scots*, in conjunction with the *Picts*, had invaded and ravaged the *Roman* provinces in this island, since he adds, that the provincials were struck with so much the greater terror of these enemies, that they were already quite wearied and spent with a great number of ravages they had made in former times. *Prætevitarum cladium congerie fessas*, &c.

From this, I conceive, it follows, that the *Scots* must have been some considerable time before this settled in the island, before they could be able

able to make so considerable a figure in *Britain* as to be taken notice of by *Ammian*, as being no less dangerous enemies of the empire in *Britain* than the *Picts* or *Caledonians*.

Now this may very well agree with the placing the coming in of *Eocha Riada* (the same as *Beda*'s *Reuda*) the first leader of the colony of the *Scots* into *Britain* about the beginning of the third age. It is like he brought over, at first, but a small number, not to give jealousy to the ancient inhabitants of these parts, the *Caledonians*; but in the space of one hundred, or about one hundred and fifty years, that passed betwixt the time of their first coming in, and their being mentioned by *Ammian*, *A. D.* 360, they might have so increased both within themselves, and by accession of new auxiliaries from *Ireland*, that the *Caledonians* or *Picts*, finding them serviceable in their wars against the *Romans* and provincial *Britains*, were easily disposed to enlarge the possessions of the *Scots* on the north-western coasts of the island, in proportion as the *Caledonians* themselves (*a*) enlarged their own bounds, by new conquests, to the south of the *Friths*. And thence it happened that the *Scots* made so considerable a figure in *Britain*, according to *Ammian*, about the middle of the sixth century. But we might have had a much more full account, both of the *Scots* and of

(*a*) Supra, p. 93, 94.

the other ancient inhabitants of *Britain*, had that book of *Ammian* been preserved, in which, as he tells (*a*) us, he had given a description of *Britain*.

ACCORDING to the antiquaries of *Ireland*, this colony of *Scots*, which was brought over and settled in *Britain* by *Eocha Riada*, began a lasting establishment in this island. *Our writers* (*b*), says *D. Kenedy, unanimously tell us, that* Eocha (he calls him *Carbre*) Riada, *was the founder of the* Scotish *soveraignty in* Britain; *but they make him only a captain, as* Bede *does, or conducter; who ingratiated himself so far with the* Picts, *by his and his childrens good service against the* Britons, *that they consented that they and their followers should continue among them.* It is true, this same writer adds a little afterwards, that these first *Scots*, who settled in *Britain*, had not laid aside *thoughts* of returning back some time or other into their mother-country *Ireland*; but their continuing ever after, they and their posterity, to inhabit *Britain*, demonstrates that they had no such *thoughts*: and this writer himself tells us (*c*), that about one hundred years after their coming, *Fergus Ulidian*, who, according to him, was great grandchild to *Eocha Riada*, and chief of the *Dalriadians* in *Ireland*, did, about the beginning of the fourth century,

(*a*) Ammian. p. 347.
(*b*) Ken. Geneal. p. 107.
(*c*) Ibid. p. 130.

strengthen

strengthen the Dalriadian *colony in* Pictland *with new supplies, as his successors continued to do from time to time*: And he informs us afterwards, (*a*) that about *A. D.* 386, *Niel* king of *Ireland* came over to the north of *Britain*, and oblig'd the *Picts to draw off what families they had in* Cantyre *and* Argyle, *and suffer the* Dalriadys *to inhabit alone that side of the country, and live separately without any mixture of* Pictish *families; to the end they might be the more secure from any insults or oppression of the* Picts, who, it seems, were become jealous of their increasing, and therefore had endeavoured to keep them under, *and dispers'd* them in different Cantons, mixed with *Pictish* Families.

I RELATE this on the credit of this Writer, who gives us these particulars of the *Dalriadys*, or *Scots* in *Britain* in these early times, as taken from the accounts of them, left by the *Irish* Seanachies. By which it appears at least, that the traditions of their antiquaries were, that the *Scots*, from their first coming into the north of *Britain*, and beginning a settlement under *Eocha Riada* their first leader, towards the beginning of the third century, had still continued, without interruption, to inhabit those parts till this time, that is, till towards the end of the fourth age.

BUT we have a more certain account from the *Roman* and *British* writers, of their continuing

(*a*) Ken. Gen p. 133.

 to

to make a considerable figure in Britain, from A. D. 360. when the name of *Scots* is first mentioned by *Ammian*, and a chronological series of their expeditions, in conjunction with the *Caledonians* or *Picts*, against the *Romans* and provincial *Britains*, as long as *Britain* remained united to the *Empire*; and down till the fifth age.

WE have already given account from *Ammian*, of that irruption of the *Scots* and *Picts* on the provincial *Britains*, *A. D.* 360. Now the *Cæsar Julian*, who was then in *Gaul*, being wholly taken up with the ambitious design of usurping the empire, and supplanting his uncle the emperor *Constantius*, put no effectual remedy to the disorders of *Britain*: So the *Picts* and *Scots* made daily new progress, and it appears by the same (a) *Ammian*, that upon *Valentinian* I's coming to the empire, *A. D.* 364. he found among other *Roman* provinces invaded by the barbarous nations in their neighbourhood, those of *Britain* exposed to the ravages, not only of the *Picts* and *Scots*, but that the example of their impunity had drawn also in upon the *Britains* other new enemies, to wit, the *Saxons* and the *Attacots*.

VALENTINIAN finding the empire attack'd all at once on so many sides, was not in condition so soon to send assistance to the *Britains*;

(a) Ammian. lib. 26, pag. 315.

so

so the *Picts* and *Scots* advanced daily in the *British* provinces, and their numbers and boldness increasing by their success, they killed *Follafaudus* (a) a *Roman* general, and *Nectarides* count of the maritime coasts. At last, *A. D.* 367, the emperor receiving daily more terrifying accounts of the progress of these enemies in *Britain*, found it necessary to confide the conduct of that war to one of the most famous generals of the empire, *Theodosius*, father to the first emperor of that name.

THEODOSIUS (b), being arrived in *Britain* with a powerful army, obliged the enemies to retire, delivered the city of *London* from the apprehensions it had been expos'd to, by the approach of these Enemies; and, in a word, forced them out of the bounds of the empire in *Britain*. The poet *Claudian*, in two of his panegyricks on the emperor *Honorius*, grand-child to this general *Theodosius*, gives the following account of this expedition in these words in (c) one of them.

> *Ille leves Mauros, nec falso nomine Pictos*
> *Edomuit; Scotumque vago mucrone secutus*
> *Fregit Hyperboreas remis audacibus undas.*

(a) Ammian. lib. 27. p. 346.
(b) Idem, pag. 347.
(c) Claudian. Panegyr. in III Consulat. Honor. Imperat. pag. 114.

And

And in the other (*a*),

Ille Caledoniis posuit qui castra pruinis.
——— *incaluit Pictorum sanguine Thule;*
Scotorum cumulos flevit glacialis Ierne.

THESE expressions are suppos'd by some learned *English* writers to import, that this *Roman* general chased the *Scots* over the Sea into *Ireland.* But we are not, I conceive, to press poetical hyperboles to the rigour of the letter; otherwise we must suppose also, that *Theodosius* pursued the *Picts* to *Thule*, and there made a great slaughter of them: whereas 'tis like, that neither *Claudian*, nor the *Romans* knew where *Thule* was situated: however, as to the *Scots*, it appears to me, that long after their first settlement in *Britain*, they still continued to live in a close union with the *Scots* in *Ireland*, as being one and the same people; and that besides those already established in *Argyle*, *Cantyre*, in the western isles, *&c.* others of them were accustomed in those early times to come over in greater or smaller numbers from *Ireland* to *Britain*, as occasion offer'd, either to enlarge the possessions of the *Scots* in *Britain*, or to march as auxiliaries in conjunction with the *Scots* in *Britain*, and, with the *Picts*, to make inroads or excursions into the *Roman* provinces, and that in case of any

(*a*) Claudian, Paneg. in IV Consulat. Honor. Imp. p. 119.

great

great defeat; as it happened in this expedition of *Theodosius*, they had always a safe retreat, some of them to the extremities of the western coasts, or islands of *Britain*; others of them, especially those that had come over only as adventurers or auxiliaries, back to *Ireland*, to wait, when the enemy retired, for a new opportunity of preying on the *Britains*.

HOWEVER, as to the poet *Claudian*'s expressions, the words *hyperboreas undas* may be at least as naturally understood of the northern friths, over which this general pursued the *Scots* and *Picts*, as of the ocean, and supposing by *Ierne* is meant *Ireland*, it was very natural for the *Scots* in *Ireland* to lament the slaughter of so great a number, *cumulos*, of their friends and kinsmen, as *Theodosius* had killed of the *Scots* in *Britain*: Besides the loss of a great number of adventurers or auxiliary *Scots*, natives of *Ireland* that came over, as it hath been observed, in these early times to join those in *Britain* in their expeditions against the provincials.

THEODOSIUS, to secure them against those irruptions of their northern enemies, fortify'd anew the northern wall, and made it again the boundary of the empire, as it had been settled 230 years before under the empire of *Antonin*, and placed (*a*) guards and garrisons on it to watch and oppose the

(*a*) Limites vigiliis tuebatur & prætenturis. *Ammian.*

the enemy's motions. But the most remarkable action of this general in *Britain*, was the erecting all the territories betwixt the southern wall in *Northumberland*, and the northern at the *Friths* into a fifth *Roman* province in *Britain*; and calling it after the emperor, by the name of *Valentia*. I abridge those accounts which may be treated of more at length in the second part of this essay. *Theodosius* left the island, and returned in triumph, *A. D.* 370, to the emperor.

A. D. 383, *Maximus*, having usurped the empire in *Britain*, before he left the island, repulsed with great vigour, and overcame the *Scots* and *Picts*, according to *Gregory* (*a*) of *Tours*, and the chronicle of *Tiro Prosper* (*b*); and this is all the ground I find in ancient writers of the subversion of the *Scotish* state by *Maximus*, which is set down at such length in *Fordun*: but their defeat by *Theodosius* looks more like a subversion, than what happen'd under *Maximus*, who, upon his usurpation, passed immediately over to *Gaul*, and surprized the emperor *Gratian*, having carried over with him all the regular troops from *Britain*.

A. D. 398, the *Scots* and *Picts*, having made use of the opportunity of *Maximus*'s carrying along with him to *Gaul* the flower of the *British*

(*a*) Greg. Turon's hist.
(*b*) Tiro Prosper. in antiq. lect. Canis.

youths

youth and best troops, had made such great progress in ravaging the *British* provinces, that these provinces were almost quite ruined, and lived in perpetual dread and terror of the *Picts*, who were joined, not only by the *Scots* in *Britain*, but by new levies of *Scots* in *Ireland*. This account of the miserable condition of these provinces being brought to *Stilicho* the *Roman* general, under *Honorius* the emperor, he sent over new forces to *Britain* against the *Scots* and *Picts*; and caused the northern wall to be fortified anew against their irruptions. All this is in short related by *Claudian* (*a*), where he brings in *Britain* lamenting its perishing condition, till *Stilicho* sent over those forces to its assistance.

Me quoque vicinis pereuntem gentibus, inquit
[Britannia]
Munivit Stilicho, totam cum Scotus Iernem
Movit, & infesto spumavit remige Tethys.
Illius effectum curis, ne bella timerem
Scotica, ne Pictum tremerem, &c.

But these auxiliary forces did not remain long in *Britain*; for *A. D.* 402, among the several troops which, by *Stilicho*'s order, came to join him before the battle of *Pollentum* against the *Goths*, *Claudian* marks among others the *Roman* troops, that guarded the wall in *Britain* in the extremity of the island against the irruptions of the *Scots* and *Picts*.

(*a*) Claudian. lib. 2. de Laudibus Stilichonis.

Venit

Venit & extremis legio Britannis,
Quæ Scoto dat fræna truci, ferroque notatas
Perlegit exanimes Picto moriente figuras (a).

The poet here, by an ordinary metaphor, calls the forces that guarded the frontiers of the *British* provinces, a legion, though there used to be always more than one legion placed there to oppose these northern enemies. However, the removal of these troops gave these enemies a favourable opportunity of breaking in upon the provinces.

A. D. 409, the *Britains*, after calling in vain for assistance against these enemies from the *Romans*, and encouraged, says *Zozimus* (b), by letters from the emperor *Honorius*, to do the best they could for themselves, resolved at last to shake off their dependence on the empire, and endeavour to defend their country with their own forces; but they soon found the dismal effects of their presuming too much on their own forces, as appears by the relation of *Gildas* and of *Bede*.

But before I proceed farther, it is necessary to take notice of some expressions of these two last historians, which some learned *English* and *Irish* writers have endeavoured to wrest against the

(a) Claudian. de bello Getico, pag. 107.
(b) Zozim. hist. lib. 6. pag. 376 & 381.

ancient

ancient settlement of the *Scots* in *Britain*, in the manner that I have here accounted for it.

AND 1°. 'tis to be observed, that *Bede*, after having in the first chapter of his history given a short account of the first coming of the *Picts* and *Scots* into *Britain*, as being next to the *Britains*, the most ancient inhabitants of this island; he never mentions again either the one or the other of them, till the twelfth chapter, when, upon the occasion above-mentioned of the *Britains* shaking off *A. D.* 409. all dependence upon the empire, and resolving to defend their country by their own forces, they became an easy prey to the northern inhabitants of the island, the *Scots* and the *Picts*, the terror of whom forced the *Britains* at last to call in the *Saxons* to their aid; which gave occasion to *Bede* to mention again the *Scots* and the *Picts*.

FROM this we may learn (and 'tis of importance to take notice of it for many other occurrences in the history of these northern people) how weak the arguments are, which are drawn from the bare silence of *Bede*, concerning the transactions among the *Scots* and the *Picts*; or indeed, concerning any of the inhabitants of *Britain*, excepting the *Saxons* or *English* alone. For whosoever will read *Bede*'s history with attention, will easily find, that after the *Saxons* or *English* (the great object of his history) were come and settled in the island, he scarce ever mentions either the *Scots* or the

the Picts, or even the old Britains; but upon occasion of the Saxons, and of some transaction among those ancient people, necessary to give light into the history of the Saxons. Thus, as it would be a very false conclusion to argue from the silence of Bede, that there never were in Britain any such people as Caledonians, because Bede never mentions them, or that the same people known by the name of Picts, and the Scots, from their first entry into this island, had lain wholly unactive and made no figure in Britain till A. D. 409; whereas the contrary is evident by the certain testimony of the Roman writers concerning the Caledonians or Picts, and by that of the same Roman and even Irish writers concerning the Scots, as we have just now made appear; so it were against the equity and candor becoming a faithful writer, to refuse to credit any other transaction among the old Britains, Picts or Scots precisely, because it is not mentioned by Bede. However, it must be acknowledg'd at the same time, that the Scots, and all the other inhabitants of Britain, owe very great obligation to Bede for the knowledge of a great many ancient accounts of their history, of which, without Bede's mentioning them, they had remained wholly ignorant: tho' he generally does not mention them, but as far as they interfere with the church history of the Saxons, or English, which is all that Bede promises by the title of his book, Historia ecclesiastica gentis Anglorum.

3° GILDAS

2° GILDAS, ſpeaking of the *Picts* and *Scots*, calls them (*a*) *Tranſmarinæ gentes*. From which expreſſion biſhop *Uſher* and Dr. *Stillingfleet* would conclude, that the *Scots*, who invaded the *Britains*, were as yet; that is, about *A. D.* 422. all of them inhabitants of *Ireland*, and none of them hitherto ſettled in *Britain*; but beſides, that *Gildas*, in this place, calls equally the *Picts*, as much as the *Scots*, *tranſmarine*, or a people from beyond the ſeas; tho' no body doubts, but the *Picts* were long before ſettled in the Iſland. *Bede*, who in the firſt chapter of his hiſtory, had deſcribed the *Scots* among the ancient inhabitants of this iſland, reckoning the *Britains* the firſt, in the next place the *Picts*, and the *Scots* the third people who ſettled in *Britain*; accordingly explains this expreſſion of *Gildas*, and informs us, that the *Picts* and *Scots* are called *Tranſmarinæ gentes*, people from beyond the ſeas, (*b*) *not that they dwelt out of the iſland of* Britain, *but that their habitations in the iſland were ſeparated from thoſe of the* Britains *by the two arms of the Sea, or the friths of* Clyde *and* Forth.

(*a*) Gild. cap. 11.

(*b*) Tranſmarinas autem dicimus has gentes [*Pictorum* & *Scotorum*] non quod extra Britanniam eſſent poſitæ, ſed quia a parte Britonum erant remotæ, duobus finibus maris interjacentibus, quorum unus ab orientali mare, alter ab occidentali, Britanniæ terras longe lateque irrumpit, quamvis ad ſe invicem pertingere poſſint, &c. *Bed hiſt.* lib. 1. c. 13.

3. *Usher* and *Stillingfleet* seem to triumph upon another expression of (a) *Gildas* copied by *Bede*, (b) *Revertuntur impudentes grassatores hyberni domum* And where could be, say they, the home of the *Hyberni*, but *Hybernia* or *Ireland?* Whence they infer, that the *Scots* were as yet about *A. D.* 447. still inhabitants of *Ireland.* But in the first place, it ought to be considered, that in the language of *Bede* and of other writers of those times, the names *Hyberni* and *Scoti* were as yet synonymous, and given to the same people inhabitants of *Ireland* and *Britain*; and that the name *Hyberni* was made use of in those early times to express, not only the inhabitants of *Ireland*, but those also of *Britain* that had their origin from *Ireland*, that spoke the same language, and were as yet look'd upon as the same people, though separated by their habitations, in the same manner as the term *Saxones* was applied, both to the inhabitants of *Britain* and to those of *Germany* from whom they had their origin. And for a proof of the promiscuous usage of the names *Hyberni* and *Scoti*, these very same people, who are here (*cap.* 14.) called *Hyberni*, are called by the same *Bede*, *Scoti*, both at their setting out upon this expedition (*cap.* 12.) and in his chronicle. And as to the application of the name *Hyberni*, or *Irish*, to the *Scots* in *Britain*, besides other examples, we find as far down as the fourteenth age

(a) Gild. c. 19.
(b) Bed. lib. 1. c. 14.

the name of *Irischery* (a) given to the *Highlanders* of *Scotland*, because of their origin from *Ireland*, and of the *Irish* language that they still continue to speak.

In the second place we have already observed, that the *Scots*, who were settled in *Britain*, were, in their expeditions against the old *Britains*, frequently assisted by auxiliaries or adventurers that came over from *Ireland*, both in order to strengthen the forces of the *Scots* in *Britain*, and many of them no doubt in hopes of prey and carrying off captives, which, when the expeditions were over, some of them carried along with them back to *Ireland*, whilst others remained to fortify and augment the colony of the *Scots* in *Britain*; and that upon any great defeat, as it happened in the expedition of the general *Theodosius*, many of them used to retire to the extremities of the north-western coasts or neighbouring islands of *Britain*, or even to *Ireland*. Wherefore, to answer now the question of these learned writers, where should the home of the *Hyberni* or *Scoti* be but in *Ireland*? If they were of the *Scots* already settled in *Britain*, they passed home to their own dwellings in and about *Argyle*, and the north-western coasts of *Britain*. But if they were only adventurers, that came over either as auxiliaries, or to prey upon or carry off captives from the *Britains*, most of

(a) Archdeacon *Barber* in the life of K. *Robert the Bruce*.

them went home again to *Ireland*, others perhaps remained with their friends in the north of *Britain*, ready to march with them upon a new expedition, as they should find opportunity (*a*). *Non post multum temporis reversuri.*

But I wonder, that these learned men reflect not upon the little appearance there seems to be, of armies of men coming so often from (*b*) *Ireland* over so dangerous a sea, and the rapid tides that run between *Ireland* and *Britain*; and that upon their *corroughs*, *curucæ*, as *Gildas* calls them: and what a number of those *corroughs* was requisite to transport armies of men, if they were such as the *corroughs* made use of as yet in some places of *Scotland*, which can contain conveniently but two men at once? One would think it more natural to understand by the sea, which they had to pass, the *Friths* of *Clyde* or *Forth*, in some places not very broad, and where the *corroughs* would run no great risk, than a rapid part of the ocean; and that the quality of the vessels, *curucæ*, in which *Gildas* tells us they us'd to transport their troops, would rather serve for a new proof, that these *Scoti* or *Hyberni*, that so often infested the *Britains*, were inland inhabitants of *Britain*, who were separated from the *Britains* only by the *Friths*, which they easily passed over. And this is farther confirmed

(*a*) Gild. & Bed. ibid.

(*b*) Anniversarias predas cogere solebant. Bed. ibid.

by

by *Gildas* (*a*) telling us, that the *Scots* came *trans Stiticam vallem*, as it was in the former editions, instead of *Sciticam*, over the valley which the *Frith* of *Clyde* made betwixt the habitations of the *Scots* and *Britains*; for as it hath been elsewhere (*b*) observed, *Sciticus* and *Scoticus* are used for the same: but I cannot understand how the passage from *Ireland* to any part of *Britain* can be called *vallis*, a valley, whether it be called *Scitica vallis*, or *Tithica* as Dr. *Gale*'s edition hath it.

3°. Dr. *STILLINGFLEET* expatiates upon the injurious names of *impudentes grassatores* and the like, that *Gildas* gives to the *Scots* and *Picts* that ravaged the *Britains*, and draws inferences from them against the *Scots* being settled in *Britain*. But in the first place, I hope, *Gildas* calling the *Scots* invaders or pillagers of the *Britains*, (or if he will, robbers) does not make them outlandish, since there are inland as well as outlandish plunderers or pillagers. Whilst *Scotland* and *England* were under two distinct soveraigns, every body knows what havock they used to make reciprocally upon the one and the other kingdom: and carry home prey and captives with them, tho' they were both inland inhabitants of the same island; and as to the injurious names that *Gildas* gives to the *Scots*, I would be very sorry to imitate Dr. *Stillingfleet*, in drawing

(*a*) Gild. c. 15.
(*b*) Supra, p 536. &c.

consequences from the names that the same *Gildas* gives to the *Saxons*, nor will I be so uncivil as even to translate (*a*) *Gildas*'s words, where, speaking of the first recruit that was sent to the *Saxons* into *Britain*, he thus expresses himself, *Supra dicta genitrix* (meaning the country of the first *Saxons* or *English*) *primo comperiens agmini fuisse prosperatum, item mittit satellitum canumque prolixiorem catastam, quæ ratibus advecta, adunatur cum manipularibus spuriis.* It ought to be consisider'd here, that *Gildas* beholding his country, so flourishing of old, put by the *Saxons* to fire and sword; and the old *Britains* his countrymen either massacred, or reduced for refuge to fly into corners of the island, or into foreign countries, was equally exasperated against the *Saxons*, as being the immediate authors of these calamities, and against the *Scots* and *Picts*, whose invasions had obliged the *Britains* to call in the *Saxons*. And therefore he never speaks of the one or the other, but in the bitterest terms that the anguish of his heart could suggest. An impartial writer, to judge aright, ought to have regard as well to the circumstances, passions, and temper of an author, whom he quotes, as to the letter of his expressions; and that is all I shall say.

THIS being premised to return to the chronological account of the *Scots* in *Britain*, I shall only

(*a*) Gild. c. 23.

ly touch the last invasions of the Scots and Picts, and refer the reader to *Gildas*, and *Bede*'s narrations for a more full account of them.

A. D. 421. the *Britains*, who had shaken off their dependence on the empire, *A. D.* 409. finding by experience they were not able to defend their country against the *Scots* and the *Picts* (*a*), after having groaned some years under the oppression of these enemies, were forced to make new application to the *Romans*, who sent over to them forces, which overcame the *Scots* and *Picts*, and caused the northern wall between the *Friths* to be repaired, and left the *Britains* to do for themselves.

A. D. 42(. (*b*) the *Scots* and *Picts* leaving the wall, broke in over the *Friths* upon the *Britains*, which obliged them to have recourse again to the *Romans*; who sent over new forces, who, after repulsing the enemies, caused the *Northumberland* wall to be repaired, and took leave of the *Britains* for the last time. Upon which the *Picts* took possession of all the extremities of the *Roman* part of the island, that is, of all the territories that composed the province of *Valentia*; and no doubt the *Scots* also made use of this opportunity to enlarge their bounds in the north of the island; and both the *Picts* and *Scots* joined to attack the *Northumbrian* wall: and thus these northern enemies continued to pillage and op-

(*a*) Gild. cap. 12. Bed. lib. 1. c. 12.
(*b*) Gildas & Bed. ibid.

 press

press the *Britains*, till they, after seeking in vain new succours from the *Romans*, called in at last the *Saxons* to their aid, who soon after turn'd their arms against them, pillaged the country, and took possession of it, and forced the *Britains*, some of them to retire to corners of the island, others to abandon it.

By this short account of the *Scots* in *Britain* in the earliest times, it appears at least very probable, that from their first coming in under *Eocha Riada* in the third age, they still remained inhabitants of *Britain*, and made a considerable figure during the fourth and fifth ages. And tho' in their expeditions against the *Romans* or provincials, they generally march'd in conjunction with the *Picts*, and had oft-times their own forces augmented by auxiliaries and new recruits of the *Scots* from *Ireland*; 'tis no ways likely, that they could have subsisted all this time without some kind of government of their own in *Britain*, nor could that subsist without leaders or chiefs, one or more, both for uniting them when at home, and leading and conducting them in their expeditions; and since they came from *Ireland* where there were many lesser kings, I do not see why these leaders or chiefs of the *Scots* in *Britain*, might not have been called kings as well as some of those of *Ireland* to whom that title is given, or even as some of those of *England* during the heptarchy, or those of the *Britons* or *Welch* in *Wales*, or in the west of *Scotland*. So that the expression we will find in the latin chronicle (a) in metre; *that the Scots in* Britain, *till the time of Fergus the son of* Erc, *lived without a king,* cannot reasonably be taken in the rigour of the letter, as if absolutely the *Scots* in *Britain* had not such lesser kings, as there were many in *Ireland*; but that his meaning is, that the possessions of the *Scots* in *Britain* were not before *Fergus* son of *Erc*, united into one state, and had not a formed government; in a word, that the *Scots* before the time of *Fergus* son of *Erc*, had no soveraign king over all the *Scotish* inhabitants of *Britain*, such as *Fergus* son of *Erc* and his successors were.

FOR it was this *Fergus*, as we shall presently shew, who united all the *Scotish* inhabitants of the western parts and isle of *Britain*, together with the new colonies of *Scots*, that he brought along with him from *Ireland*, into one body of people; who extended their bounds in *Britain*, who freed them from all dependence on the *Picts* and on the *Scots* in *Ireland*; who erected their possessions in *Britain* into a soveraignty or independent monarchy, polished them by laws, and settled order and subordination among them; and first took upon himself the soveraign authority, and (as *Fordun* the most ancient of our historians, speaking of his first king *Fergus*, expresses it) *Fergus* made himself *the first king over the* Scots, or as *Winton*,

(a) Append. n. 6.

who

who never saw *Fordun*'s history, expresses it in the language of his time.

> He yat was callit Fergus-more (*a*)
> In ye (*b*) thyrd buke ze hard befor
> Wes Fergus Erchs son, yat thre yhere
> Maid him beyond the Drwm to Steir
> Oure all the hychtis ever ilkane
> As yai ly fra Drumalbane (*c*)
> Tyll Stanemore (*d*) and Inchegal
> Kyng he maid hym (*e*) oure thaim all.

ART II. *Of the first king of the* Scots *in* Britain.

ALL the *Scotish* historians, and all others that mention our kings, do generally agree, that the name of the first king of *Scots* in *Britain* was *Fergus*. But they are divided in this, whether it was *Fergus* son of *Ferchard*, called *Fergus* the first, or *Fergus* son of *Erc*, called *Fergus* the second; who, according to the most ancient genealogy of our kings, lived about thirty two generations after the first *Fergus*. All the *Scotish* historians from *Fordun* downwards, or since his chronicle was published about *A. D.* 1447. have followed his opi-

(*a*) Winton. Chron. book IV. chap. VIII. Biblioth. Reg. Lond.

(*b*) Wint. book III. chap. IX.

(*c*) In marg. MS. *Drum Albane, the back of Albania.*

(*d*) In the register of St. *Andrew*'s (whence this was taken) there is *Sluab*, *muere* or *more*.

(*e*) Himself.

nion,

nion, and own *Fergus* son of *Ferchard* for the first king of the *Scots*, and that he began his reign three hundred and thirty years before the incarnation; whereas they place the reign of *Fergus* son of *Erc*, or *Fergus* the second, in the beginning of the fifth century of christianity, as *Fordun* does.

BUT besides that, this question is already in a great measure decided against *Fordun* and his followers opinion, by all that hath been brought to prove, that the *Scots* were not settled even in *Ireland*, much less in *Britain*, till after the time of the incarnation, and so could have no king of their nation before that time, in either of these countries: besides this, I say, *Fordun* himself, the most ancient of our writers that calls *Fergus* son of *Ferchard* first king of the *Scots*, wrote near one hundred years after the time, that 'tis said, that the monuments and records of our history were destroyed or carried off by king *Edward* I. and he brings no document or proof from any credible authority to support his opinion, as we shall see elsewhere.

WHEREAS all the remains, without exception, which we have of our ancient histories or records, written, extracted or abridged from them, whilst they were yet subsisting, before the year 1291. all these remains, I say, far from authorizing *Fordun*'s new scheme, do all unanimously contradict it and agree, that *Fergus* son of *Erc* was the first king of the

the *Scots* in *Britain*. I have already (*a*) given an account of these monuments or remains of our ancient history, and they are all I ever met with concerning our ancient kings written before the year 1291. and each of them, that gives any account of the beginning of the *Scotish* monarchy in *Albany*, places *Fergus* son of *Erc* the first king, and that in plain terms; so as there needs no more but to set down their words without any commentary.

I SHALL not here alledge for a proof of *Fergus* son of *Erc*, his being reckoned, in the twelfth age, the first soveraign king of the *Scots* in *Albany*, the testimony so plain of the first piece set down in the appendix to this essay, entituled, *De situ Albaniæ*, which was formerly quoted by *Camden*, (and upon his authority by other *English* and *Irish* writers) because, as I have already observed (*b*), it appears to me, that the author of it was no *Scotsman*; but that it is probably a production of *Giraldus Cambrensis*. The reader, if he pleases, may see it in the appendix (*c*), beginning by these words, *Fergus filius Eric, ipse fuit primus qui de semine Chonare suscepit regnum Albaniæ, &c.* This piece wants no commentary, being clear upon the point, whether *Girald* had this with the rest of his informations

(*a*) Supra, p. 598. &c.
(*b*) Supra, p. 681.
(*c*) Appendix, num. I.

from

from *Andrew* bishop of *Carenes*, he does not tell us. However, leaving this to the reader's judgment, I come to the testimony of *Scotish* writers.

I. THE first testimony that I shall bring, is from that ancient abstract of our chronicles, intituled, *Chronica regum Scottorum*, *num.* 4. in the appendix and already (*a*) describ'd. It begins thus, *Fergus filius Eric fuit primus qui de semine Chonare suscepit regnum Albaniæ, id est, a monte Drum Albain usque ad mare Hyberniæ, & ad Inchegall. Hic regnavit tribus annis. Domangart filius ejus quinque annis. Congal filius Domangart*, &c. and so continues to give the series of our kings, with the years of their reigns, down to king *William* in the twelfth age, when it was abstracted from our old chronicles, whilst they were yet in being. This abstract ends in the MS. with king *William*'s genealogy up to *Noah*, as it was then received. According to this genealogy, *Fergus-mor-mac-Erch* first of our kings, was in the thirteenth degree from *Conare* son to *Mogoloma*. The son of this *Conare* was *Eocha Riada*, who is thought to be the *Reuda*, mentioned by *Bede*, the leader of the first *Scotish* colony to *Britain*.

II. THE second testimony is from a very authentick record, an ancient register or chartulary of the church

(*a*) Supra, p. 605.

church of St. *Andrew's*, written in the beginning of the reign of king *Alexander* III. about the year 1251. whilst our ancient chronicles were yet to be seen. In this register, there is a series or chronological (*a*) catalogue of the kings of *Scots*, down till the reign of *Alexander* III. whereof I have given an account already (*b*). And this series, inserted in that church register, was preserved from the general disaster which fell out forty years afterwards, as were generally all other church registers, records and libraries.

Now this series of our kings contains, in as express terms as the former testimonies, an account that *Fergus* son of *Erc* or *Erch* was the first king of the *Scots* in *Britain*; for it begins thus, 1. *Fergus filius Erch primus in Scotia regnavit tribus annis ultra Drumalbain usque Sluagmuner & usque ad Inchegall*; 2. *Douengbart filius Fergus quinque annis regnavit*; 3. *Congall filius Douengbart*, &c. And thus continues down the series of the kings of the *Scots*, till *Alpin* son of *Eocha* the twenty third king. After him he sets down the catalogue of the *Pictish* kings, to the number of sixty. And then follows out that of the kings of *Scotland*, from *Keneth* son of *Alpin*, down till king *Alexander* III. and gives a short

(*a*) In append. n. 5.
(*b*) Supra, p. 606.

account

account of each king, such as we find in other ancient short chronicles of these times.

III. A third proof of *Fergus* son of *Erch*, his being the first king of the *Scots* in *Britain*, is furnish'd us by *James Gray* publick notary and secretary to the Archbishops of St. *Andrew*'s, *William Schevez*, and prince *James* duke of *Ross*, brother to king *James* IV, in the copy he hath given us in his collections (mention'd (*a*) elsewhere) of the series and succession of our kings, transcrib'd, as we remarked already, from some chronicle or record written during the reign of king *William*, and which is, (allowing difference in the expressions of no moment, and faults of copyists) as to the substance, entirely conformable to the forsaid extract of the register of St. *Andrew*'s. This transcript begins thus, *Fergus filius Herch primus regnavit in Scotia tribus annis ultra Druthin Alban usque Sluaghmorre & usque Inchgall. Dovenghard filius Fergus 5 annis regnavit. Congal filius Dovengard*, &c. in the very terms of the St. *Andrew*'s register, except a wrong reading or transcribing the name *Drumalban*. So the agreement of this transcript of *James Gray*, with the extract of the register, mutually corroborates one another, and, being written at so different times, the one about the middle of the thirteenth age, the other towards the end of the fifteenth, their agreement proves, that they both

(*a*) Supra, pag. 627.

had

had their accounts from the same source. But 'tis observable in *James Gray's* account of the succession of our kings, that having perused *Fordun*'s history, and being otherwise prevened by the common notions that the *Scots* had in his days of *Fergus* the son of *Ferchard*, his being the first king and founder of the monarchy; accordingly, before he sets down the account of our kings, he prefixes a *Notandum* of his own conformable to the then common notion of the antiquity of the monarchy in the *Scotish* line. *Notandum*, says he, *quod regnum Scotiæ incepit ante incarnatiomen domin.* 443. *annis:* yet being in a publick station, and accustomed to draw up acts, or transcribe them faithfully, such as he found them, he caused to be transcribed, without alteration, this account of the succession of our kings, such as he found it in ancient records, however opposite it was to his own, and to the common opinion of the *Scots* in those days, and ever since *Fordun*'s chronicle had been published.

IV. It will no doubt appear a strange paradox to bring the fourth testimony for *Fergus* son of *Erc*, his being the first king of the *Scots* in *Britain*, from *John Fordun*. Since the whole design of the second book of his chronicles, is to give us the history of *Fergus* son of *Ferchard*, as first king of the *Scots*, and of forty-five other kings of *Scots* that succeeded him before *Fergus* son of *Erc*. But such is the force of truth, on minds that are not wholly corrupted by a formed design to invent and impose,

impoſe, but only byaſſed by the popular opinions and prejudices of the times and circumſtances in which they live (which we ſhall ſee elſewhere was *Fordun*'s caſe) that they will not abſolutely ſmother all ancient teſtimonies, tho' oppoſite to the opinions they are imbarked in; but rather, in quoting them, endeavour to reconcile their own opinions with them. *John Fordun*, in his ſearches for memorials of our hiſtory, had no doubt ſeen theſe ancient abſtracts of our ancient chronicles I have quoted above, or others equivalent, and read in them the words I have ſet down, (*a*) *viz.* that *Fergus* ſon of *Erc* was the firſt king of the *Scotiſh* race; that he reigned from *Drum Albayn* to *Inchgall*, and that he reigned only three years, which are the words of the extracts above mentioned: but if they be let paſs without a commentary, and be taken in their literal meaning, they are enough to ſubvert the whole fabrick of *Fordun*'s forty-five kings before *Fergus* ſon of *Erc*.

Wherefore, to obviate that inconveniency, *Fordun* ſuppoſes a ſubverſion of the *Scotiſh* monarchy in the fourth age, upon the grounds we ſhall elſewhere examine, and by conſequence a reſtoration of the monarchy by *Fergus* ſon of *Erc*, which gives *Fordun* a kind of ground to call this *Fergus* firſt king of the *Scots*, *viz.* after their reſtoration: and adds, that towards the latter end of his reign, which he ſuppoſes laſted ſixteen years; he gained ſome lands (he owns he knows not how)

(*a*) Fordun lib. 3. c. 2. pag. 173. edit. Hearn.

beyond *Drumalbayn*, and was the first king of the *Scotish* race, that reigned three years in the *Pictish* land, from the hills to the *Scotish* sea. But all this varnish will not cover the conformity of his expression, with those of the extracts from our old chronicles which I have related, nor hinder them, if taken alone, from having the same meaning among all unprejudiced persons. The words are these [*Fergus filius Ereb*] *tribus* [ultimis] *annis ultra Drumalbayn, hoc est, ultra dorsum Albaniæ primus regum Scotici generis* [in terra Pictorum] *a montibus ad mare* [Scoticum] *regnavit.* What is here inclosed in crotchets, are *Fordun*'s interpolations of our old chronicles, to adapt them to his systheme.

But a manifold proof of *Fergus* son of *Erc*, his having been the first king of the *Scots* in *Britain*, is drawn from the short chronicle of the *Scots* in latin *rhythm*, or verses, inserted at the end of most of the copies of the *Scotichronicon*; as an ancient abridgment of our history, printed in the appendix num 5. I have given an account (*a*) of it already, to which I refer the reader. The first part of this short chronicle ends with the death of king *William*, and with the eighth chapter, and was written about the time of king *Alexander* II or III, as appears by the beginning of the ninth chapter.

(*a*) Supra, p. 608.

V. The

V. THE first proof drawn from this chronicle of *Fergus* son of *Erc*, his being counted the first king of *Scots*, is taken from the fifth chapter; where the author supposing, according to a tradition already received in those days, that the *Scots* came to *Britain* before the incarnation, informs us, that they lived in *Argyle* a very long time according to the law of nature (so he expresses it) but without any king, till one, called *Fergus*, brought over from *Ireland* the famous stone to *Argyle*, and became the first king of the *Scots*.

(a) *In tamen Ergadia vixit per tempora multa*
Hæc gens [Scottorum] *sub lege naturæ, sed sine rege,*
Donec ad Ergadiam tulit audax nomine quidam
Fergusius lapidem, de quo fit mentio pridem:
Hic primus rexit Scotos, lapidem quia vexit:
Quem Scoti lapidem sanxerunt ponere sedem.
Regibus inde suis tantum, sed non alienis.

THAT this *Fergus* was the son of *Erc*, the whole series of this chronicle, continued in the next and following chapters, sufficiently demonstrates; for he begins the next chapter immediately following the verses above set down, by telling us, that this *Fergus was the first that reign'd in Argyle*, and that he reigned *three years*, that *he was succeeded by* Donegard *who reign'd five*, and *he by* Congall, &c. all which characters, as they agree to this *Fergus* son of *Erc* and to no other; so they

(a) Chron. Rythm. *cap.* 5.

 per-

perfectly agree with the three former catalogues of our kings in every thing, in which they differ from *Fordun* and his followers new catalogue of our kings immediate successors to *Fergus* son of *Erc*. These are the words of this short chronicle, cap. 6.

Primus in Ergadia Fergus rexit tribus annis
Post Donegard quinis, Congal quater octo bis, &c.

VI. A second proof is drawn from what the author of this chronicle tells us, *cap. 6.* that the *Scots* reigned in *Britain* together with the *Picts* 332, or 312 years three months: for the verses following will bear either of those explications.

[Scoti] *Hi cum prædictis regnarunt tempore Pictis*
Quod trecentenos quater octoque continet annos,
His annis & tres debetis jungere menses. cap. 6.

Now its certain that by the middle of the ninth age, the *Picts* ceased to make a distinct people and kingdom by their union and subjection to the *Scots*; so counting backward from this union, the number of years here assigned, will not reach back farther than the time of *Fergus* son of *Erc*, in the fifth or sixth age, and comes many ages short of *Fergus* I. who is supposed to have lived 330 years before the coming of *Christ*, that is, near twelve hundred years before the union of the *Scots* and *Picts*.

VII.

VII. 3° This short chronicle assures us, that king *Alexander* III. was the fifty first king of the *Scots*.

ALEXANDER III.

(*a*) *Qui quinquagenus regum fuit ordine primus.*

And this supposes clearly, that *Fergus* son of *Erc* was the first king, there being just fifty-one kings in this author's account, as well as in that of the above-mentioned *chronica regum Scotorum*, and in that of the register of St. *Andrew*'s, from *Fergus* son of *Erc*, down to king *Alexander* III. This same author calls afterwards, *c.* 10. king *John Baliol*. the fifty-second king.

Before I leave this *Chron.Rythm.* or short chronicle in latin verses, 'tis of importance, towards preventing any mistake by alterations in it, to observe, that in several copies of the *Scotichronicon*, at the end of which, this *Chron.Rythmicum* is to be found, there is, besides other additions, an interpolation at the end of the seventh chapter, containing some latin verses for the most part extracted out of different places of *Fordun*'s chronicle, and put together in this interpolation without any suit or coherence; and the whole so oddly and unskilfully inserted in the *Chronicon Rythmicum*, that tho' we had not a fair and genuine ancient copy of it, without any interpolation in the MS. *Scotichronicon* in Vellum, of the *Scotish* college at *Paris*; the interpolation would visibly appear to any that reads the whole piece with attention to the sense and coherence.

(*a*) Cap. 9.

FOR the sixth chapter of this *Chron. Rythm.* to which is subjoin'd this interpolation, finishes the short account of the succession of our first kings, by telling us, that *Kenneth* son of *Alpin*, reign'd seven years over the *Scots*, before he subdued the *Picts*; and then, after adding the number of years that the *Pictish* and *Scotish* kings reign'd together in *Albany*, which ends this sixth chapter, the seventh chapter, which immediately follows, continues on naturally to tell us, how long this king *Kenneth* reigned after he overcame the *Picts*; and so continues down the succession of our kings where the sixth chapter left off from this king *Kenneth*, till *Malcolm Keanmor*'s children descended, partly of the *Scottish*, partly of the *Saxon* blood, by queen *Margaret* their mother.

NOW 'tis betwixt the sixth and this seventh chapter, which follow so naturally one another, that the unskilful interpolator has placed his additions, taking 1°. out of *cap.* 35. *lib.* 2. of *Fordun*, the verses *Christi transactis tribus annis atque ducentis, &c.* giving account of the first planting of christianity in *Scotland*. 2°. To these he hath added new verses of his own fabrick, containing the coming in of *S. Palladius*, according to *Fordun*'s account of it. 3°. He joins to those, without any coherence, *Fordun*'s verses (*lib.* 2. *cap.* 12.) *Albion in terris rex primus germine Scotus*, &c. describing *Fergus* son of *Ferchard* as first king of the *Scots*: and this in plain contradiction to the *Chron. Rythm.* to which he hath tack'd them: whether with a design to elude, or embroil the distinct account and manifold testimonies it contains of *Fergus* son of *Erch*, his being the first king of the *Scots*, I leave to others to judge.

But to return now from this digression: these are all the monuments written before the year 1291, that give any account of the succession or series of the kings of the *Scots*, that hitherto I have had occasion to meet with. And it is not improper to take notice, that they are almost all of them written in different places, by different authors, and on different occasions, without communication; and yet all agree together exactly in the same names, order, and number of kings; and in placing *Fergus* son of *Erc* as the first of them; and equally differ from *Fordun* and his followers.

Perhaps this essay may give occasion to the curious and learned of our country or elsewhere, to discover and remark other ancient pieces of the same tenor. But I dare confidently affirm beforehand, that in no genuine writer before the year 1291, and our contests with king *Edward* I. about the year 1300, will be found any certain account of the first forty kings; or of any soveraign kings at all of the *Scots* in *Britain* before *Fergus* the son of *Erc*. And now I refer it to the judgment of any impartial man, whether the authority of the monuments I have here made use of, however short and lame they may appear, all written by authors who had before them our genuine ancient writers as yet in being, and who extracted with simplicity from them a short account of the beginning of the *Scotish* monarchy and succession of the kings; whether, I say, authors, so well inform'd and so void in all appearance of prejudice and design, their testimony be not preferable to the contradictory accounts given of the monarchy, and of our ancient kings by posterior authors, deprived of the help of our genuine ancient chronicles, and byassed by so many prejudices.

VIII. To confirm what the monuments, I have already cited, unanimously affirm of *Fergus* son of *Erc*, his being the first king of the *Scots* in *Albany*, I shall as yet bring for an eighth testimony, the authority of one author, who, though he lived after *Fordun* or about his time, yet he never saw his work, which was not as yet publish'd, or, at least, generally known till about *A. D.* 1447, or 1448. probably after this author's death. This is *Andrew Winton* prior of *Lochlevin*, who wrote his chronicle (of which (*a*) we have already given an account) towards the end of the reign of king *Robert* III, or during the captivity of king *James* I. This author, tho' he believed according to the tradition received long before his time, that the *Scots* were settled in *Britain* before the incar-

(*a*) Supra, p. 622.

nation

nation, and writing about one hundred years after the opinion (first vented during our debates with king *Edward* I. about the independency) of the *Scots* having had ancient kings in *Britain*, even before the incarnation, had, by length of time, and as being honourable to the nation, spread itself and gained credit among the generality; tho' *Winton*, I say, writing in that juncture, was much inclined to believe the *Scots* had kings before the incarnation; 1°. yet not only when he sets down (*a*) the old genealogy of the *Scotish* kings, from *Simon-Breac* downwards, he reckons, among the rest of the names of the ancestors of our kings, that of *Fergus* son to *Ferchar* or *Feraret* in the genealogical line, without taking any the least particular notice of him, as he doth of the famous men among them; such as *Simon-Breac*, and *Fergus* son of *Erc*, and without the least insinuation of this *Fergus* son of *Ferchar*, his ever having been the first king or a king of the *Scots* at all, no more than any of the rest. But 2°. when he comes down with the genealogical line to *Fergus* son of *Erc*, he (*b*) calls him expresly the first king of the *Scots* in *Britain*, and looked upon that as so constant and certain an historical truth, that he repeats it no less than three times, in three or four different places of his chronicle.

(*a*) *Winton's Chronicle* in Biblioth. Cotton. Nero D. XI lib. 3. fol. 30.

(*b*) Winton ibid, lib. 3. fol. 30. lib. 4. fol 37, 38, 43.

WHAT

WHAT is remarkable, and shews how much it was fixed in the minds of the *Scots* as yet in *Winton*'s time, that *Fergus* son of *Erc* was the first king, is, that *Winton* himself overswayed by the prevailing new opinion of the *Scots* having had kings three or four hundred years before the birth of Christ, or rather before the *Picts*, who he supposeth began to reign two hundred years before the incarnation, on the one hand; and on the other hand, being assured that the first king of the *Scots* was *Fergus* son of *Erc*, and that there were but ten generations *(a)* betwixt this *Fergus* and *Kenneth Mac Alpin*, who lived above eight hundred years after the birth of *Christ*; after a fruitless effort in two places in his chronicle to reconcile this contradiction; at last finding it impossible to make ten or eleven generations in those times fill up twelve hundred years, he chooses rather to bring down the beginning of the *Scotish* monarchy to more modern times, and to grant that the *Picts* were already settled, and their monarchy subsisting in *Britain* when the *Scots* came into it, than to doubt of *Fergus* son of *Erc*, his being their first king. This shews how certain this was as yet even in *Winton*'s time, and that he had never seen *Fordun*'s chronicle; otherwise he could not have failed to mention at least the distinction of two

(*a*) Winton. lib. 3. fol. 7. lib. 4. fol. 43, *Vide Appendix*, No. 3.

Fergus's

Fergus's I. and II. which, if it had been grounded, would have ſolved all his difficulties.

Thus *Winton*, in the firſt draughts or editions of his chronicles, ſuch as it is in all the MSS. of it that I have ſeen in *Scotland* or *England*, excepting one, the moſt valuable of all, which belongs to the king's library at *London*, whereof I have already (*a*) given an account, it contains the laſt review made by himſelf of his chronicle, with ſome conſiderable additions and corrections. In this not only he ſtill perſiſts to make *Fergus* ſon of *Erch* firſt king of the *Scots*, but what the ordinary copies of his chronicles do not contain, he informs us, no doubt from the records of St. *Andrew's*, to which he belong'd, and conformably to the accounts of all the above-mentioned writers that had been publiſhed till his time; that (*b*) Fergus *ſon of* Erch *firſt king of the* Scots, *reigned three years from* Drumalban *to* Inchgall; Douengart *his ſon five years, to whom ſucceeded his ſon* Congal, *&c.* and continues on a chronological ſeries of our kings, with their genealogy and years of their reigns, till *Eocha - rinneval* call'd by our moderns, after *Fordun, Eugen.* V.

And now we have ſeen by the agreeing teſtimonies of all our ancient writers, without exception,

(*a*) Supra, pag. 624.
(*b*) Append. n. vii.

not

not only of those who wrote before the year 1291; but of all of them that we have remaining before the publication of *Fordun*'s history, under the reign of king *James* II, that *Fergus* son of *Erch* was still believed to have been the first king of the *Scots*, and that, till the history of *Fordun* was publish'd, we have not one word, in any writer extant, of *Fergus* the son of *Ferchard* his being the first king, or a king at all of the *Scots*, nor in the old genealogy of our kings any particular notice taken of his name, except by *Fordun*, no more than of so many other names in that genealogy.

It is farther worth observing, that the tradition of the *Scotish* monarchy's beginning by one *Erc*, or the son of *Erc*, was so rooted in the minds of the *Scots*, that even in their instructions to their commissioners at *Rome* (*A. D* 1300) during the debate with king *Edward* before the *Pope* (where we find the first notions of kings of *Scots* before the incarnation) they visibly point at one *Erc* as the founder of their monarchy. 1°. By deriving from *Erc* and *Gatheyl* the name of their first settlement in *Britain*; and 2°. by their naming no other king of *Scots* but *Erc*, whom they bring in both the first king of the *Scots* in *Britain*, in the highest antiquity, and again as a king of the *Scots* about the end of the fourth, or beginning of the fifth age, where our moderns place the restoration of monarchy. And thus far as to the authorities of *Scotish* writers before *Fordun*, who all agree that *Fergus* son of *Erc* was the first king of *Scots*.

It would have perhaps appeared invidious, to have brought the testimonies of *English* or *Irish* writers to prove this delicate point; for which reason also I have not alledged the testimony, so clear for this purpose, contained in the description (*a*) of *Albany*, and quoted by *Camden* and others, because I suppose *Giraldus Cambrensis* was author of that description; and therefore, having sufficient proofs from the *Scotish* ancient writers, I have designedly abstained from quoting the others, and shall refer my reader, if he desires farther information and other proofs, to archbishop *Usher's Antiquitates Britannicae* (*b*), *Flaherty*'s *Ogygia* (*c*), &c. and others of lesser note among the *Irish*, and of the *English* to *Camden*'s *Scotia*, to the history of church-government of *Britain*, &c. by Dr. *Loyd* bishop of St. *Asaph*, and Dr. *Stillingfleet*'s antiquities of *British* churches; in all which they will find this argument treated most part from testimonies drawn from *Irish* writers, which, tho' I have not made use of in examining this question, yet I am perswaded they may be very serviceable to the *Scotish* history.

(*a*) Appendix, num. I.
(*b*) Usher. Antiq. Brit. p. 319, 320. &c.
(*c*) Ogygia, p. 465. &c.

But

But in order to that, it ought to be observed, 1°. that a great difference is to be made betwixt the histories or annals of *Ireland*, containing accounts of transactions passed since king *Leogaire* and St. *Patrick*'s time, and those pretended old histories of the *Irish*, which, they gave out, were written by their seanachies before the times of christianity, or even before they received the gospel with the use of letters. As to these last, we have endeavoured to shew elsewhere (*a*) at length, that these pretended ancient histories being built upon the dubious foundation of the *Bards* traditions, there's no weight to be laid upon them: whereas the first, that is, their historical accounts written since they received christianity, deserves much more credit.

2°. A great difference ought also to be made among the *Irish* writers, even since they had the use of letters, betwixt those of their histories or annals that contain the accounts of the succession of kings, bishops and other such publick transactions within or without that kingdom; such as *Tigernac*'s annals, the *Ulster* annals, the *Synchronism*'s of *Flann*, where they relate matters that happen'd since king *Leogair*'s time on the one hand, and on the other, the uncertain rapsodies of genealogies, some of the legends of saints, written

(*a*) Supra, Book II. Sect. 1. chap. 1. per totum.

by

matters relating to *Albany*, when equally ancient, and near the times of the transactions; yet I cannot but here renew again my earnest wishes, that those of the *Irish* writers who treat of transactions in *Albany*, such as *Tigernach*, the *Synchronisms*, the *Ulster* annals, and such like, were faithfully published in a fair and literal translation; if they cannot be printed (as the *English* have done their *Saxon* monuments of history) in the original language, with a literal translation joined to them. And I doubt not but the history of the *Scots* would receive light by their so doing, as the *Irish* would gain credit to their own history, and honour to the authors of such a laudable undertaking: and it was particularly for this reason that I insisted so much on this subject, in the former dissertation.

ART. III. *Of the time of the beginning of the reign of* Fergus *son of* Erc, *and proper* Epoch *of the monarchy of the* Scots *in* Britain.

FORDUN hath placed the beginning of this *Fergus*'s reign, and of the restoration, as he calls it, of the *Scotish* kingdom in *Britain* in the year 403. Our other historians, ever since, have generally followed him in that date: only *Boece*, and some of his followers, in order to give this *Fergus* time to accompany *Alaric* at the sacking of *Rome* in 409, hath placed this restoration some few years later.

But this *Epoch* of *Fergus*'s reign settled on bare conjecture, as we shall shew elsewhere, is contradicted both by the account that *Fordun* himself, as well as all our ancient and modern writers, give of the genealogy of our kings, and by all the monuments remaining of our ancient annals before *A. D.* 1291. All which suppose or prove plainly, that the beginning of the reign of *Fergus* son of *Erc*, was about one hundred years later than *Fordun* hath placed it.

According to the genealogy of our kings, received by *Fordun* and all our other writers, there are but two generations or persons betwixt this *Fergus* and king *Aydan*, his great grandchild; to wit, *Dongard*, who was son to *Fergus*; and *Gauran*, who was son to *Dongard*, and father to king *Aydan*. Now, according to *Fordun*'s account, *Fergus* began his reign *A. D.* 403, and died *A. D.* 419; and king *Aydan*, his great grandchild, died *A. D.* 605: so there would be only three generations to take up near two centuries, *viz.* one hundred and sixty-eight years from the death of king *Fergus*, to that of king *Aydan*; which, in the first place, would be against the common received rule of counting three generations to one hundred years, or of allowing thirty years to each generation: in the second place, it would be absolutely contrary to the experience of all that hath ever happened in *Scotland* since, where there have always been in

Genealogical and Chronologi

COL. I.

According to more ancient MS. *Ch*

Began to Reign.	*Order of* SUCCESSION.	*Reigned Years.*
*A.D.*503	1 Fergus, *Son of* Erc	3
506	2 Dongard, *Son of* Fergus	5
511	3 Congal, *Son of* Dongard	24
535	4 Gabhran, *Son of* Dongard	22
557	5 Conal, *Son of* Congal	14
571	6 Aydan, *Son of* Gabhran	34

ies of the Kings of Scots, from Fer

r Catalogues. | | Acco

	Series of Generations.		Began to Reign.	Order of
16	Fergus		A.D. 403	1 Fergus
			419	2 Eugeni
11	Dongard	1	452	3 Dong
			457	4 Constan
35			479	5 Congal,
57	Gabhran	2	501	6 Gonran
			535	7 Ethod,
71			558	8 Conal,
			567	9 Kynatel
05	Aydan	3	569	10 Aydan,

f *Erc*, to *Aydan* Son of *Gavran*.

O. L. II.

n Fordun, *and his Followers.*

N.	*Reigned Years.*	*Died.*	*Series of Generations.*
	16	*A. D.* 419	Fergus
gus	34	452	
gus	5	457	Dongard 1
ergus	22	479	
gard	22	501	
ngard	34	535	Gonran 2
gal	23	558	
al	10	567	
ngal	1 3 mths.	569	
ran	35	605	Aydan 3

In the genealogy of our kings, at least six generations for every two centuries. And from the death of king *Aydan*, A. D. 605, till that of the late king *James* VII. *A. D.* 1701, there are thirty-six generations, and only one thousand ninety-six years, or about eleven centuries, which is more than three generations for every century: which shews, that there can be no more than one hundred years allowed for the three generations of *Dongard*, *Gauran*, and of *Aydan*; and by consequence, that according to the genealogy owned by all, as well as the fixed *Epoch* of king *Aydan*'s death, *A. D.* 605, and conformable to the experience of all succeeding ages, the beginning of the reign of king *Fergus* II. can be placed no higher than the beginning of the sixth century, or about the year 500 of Christ. But all this will better appear by the genealogical table here inserted (*a*).

It would seem that *Fordun*, or those who furnished him with memoirs, had been aware of this difficulty; and therefore, to obviate it, or rather to hinder it from being taken notice of, care is taken to intermix, with the real kings, in the interval betwixt *Fergus* and *Aydan*, the names of three supernumerary kings, besides one *Kinatill*, viz. *Eugenius*, *Constantin*, and *Ethodius*, (of all whom there is not the least mention in the more ancient chronicles or catalogues of our kings) and to each of them are given long reigns, to help

(*a*) Vide Genealogical Table.

to spin out the two centuries; for which reason there are also several years added to the reigns of some of the real kings: but this cobweb device is easily dissipated, and can be of no use to the purpose, as long as the old genealogy (which could not be so easily altered) remains still the same, even in *Fordun*'s account, and in that of all our writers, and king *Aydan*, but in the third degree from king *Fergus*, the intermixing these new kings with the additional number of years of the reigns (which serves only for a blind, that is easily seen through) will in no manner mend the matter, and still the same difficulty remains, of making three generations fill up two centuries, which in all succeeding ages have required at least double that number of generations, as it were easy to prove it by induction, or examples of every two ages or centuries since king *Aydan*'s, till the present times.

To render this yet more evident, there needs only to lay aside the seventy-nine years of reign which *Fordun*, or those that helped him with memoirs, thought fit to assign to the three supernumerary kings, (*Eugenius*, *Constantin*, and *Ethodius*) and cut off the twenty-four years, which they have added to lengthen the reigns of *Fergus* and *Gauran* beyond what the ancient catalogues give them. These two numbers of years (seventy-nine and twenty-four) put together, make up above one hundred years: now retrenching them, and reckoning

koning back from king *Aydan*'s death, *A. D.* 605, (which is a fixed *Epoch* on which all parties, *Fordun*, as well as others, agree) there will not remain one full century from the death of king *Aydan*, A. D. 605, till the beginning of *Fergus*'s reign, which therefore must necessarily be placed after the year 500, or the beginning of the sixth century, and about one hundred years after the year 403, to which *Fordun* had fixed it.

It is no less evident, by all the ancient abstracts of our chronicles, written before the year 1291, that king *Fergus*'s reign can be placed no higher than about the year 500; for according to the three ancient catalogues of our kings, to wit, that of the *Chronica Regum Scottorum*, that of the register of St. *Andrew*'s, that of the chronicle in *Latin* verse, and those of *Winton* and *Gray*, counting all the years of the king's reigns, from the death of king *Aydan*, A. D. 605, up to the beginning of king *Fergus*'s reign, it will be found, according to these chronicles or catalogues, that the first of king *Fergus* amounts no higher than to the year 503: for these catalogues or chronicles, (allowing a few faults in the numbers, ordinary to copyists) bear unananimously that, 1°. *Fergus*, son of *Erc*, reigned three years; 2°. *Dongard*, son of *Fergus*, five years; 3°. *Congal*, son of *Dongard*, twenty-four years; 4°. *Gauran*, son of *Dongard*, twenty-two years; 5°. *Conal*, son of *Congal*, fourteen years; 6°. *Aydan*, son of *Gauran*, thirty-four

 years

years, and died *A.D.* 605. Now counting up the years of the reigns of these kings, they amount to one hundred and two years, which being deduced from six hundred and five, the fixed *Epoch* of the death of king *Aydan*, there remains just five hundred and three, as another fixed *Epoch* of the beginning of the reign of king *Fergus* son of *Erc*; and by consequence of the monarchy of the *Scots* in *Britain*: and this just answers the calculation of the *Irish* (*a*) chronicles, whose conformity in this, to the most ancient monuments that we have, mutually confirms one another.

(*a*) Usser. Britan. Eccles. Antiq. p. 32[illegible]

CHAP. III.

CHAP. III.

Of the different steps and degrees by which the high antiquities of the Scots *grew up by length of time, in the several hands through which they passed, into the plan of history, in which they were afterwards delivered by the modern writers of both nations.*

HAVING examined, in the first and second dissertation of this second section, the grounds of the remote antiquities of the *Scots*, both in *Ireland* and *Scotland*, and endeavoured to fix the true *Epoch* of their coming in, and of their first settlement in both these kingdoms; to finish the matter, it remains to answer a vulgar objection which may occur against all I have said; the clearing of which will, I hope, give me occasion far from abating any thing of what I have advanced, to add on the contrary a new confirmation to it, and set the whole in a better light.

IT may be objected then against what I have said, that if the remote antiquities of *Ireland* and *Scotland* had been so groundless in their origin, and the *Epoch* of the first settlement, and beginning

ning of monarchy of the *Scots* in these countries, not more ancient than I pretend, it seems not possible that the story of the antiquities of both countries, and of the ancient settlement of the *Scots*, could ever have grown up into such a detail of facts, so apparently regular a succession of kings, attended with genealogies, fixed dates, and the other outward appearances of authentick ancient history, nor be delivered with such an air of assurance, as we see that of *Ireland* is by *O Flaherty*, and that of *Scotland* by *Boece* and *Buchanan*.

THO' this objection or difficulty be already in a great measure answered by all that we have said at so much length of these remote antiquities, and shewn that they have no solid grounds, but rather the characters of invention, and of being the work of posterior times; yet to put the whole in greater evidence, I conceive it would not be amiss to endeavour to trace down, as far as the subject will bear, the several steps by which the remote antiquities of both nations have grown up, by degrees and length of time, from the first invention of them, into the detail of circumstantiated facts and form of history, in which their modern writers present them.

BUT as to the remote antiquities of *Ireland*, having in the former dissertation entered, I am afraid, into too great a detail of them for a stranger, though with no other view than to endeavour to ſet in a due light the firſt foundations of the remote antiquities of my own country, I ſhall enquire no farther into thoſe of *Ireland*, but leave that to the learned, impartial and judicious writers of that kingdom, who, by a perfect knowledge of their ancient language, and by the acceſs they may have to all that remains of the more ancient and valuable of their hiſtorical monuments, are alone equal to ſuch a task. I ſhall therefore content myſelf to examine here the progreſs of theſe remote antiquities among the *Scots* in *Britain*; which, as it will give me an opportunity to diſcuſs ſome things more fully than I could do in the former part of this diſſertation, ſo I hope that what I am to add here, will remove ſome popular objections, and ſerve for a new confirmation to the whole.

To put this ſubject in a clear light, it may be uſeful to begin, by laying before the reader the double ſcheme of the hiſtory of the *Scots* before *Fergus* ſon of *Erch*: 1°. Such as it was in reality, as I have endeavoured to prove, from what remains we have of our ancient writers. 2°. Such as *Boece* and *Buchanan* have publiſhed it, which is what I call the remote or high antiquities of the *Scots* in *Britain*.

The firſt ſcheme may be reduced to theſe four heads; 1°. That the *Scots* were not ſettled even in *Ireland* till about, or after the times of the incarnation (*a*).

carnation (*a*): 2°. That the *Scots* were not settled in *Britain* till about the third age of christianity (*b*). 3°. That the *Scots* in *Britain* had no soveraign kings of their own nation before *Fergus* son of *Erch* (*c*); and that the reign of *Fergus* son of *Erch*, and by consequence the beginning of the *Scotish* monarchy in *Britain*, is to be placed no higher than about the end of the fifth, or beginning of the sixth century (*d*).

The second, and opposite scheme, or that of the *Scotish* high antiquities, may be reduced to the following heads; 1°. The *Scotish* monarchy in *Ireland* began by *Simon Breac*, about six hundred years before the incarnation. 2°. The *Scots* came to *Britain* about four hundred years before the incarnation. 3°. The *Scots* in *Britain* had kings before the incarnation, and their monarchy began three hundred and thirty years before the birth of Christ. 4°. *Fergus* the son of *Feredac* or *Fercart*, was the first king of the *Scots* in *Britain*, and had about thirty-eight kings his successors, who reigned during about seven hundred years in the north of *Britain*, till the overthrow of the *Scotish* monarchy about the end of the fourth century; of each of which kings reigns our modern historians give a circumstantial chronological account.

(*a*) Vide Dissert. I. p. 401, &c. and p. 506, &c.
(*b*) Supra, p. 638, &c.
(*c*) Ibid. p. 676.
(*d*) Ibid. p. 689.

5°. *Fergus*

5°. *Fergus* the son of *Erch*, called *Fergus* II. restored the *Scotish* monarchy, and began his reign about the beginning of the fifth century, *A. D.* 403.

To come then to the purpose, and describe the several additions and alterations that were made in different ages, by different hands and occasions, in the first simple scheme of the *Scotish* antiquities before *Fergus* son of *Erch*, till they grew up into that high fabrick whereof *Fordun* laid the plan, which *Boece* finished, and *Buchanan* adorned; I must, in the first place, do that justice to my countrymen to acknowledge, that, except in the last additions, whereof the first authors, I mean of the books under the name of *Veremund*, &c. were, no doubt, guilty of forgery (as I have shewn (*a*) elsewhere.) All the rest of the additions or alterations were made rather out of ignorance of ancient history, and too great credulity, from the motive of raising the honour and prerogatives of their country beyond others; and rather upon conjectures and grounds that seemed at least probable enough, in the several occasions and circumstances that gave rise to them, than upon any formed design to alter the truth, or to invent: and if we consider, with more attention, the several degrees of growth of these high antiquities, in the hands of our writers of different ages, we will find that

(*a*) Supra, p. 234, &c.

each

each new addition to the firſt invention of them (which was wholly due to the bards) was in ſome manner but a conſequence of the former; each new one leaving as it were behind it a demand of a new ſupplement, till the fabrick of theſe high antiquities was completed, by degrees, in the order, and with the dimenſions in which our modern hiſtorians preſent it.

§. 1. *Firſt ſtep or foundation of the high antiquities of the* Scots *in* Britain: *the opinion of the* Scots *having been ſettled in* Ireland *ſeveral ages before the incarnation.*

THIS firſt ſtep, or the firſt invention, is wholly due to the bards in *Ireland:* the *Scots* being ſettled there about, or after the times of the incarnation, and becoming the leading men in that iſland, and being by degrees cemented into one body of people with the ancient inhabitants, the time of their firſt coming in, wore out of the memory of men in ſome ages, (and a few ages ſufficed, for that in a country where as yet there was no uſe of letters, nor written records) it is like, that the bards, to flatter the *Scots* in *Ireland,* as the governing party, and gain their favour and rewards, began to ſet them out in their rythms as very ancient inhabitants of the iſland, come into it time out of mind: and having afterwards, as we have obſerved, eſpecially after they had ſome knowledge of the ſcripture, gotten ſome hints of long genealogies, they

they drew up genealogies for the leading men of the *Scots*, and led them up first to the supposed first heroes and founders of the *Irish*, and from thence up to *Noah* and *Adam*. Having also gotten some notion of chronology, they seem to have at first fixed the time of the coming in of the *Scots* to about six or seven hundred years before the incarnation, as we have elsewhere shewn; and the *Scots* in *Britain*, having received these first draughts of the genealogy and chronology from the *Irish*, have preserved them much in the same state in which they were at first broached, having no national concern, as the *Irish* had, to alter (a) them, in order to make their settlement in *Ireland*, and their monarchy remount to a higher antiquity.

§. 2. *The settlement of the* Scots *in* Britain *placed before the incarnation, but no kings till* Fergus *son of* Erch.

THE story of the *Scots* settlement in *Ireland* six or seven hundred years before the incarnation being generally received, it was the more easy to think that their first settlement in *Britain* was also very ancient: that the *Scots* coming in at first to *Britain* by degrees, insensibly, and in small numbers, and not in bodies of men, the memory of the time of the coming in of the first of them

(a) Supra, p. 479, &c.

might

might in some ages be quite worn out. And they being originally the same people with the *Scots* in *Ireland*, and the ancient settlement of these last in *Ireland* being generally received, it was the more likely that the settlement of those in *Britain* must have been ancient also; that the passage from *Ireland* first to the western islands, or to *Kintyre*, *Lorn*, *Argyle*, and other western coasts of *Britain*, the first possession of the *Scots* in this island, was more short and easy.

Now the first *Scots* being come into *Britain*, as we suppose, in the third (*a*) age of christianity, though they made no figure there till the fourth; their descendents in the seventh or eighth age, after ten or twelve generations, ignorant of the precise time of their coming in, and knowing only that they were settled in *Britain* time out of mind, would naturally be inclined rather to augment, than diminish their antiquity in the seats which they then enjoyed (ancient possession being an honourable title) when the question was about the time of their settlement. Wherefore we must not wonder, that *Bede*, who had his informations from some *Scotish* monks in the eighth age, when he wrote his history, seems to have believed, on their credit, that the (*b*) *Scots* were settled before the times of the incarnation, not only in *Ireland*, but even in

(*a*) Supra, p. 638, &c.
(*b*) Bed. l. 1. c. 1.

Britain:

Britain: and for the same reason (*a*) *Nennius* also, a *British* writer of the ninth age, seems to place the coming in of the *Scots* to *Dalried* (the ancient name of their possessions in *Britain*) about five hundred years before the incarnation, that is, about an age or two after their first coming to *Ireland*, according to the *Irish* tradition, not as yet altered in his time.

THIS opinion of the ancient settlement of the *Scots* in *Britain*, being once received among them, was too honourable to be abandoned, and much more likely to be improved, than examined in such ages, as the ninth, tenth and eleventh: and accordingly we find, that in the twelfth and thirteenth following ages, it was not only held among the *Scots* as certain, but the time of the *Scots* first coming into *Britain* condescended upon, to have been about the year four hundred and forty-three before the incarnation, according to the *Latin* (*b*) chronicle in verse, in the following passage.

Bis bis centeno quater endeca, sed minus uno
Anno, quo sumpsit primos Ergadia Scotos
Ut referunt isti fuit incarnatio Christi, &c.

And here I cannot but take notice of a mistake (I shall give it no other name, out of respect to so truly learned a person) that *Usher* (*c*), and others,

(*a*) Nennius, c. 9.
(*b*) Append. n. 6. c. 6.
(*c*) Brit. Eccl. Antiq. p. 312.

copying

copying after him, to bring down as low as they can the settlement of the *Scots* in *Britain*, have fallen into, in applying the number of four hundred and fourty-three years, contained in these verses to the times posteriour to the incarnation: whereas by a little attention to what goes before, and what follows after, these verses in this short chronicle, it would have clearly appeared, that the author's meaning was, that the *Scots* were settled in *Britain* four hundred and forty-three years before the incarnation. I say, four hundred and forty-three years, and not four hundred and thirty-nine. For in all the best copies of this chronicle, such as that in the *Scotichronicon*, or *black book of Pasly* in the king's library at *London*, in the *Scotichronicons* of the college of *Edinburgh*, in that of *Panmure*, and in that of the *Scotish* college of *Paris* there is, *Bis bis centeno quater* (endeca) *sed minus uno*, &c. and not *quater & deca*, &c. as it seems *Usher's* copy had it. This is farther confirmed, by the following more ancient *Scotish* writers, such as *Winton* and *Gray*, who both of them copied from the records of St. *Andrew's*, and both place the first settlement of the *Scots* in *Britain*, about four hundred and forty-three years before the incarnation.

But tho' the author of this chronicle and other writers about this time, were perswaded of this ancient settlement of the *Scots* in *Britain*; yet not only this author hath not a word of any kings of of the *Scots* before *Fergus* son of *Erc*; but on the contrary, he tells us plainly, that the *Scots* lived long in *Britain* before they had kings, and both he and all the remains of our ancient histories, and all our other writers of the thirteenth age down to our debates about the independency of *Scotland* with *Edward* I. before *Pope Boniface* VIII. are positive, that the *Scots* had at least no soveraign kings of their own nation in *Britain*, before king *Fergus* son of *Erch*, and all of them place him the first monarch of the *Scots* in *Britain*, as we (*a*) have shewn elsewhere.

§. 3. *First rise or origin of the opinion of ancient kings of the* Scots *in* Britain, *before the incarnation: but nothing yet determined as to their number or names.*

WE have given some account in another place (*b*), upon what occasion the opinion of ancient *Scotish* kings in *Britain*, was at first started at the debates with king *Edward* I. before the *Pope* about our independencies, contained in the two records set down at length by the best continuators of *Fordun*; whereof the one is the memorial (*c*) sent by the states of *Scotland* to their three deputies at the court of *Rome*; the other is the (*d*) memorial or

(*a*) Supra, p. 676.
(*b*) Supra, p. 1621.
(*c*) Fordun. edit. Tho. Hearne, p. 1835.
(*d*) Ibid. p. 1883.

process of *Baldred Bisset*, the chief of these deputies: both given in to the pope, *A. D.* 1301. we have given a full account of them in the place above-mentioned.

IN these debates, as hath been observed, our deputies, like skilful and zealous advocates in a cause of the highest importance to their country, made use of all sort of arguments to defend it. They proved our independency by what could be found in the country of ancient records. They endeavoured to raise in the eyes of the *Pope*, and court of *Rome*, a high opinion of the *Scotish* nation, and of its prerogatives above the *English*, by the ancient settlement of the *Scots* in *Britain*; which in those days they made no doubt of, having then for several ages been generally received by them; from their having received christianity long before the *English* or *Saxons*; from their having still preserved their freedom, and kept possession of the same territories in the north of *Britain* for so many ages, notwithstanding their being attacked by so many enemies; whilst the south of *Britain* or *England* had so often lost its freedom, and been so frequently subjected to new masters, *Romans*, *Saxons*, *Danes* and *Normands*.

BUT king *Edwa d* I, in his letter to the pope, having brought his succession and pretended superiority over *Scotland*, down from *Brutus*, *Locrinus*, and the ancient *British* kings, which, however fabulous

fabulous, paſs'd current in thoſe days; the *Scots* would not be behind-hand with him in that neither; and therefore having, as they believed, probable grounds to go upon, the advocates of the *Scots* advance before the pope, that the *Scots* had alſo a ſucceſſion of ancient kings from before the incarnation. This is indeed the firſt time we hear of it, but the *Scotiſh* deputies advanced it with the greater confidence that, beſides the preſſing occaſion they had for it, in that juncture, not to have the *Scots* thought any ways inferior to the *Engliſh*, in ſo honourable a prerogative as that of an ancient monarchy; beſides this, the thing in it ſelf ſeemed probable enough in thoſe days.

For to ſay nothing here of our kings being deſcended time out of mind from the *Pictiſh* kings in whoſe right they had ſucceeded; it was now ſome ages ſince the opinion of the *Scots*, their having been ſettled four or five hundred years in *Britain* before the incarnation, and ſo about nine hundred years before the reign of *Fergus* ſon of *Erch*, was generally receiv'd, as (*a*) we have ſhewn, among the *Scots*: Now that the *Scots*, a people almoſt always in war with their neighbours, could be in *Britain* about eight or nine hundred years, a headleſs people, and without a king, was a thing that ſeemed no ways probable, or rather almoſt intirely incredible.

(*a*) Supra, p. 7-3.

Besides, that this memorial of the *Scots* was drawn up in great haste (*cum festinatione*) in *Scotland*, so that they had not leisure to examine things maturely, or to consult those that were most versed in the antiquities of the nation, but were obliged to set down such notions of them, as their memory or popular traditions could furnish them, or rather their secretaries, and at the same time, to give them the most favourable turn for the support of their cause that they could think of. And upon the whole, considering the ignorance the *Scots* were in (since the destruction, or carrying off the ancient documents of their history) the persuasion they were in, of their ancient settlement in *Britain*; and the little probability there was, that they could have been so many ages in *Britain* without kings; I can scarce doubt but their deputies, and those that drew up their memorials, had perswaded themselves, that the *Scots* had a succession of kings from their first settlement. And this came afterwards to be a common opinion among them, but without condescending as yet upon their names, not even upon that of the first king or founder, till *Fordun*'s chronicle was published and universally received in the fifteenth century.

But as to *Baldred Bizet*, one of the deputies, his telling the *Pope* in his memorial (*a*), that the *Scots* had thirty-six catholick or christian kings before

(*a*) Fordun. Edit. Hearne, p. 887.

fore the *English* were converted to christianity, this, I own, is a stretch I cannot fathom, or guess at the grounds on which he went, except that it shews, that he knew nothing yet certain in particular, about the beginning of the monarchy or christianity among the *Scots*: for at that rate the *Scots* would have had christian kings before the times of christianity: since even in *Boece*'s account, *Metellan*, whom he places about the time of the incarnation, was but the thirty-second king upwards from king *Aydan*, in whose time the gospel was preached to the *Saxons* or *English*.

YET there is another *Scotish* writer in these dark times, mentioned by the continuators of *Fordun* (*a*) that surpasseth in the antiquity of the *Scotish* monarchy, even *Baldred*'s memorial: for he tells us, that the *Scots* had twenty-three kings before the *Picts* came into *Britain*, which, according to this writer's accounts, happened above two hundred years before the incarnation. So that according to him, the beginning of the *Scotish* monarchy would be placed about six or seven hundred years before the incarnation; since twenty three of our kings reigns in no age, or writer, take up less than betwixt four and five hundred years.

BUT 'tis easy to observe from these high flights and incredible accounts, that when the first men-

(*a*) Scotichron. l. 4. c. 10.

tion of these ancient kings, before *Fergus* son of *Erc*, began (that is, at the end of the thirteenth or about the beginning of the fourteenth age), there was nothing yet fix'd or agreed on about them; and those incredible accounts given by those who first mention them, insinuate plainly enough, that the opinion was as yet new and undigested; advanced only at a venture, in a necessary juncture to serve a turn. It required time to make it ripen, and the labours of posterior writers to digest it, to fix the date of the monarchy, the number of kings, their names; at least that of the first and founder. All this was the work of time: but the fabrick was now begun; we shall see there wanted not hands, as occasion offered, to finish it piece-meal.

§. 4. *The number of those ancient kings first mentioned, but no account as yet of their names, not even that of the first king or founder of the monarchy, nor the time of the beginning of the monarchy as yet fixed.*

THE next step then of the growth of our remote antiquities, was the fixing the number of these ancient kings. This we have for the first time advanced transiently, rather than determined (for posterior writers stuck not by it) about twenty years after the first mention of them: we have it, I say, in the famous letter of our *Scotish* nobility, under king *Robert* the *Bruce*, to Pope *John* XXII. *A. D.* 1320. There they tell the pope, that king *Robert* was the hundred and thirteenth king of the *Scots*. Now he being in reality but our fifty-third king from *Fergus* son of *Erc*, and even in *Fordun*'s, and the vulgar account, but the fifty-seventh from this *Fergus*, they must have counted fifty-six kings before this *Fergus* II. and that is about sixteen kings more than *Boece*, *Buchanan* and our other modern writers suppose, who reckon only thirty-nine kings in all before this *Fergus*.

As for this number of one hundred and thirteen kings, it may be the nobility, or rather their secretary, reckon'd all at once, both the ancient kings of the *Picts*, and those of the *Scots*, in the number of their present kings ancestors, as they might very well do, since he was descended of them both, and was possess'd of both their rights. The *Pictish* kings, according to the best accounts of them given by the *Scots* (such as that of the register of St. *Andrew*'s) being sixty in number; and those in the *Scotish* line, from *Fergus* son of *Erch* till *Robert Bruce*, making, according to our most ancient chronologists, just the number of fifty-three. Both these together make exactly that of one hundred and thirteen kings according to this letter.

But if any will insist rigorously upon the expression of this letter of the nobility (*de ipsorum* (Scotorum) *regali prosapia, nullo alienigena interveniente*) and conclude from thence, that all these kings must have been of the *Scotish* race or line; I offer them another conjecture, for verifying the expression of the letter, and finding out the hundred and thirteen kings.

SIMON BREAC was look'd upon by all the *Scots* for many ages before, as their leader from *Spain*; who brought the fatal stone along with him, and first founded a monarchy of the *Scotish* nation. Now the *Scots*, in their letter to the *Pope*, take not the least notice of the *Scots* coming from *Spain* first to *Ireland*, and thence to the north-west of *Britain*; but suppose that the *Scots* came straight from *Spain* to *Britain*, and possess'd themselves of these territories in the west of *Britain*, where they first settled, and which they still enjoy'd with the accession of the *Pictish* dominions.

Now tho' the *Scotish* nobility, or their secretary, do not expresly name *Simon Breac* in this letter, yet he being reputed in these times their leader from *Spain*, and first monarch of the *Scots*, 'tis like the secretary may have look'd upon the fifty-four or fifty-five descents or names in the old genealogy, from *Simon* till *Fergus* son of *Erch*, as so many kings descended of *Simon* the first *Scotish* king in these parts. And this, confounding the descents of the genealogy with the succession or reigns of kings, ought not to seem extraordinary in those times of ignorance, since the learned Dr. *Stil-*

lingfleet

lingfleet (*a*) in our time, hath fallen into the same mistake, in taking a genealogical line for a succession of kings. Now the *Scots*, in their letter to the *Pope*, taking the fifty-five names, or descents, in the genealogical line from *Simon* till *Fergus* son of *Erch*, for fifty-five kings, and those added to the fifty-eight kings in the common account from *Fergus* son of *Erch* down till *Robert* the *Bruce*; both together make exactly the number of one hundred and thirteen kings, including king *Robert*. If these conjectures for the number of one hundred and thirteen kings, mentioned by the nobility, do not please: I leave to others to find out more likely grounds for it.

HOWEVER, neither in this letter, nor in any piece now extant of those times, do we find the names of these kings, not so much as that of the first, or founder, different from *Simon Breac*; for as to *Fergus* son of *Ferchard*, his being called the first king of the *Scots* in *Albany*, in the copy we have from *Fordun* and his continuators of the genealogy of our kings, in the end of king *David*'s life (*b*), and in that recited by the highlander, at the coronation of king *Alexander* III, it cannot be doubted of, but these words, *Fergus first king of the* Scots *in* Albany, meaning *Fergus* son of

(*a*) Stillingfl. Orig. Britan. Præf. pag. 10, &c.
(*b*) Fordun. edit. Hearne, lib. 5. c. 50. pag. 487. ibidem pag. 750.

Ferchard,

Ferchard, are not of these times, nor of the first hand, but are a bare interpolation of *Fordun*, or of his continuators, according to their custom of adapting ancient historical pieces to the systems they had form'd to themselves. For, in all the genuine copies of this genealogy before *Fordun*, such as that of king *William*'s time, set down here in the appendix, *num.* 4. as well as in that of *Ralf de Diceto* dean of *London*, in the same age; and in *Winton*'s copy, who lived in *Fordun*'s time, and in that of Mr. *James Gray* who lived after *Fordun*, both which were taken from the ancient records of St. *Andrew*'s; in all these, I say, there's never a word of this *Fergus* son of *Ferchard* his being first king of *Albany*, or a king at all, but his bare name is ranked with the rest of the names of that genealogy, without the least mark of distinction.

AND neither in the memorials and process of *Baldred*, and of the other *Scotish* deputies, given in by the *Scots*, *A. D.* 1301. or in the letter to the pope, *A. D.* 1320, where we have the first mention of the number of these ancient kings, is there the least word of *Fergus* I. or of any one of these first kings by name: only the instructions of the states of *Scotland*, *A. D.* 1301, mention over and again, one *Erch*, as the father of our kings. 1°. They bring him in as son to *Gathcyl* and *Scota*, as first of our (*a*) kings at the settlement of the *Scots* in

(*a*) Fordun. edit. Hearn. pag. 847.

in *Britain*, and as giving his name with that of his father, as they call him, *Gathel*, join'd in one name *Ercgatheyl*, to the country in *Britain*, which they first possess'd. 2. They place (*a*) him again a king of the *Scots*, *Erch* son to *Echad* or *Ethod*, and brother to *Eugenius* at the end of the fourth or beginning of the fifth century, about the time the monarchy is suppos'd by our modern writers to have been restored by *Fergus* son of *Erch*. This double mention of *Erch*, as the stock of our kings is remarkable, and shews us how much the tradition of our kings, being descended of *Erch*, or rather of *Fergus* son of *Erch*, was fixed in the minds of the *Scots* at that time, and that the notion of *Fergus* son of *Ferchard*, as our first king, was not yet known or invented.

Before we enter upon the improvements made in our high antiquities by *John Fordun*, who first reduced them to a system and order, we must of course set down what *Winton*, prior of *Lochlevin*, says of them in his chronicle. We have given account of *Winton* (*b*) among the rest of our writers: And tho' he wrote only some few years after *Fordun*; yet it's certain he had never seen *John Fordun*'s chronicle, which, it appears, was not pub-

(*a*) Idem pag. 854.
(*b*) Supra, p. 642.

lish'd

lish'd by *Bowmaker Abbot* of *Inchcolm*, till about the year 1448, and that after *Winton*'s time. So *Winton*, knowing nothing of *Fordun*'s new systems, was still much in the same darkness and uncertainty about our high antiquities, as the rest of the nation were in the beginning of the fourteenth age. But having made it his business to enquire into our history, and living at the end of the fourteenth age, and beginning of the fifteenth, we may learn from him, what progress the opinions already received about our ancient settlement, and antiquity of the *Scotish* monarchy in *Britain* had made, during the course of that fourteenth age, independently of *John Fordun*'s labours, and what the common opinion and sense of the *Scots* was, upon these heads before *John Fordun*'s system of our history was publish'd.

WINTON believed according to the tradition received many ages before, that the *Scots* were settled in *Britain* before the incarnation: and he fixes the *Epoch* of their coming in, about the year four hundred and forty-three before the birth of Christ, as the short *Latin Chron. in Rythm* had done: And as to the opinion of the *Scots* having had kings before the *Picts*, or from about the time of their first settlement in *Britain*, first started as we have observed, at the debate with king *Edward* I. this opinion seeming so honourable to the nation, and having had in *Winton*'s time about a whole age to ripen, and being then almost generally

rally receiv'd among the *Scots*, *Winton* goes into it heartily at first: But then being at the same time so fully persuaded, that *Fergus* son of *Erch* was the first king of the *Scots*, that (*a*) he repeats it over and over three or four several times in his chronicle; and finding on the other hand, that there were only ten (*b*) generations or descents betwixt *Fergus* son of *Erch* and *Kenneth Mac Alpin*, who began his reign *A. D.* 842, and overcame the *Picts*; and that it was impossible that these ten generations could last twelve hundred years, as they must have done, if *Fergus* son of *Erch* had begun to reign over the *Scots* from their first settlement in *Britain* in his account, more than four hundred years before the incarnation; *Winton* is at last with reluctancy forced to part with the notion of the *Scots*, having had a king from their first settlement; and yet being sure that the name of their first king was *Fergus* son of *Erch* (whom he calls always *Erth*, as it was the custom of that age to write) as it was true, he at last begins first to doubt, and then inclines to believe, that king *Fergus*'s reign was not of so old date, and in short leaves the difficulty to be resolved by others.

It is evident by the perplexity *Winton* was in, to reconcile *Fergus* son of *Erch*, his being the first

(*a*) Winton's Chronicle, MS. in Bibl. Cotton. fol. 30. fol. 37, 43.

(*b*) Appendix, num. 7.

king

king of the *Scots*, with the notion of kings of *Scots* from their firſt ſettlement before the incarnation, and before the *Picts*, that *Winton* knew nothing of any other king *Fergus*, but *Fergus* ſon of *Erch*, who was but ten generations before *Kenneth Mac Alpin*; and that in *Winton*'s days, that is, about the end of the fourteenth age, *Fergus* ſon of *Feradac* or *Ferchart*, called king *Fergus* I, was not as yet known as a king of *Scots*, either by *Winton*, or commonly among the *Scots*; and by conſequence, that *Fordun*'s chronicle, where we meet, for the firſt time, with the diſtinction of two kings, firſt and ſecond of the name of *Fergus*, was not yet generally known in the kingdom, nor had ever been ſeen by *Winton*, having never been publiſh'd in all appearance till it came out with additions, during the reign of king *James* II. as hath been already remarked.

And as to *Winton*, he was ſo far from looking on *Fergus* or (as he calls him with the oldeſt copies of the genealogy) *Fergo* or *Forco* ſon of *Feradach*, as the firſt king, or a king at all, of the *Scots*, that he ſets down his name, as all the oldeſt copies of the genealogy do, confuſedly among the reſt of the names (*a*) of that genealogy of our kings, without taking the leaſt notice of him, more than of the reſt. Now had *Winton* gotten but a

(*a*) Winton, Book III. fol. 30. MS. Colon. —— Bibl. Reg. Lond. lib. 3. c. 10.

hint

hint of this first *Fergus* son of *Ferchard*, his having been a king of *Scots*, he had instantly disintangled himself, and had been able to reconcile his belief of the *Scots* having been settled four hundred years before the incarnation, with their having had kings, and the first of them a *Fergus* from the beginning (and so to have raised their antiquity higher than that of the *Picts*, which he and our other writers chiefly aimed at) since there were no less than forty-five generations, betwixt this first *Fergus* son of *Ferchard*, and *Kenneth Mac Alpin*, which were more than enough to fill up twelve hundred years, and so would have reconciled all matters, and solved all *Winton*'s difficulties. But this discovery was left to *Fordun*, whose labours in advancing the fabrick of our remote antiquities, and giving them a form, require to be treated of at more length.

§. 5. John Fordun's *labours in the remote antiquities of the* Scots. *These antiquities reduced into a fixed plan and chronological order.*

We have already (*a*) given a general account of *John Fordun*, and more than once spoken of his labours in the *Scotish* history: we are now to treat of his bringing it to that fixed plan and order, which hath been followed by all our later writers, especially in what concerns our high antiquities,

(*a*) Supra, p. 201, &c. 225, 632, &c.

or

or the hiſtory of the *Scots* before *Fergus* ſon of *Erch*, commonly called *Fergus* II.

To do juſtice to *Fordun*, it appears by what we have ſaid elſewhere of him, that none ever applied to hiſtory with more zeal for his country, nor with a better intention than *Fordun*, nor hath been at greater pains to find out materials, or to digeſt them in a more regular form, conſidering the times in which he wrote. For as to the ſubſtance of his chronicle, it muſt be conſidered, that *Fordun* wrote in an age when there was little or no critical learning, and very little diſtinction made betwixt certain and fabulous monuments of hiſtory; when uncertain popular traditions, and dubious legends, for want of better materials, were often employ'd as documents of hiſtory; when certain national preventions in favour of our remote antiquities run ſo high, that a miſtaken zeal for what was thought in thoſe days honourable to the country, and an apprehenſion to ſhock the better part of the nation, hindered *Fordun* from diſcuſſing matters, and ſo overſwayed him, as it hath done many others, that he believed that the dignity of the crown and kingdom was concern'd in ſupporting by all means the current popular traditions of our remote antiquities, which were become daily more in vogue, ſince the debates about our independency with king *Edward* I.

HENCE

HENCE it happened, that the antiquities of the *Scots* made a new and considerable progress and figure in passing thro' *Fordun*'s hands. For what had been only advanced by conjecture in times past, especially at the debate about the independency, and that only to serve a turn, and on bare probabilities, or advanced confusedly in different former ages, without order and connexion, as well as all the popular traditions about the ancient settlement of the *Scots* in *Britain*, the antiquities of the monarchy, *&c.* all this was by *Fordun* digested into a following series of history, reduced to chronological order, and supported with all the documents he had met with in his searches, fit for his purpose: documents indeed much of the same character, as the facts they were brought to support: but documents, after all, and vouchers, much of the same nature and credit as those brought by the writers of our neighbouring countries for antiquities of the same nature; by the *British* or *Welch* for their *Brutus*, and the long tract of his ancient successors; by the *Irish* for their *Milesius* and his successors before christianity, for their ancient litterature, and their other remote antiquities.

WE are now to consider *Fordun*'s performances more in detail, the grounds he had to go upon, the method which he followed, and the means he was oblig'd to make use of, to put in a more regular order the new plan of the fabrick of our remote antiquities, contained in the first, but chiefly in the second, and beginning of the third book of his chronicle.

As to his first book containing the story of the *Scotish* high antiquities, from *Geythelos* or *Gathelus*, till *Fergus* son of *Ferchart*, the substance of that (except what concern'd *Fergus* as a king) had been advanced, and by degrees received among the *Scots* long before *Fordun*; as we have already observed (*a*). And *Fordun* only enlarged on the same bottom, improved into better order these vulgar traditions, and fixed them to certain periods of chronology. It is chiefly in the last chapters of his first book, in his second, and in the first chapter of the third, that the *Scotish* remote antiquities received from him their greatest increase and improvement, and were brought to a more regular form and consistency.

We have seen in the four foregoing paragraphs, the several steps or degrees of the growth of those antiquities, which, like a large fabrick, received new dimensions or additions from the several ages and different hands, through which they had passed, but nothing fixed or regular till *Fordun*. The first foundation of them, to wit, the opinion of the *Scots*, their having been settled in *Ireland*, long

(*a*) Supra, p. 707, 733.

before

before the incarnation, had been laid many ages ago. The first superstructure upon that, to wit, of the *Scots* having been settled in *Britain* about four hundred years before the incarnation, was raised before the twelfth age. The first additions to that, to wit, of the *Scots* in *Britain*, their having had kings from their first settlement, was first started at our debates with king *Edward* I. about independency; and by the circumstances of the times and other reasons mentioned already in its proper place, soon gain'd credit among the *Scots*. The number of their ancient kings was named by conjecture, about twenty years afterwards, in the famous letter of the *Scots* nobility, to pope *John* XXII.

It remain'd now for *Fordun*'s task in this fabrick, 1°. to reduce former superstructures into symmetry, by digesting the whole into distinct epochs, and a chronological order. 2°. to fix a certain epoch for the beginning of the *Scotish* monarchy in *Britain*. 3°. To reduce the number of their ancient kings, within a more plausible compass, to wit, to that of forty-five. 4°. To assign their names. 5°. At least to give us the name of the first king and founder of the monarchy. 6°. To give a chronological account of their reigns, at least such as he had given of the *Picts*, and as he gave afterwards of the *Scotish* kings from *Fergus* II. downwards. 7°. In order to support the credit of the story of the kings of *Scots* in *Britain* before *Fergus* son of *Erch* against the plain testimonies of all the above-mentioned remains of ancient monuments of the *Scots*, before the twelfth age, and the debates about our independency with *Edward* I. and others of a like purport, *Fordun* had to give a plausible reason, why in all these ancient remains of our history, *Fergus* son of *Erch* is reckon'd the first king of the *Scots* in *Britain*; which assertion alone, if not obviated or cleared, overturns at once all the system of the high antiquities of the *Scots*, or of their forty or forty-five kings before *Fergus* son of *Erch*, or *Fergus* II. Now *Fordun*, being perswaded of the truth of this system, look'd upon all that he met with of these remains, contrary to it, in his searches, barely as objections or difficulties, which he had to answer or remove by explications or distinctions. We have already had occasion to observe one means made use of by *Fordun* to that purpose; but another and more universal answer, was to find out or discover a dissolution of the ancient *Scotish* monarchy, founded by *Fergus* I. son of *Ferchard*, and continued down till it was ruined, towards the end of the 4th age of christianity, and a new erection or foundation of it by *Fergus* II. son of *Erch*, in the beginning of the fifth age; by which this *Fergus* son of *Erch* might be justly called the first king of the *Scots*, to wit, after the restoration of the monarchy.

We are now to give an account of *Fordun*'s proceedings in the execution of this task, consisting

historical fact many ages before his time, and that of an ancient christianity among these *Scots*, being no less honourable to the nation, had been also received among them long before *Fordun*'s days: tho' he is the first that we know of, who assigned to the conversion of the *Scots*, the fixed date of *A. D.* 203. and that quotes for this the verses.

Christi transactis tribus annis atque ducentis
Scotia *catholicam cœpit habere fidem.*
Roma *Victore primo papa residente*
Principe Severo martyr et occubuit.

And tho' the expression, *Victore primo*, demonstrates, that those verses are posteriour to the eleventh age, when pope *Victor* II. lived, and their barbarous composition shews, that they are yet later, yet they past for good authority in *Fordun*'s time, and apparently before it.

Now those two facts of the early settlement, and early conversion of the *Scots*, being received as historical truths that no-body called in question, when *Fordun* wrote, he meets in *Bede* and *Sigibert*, with the famous passage of *Prosper*'s chronicle, bearing that more than two hundred years after this first suppos'd conversion of the *Scots*, *A. D.* 431. (*a*) Palladius *was ordained by*

(*a*) Ad Scottos in Christum credentes ordinatur a papa Cælestino Palladius, & primus episcopus mittitur. *Prosp. Chron.*

pope

pope Celestin, *and sent the first bishop to the* Scots, *who believed in Christ.* *Fordun* made no doubt, but these *Scots* believing in *Christ*, *credentes in Christum*, were the *Scots* of *Britain*. They had been in his opinion converted two hundred years before, and St. *Patrick* was not yet sent to convert the *Scots* of *Ireland*. The consequence in *Fordun*'s judgment seemed evident; that during the two first ages of the christianity of the *Scots*, from *A. D.* 203, till *A. D.* 431, when *Palladius* the first bishop was sent to them, the *Scots* had lived without bishops; and since they had persevered in the profession of christianity, being still *credentes in Christum*; and that the profession of christianity could not be kept up during all that time, without doctors of faith, and pastors or ministers of the word and sacraments; and it being a certain truth, that in the absence or default of bishops, none were qualified to exercise those sacred functions but priests or monks elevated to the dignity of priesthood; from all this, as from unquestionable principles in *Fordun*'s judgment, he draws this famous conclusion: that (*a*) *before* Palladius's *coming, the* Scots *had for doctors of faith and ministers of the sacraments, priests only, and monks following the rite of the primitive church.*

(*a*) Ante cujus [Palladii] adventum, habebant Scoti fidei doctores, ac sacramentorum ministratores, presbyteros solummodo, vel monachos, ritum sequentes ecclesiæ primitivæ. *Fordun. lib.* 3. *cap.* 8. *edit. Th. Hearne, p.* 184.

This passage of *Fordun* at the new reformation of *Scotland*, became the corner-stone or fundamental charter of presbyterian government in that kingdom, as containing the most ancient account of church government, from the first establishment of the christian religion among the *Scots*. The same passage hath been ever since appealed to, by the successors of our first reformers in all the debates they have had with the episcopal party, concerning the government of the church. It hath also been employed by the most learned antagonists of episcopal government among foreigners, as one of their principal arguments: for as a learned (*a*) bishop of the church of *England* hath observed, *In that laborious collection of* Blondel, *under the title of an apology for St.* Hierome, *that writer, with all his vast reading, could not find one undoubted example of a church of the presbyterian way in ancient times, but only that of the* Scots.

We may have occasion in the second part of this essay, to discuss this passage more fully, together with those of *Bede*, concerning S. *Columba*, and those of the *Keledees*, which are brought to strengthen *Fordun*'s passage; but to say a word

(*a*) Bp. of St. *Asaph's* Governm. of the Ch. of G. B. preface, pag. 5.

here

here of this last, will not be out of the way, since it will serve to make *Fordun*'s method to be more fully understood.

THIS famous passage of *Fordun*, *Ante cujus* [Palladii] *adventum*, &c. is a consequence which *Fordun* draws from two premises, whereof the one is absolutely groundless, and the other at least extremely dubious, tho' both of them were held for certain by *Fordun*. The first is, that the *Scots* in *Britain* were converted to christianity, *A. D.* 203. But we have no ground to believe that the *Scots* were come into *Britain*, *A. D.* 203. as hath been already shewn (*a*), and that the most that can be advanced with any probability or ground, is that the *Scots* began during the third age to come over from *Ireland* into *Britain*, under their first leader *Eocha Riada*, call'd *Reuda* by *Bede*. So there could be no conversion of the *Scots* *A. D.* 203, in *Britain*, where they were not as yet settled; nor by consequence any occasion as yet for pastors or ministers of any kind among them. So all the inferences drawn from *Fordun*'s passage, *ante cujus*, &c. being built on the supposition of a profession of christianity, or christian church among the *Scots*, during above two hundred years before the mission of *Palladius*, are absolutely groundless.

(*a*) Supra, p.

THE

THE other premiſe ſuppoſed by *Fordun*, is, that the *Scots* to whom *Palladius* was ſent the firſt biſhop, *A D.* 431. by pope *Celeſtine*, were the *Scots* of *Britain*. It may indeed be ſaid, that *Palladius* was ſent to the *Scots* in general, that is, to the nation of the *Scots* wherever they were ſettled, and ſo thoſe of *Britain* might be comprehended; and 'tis not unlike, as we may have occaſion to obſerve elſewhere, that this holy biſhop, not being well received by the *Scots* of *Ireland*, and coming over to *Britain*, where he died among the *Picts*, may have probably announced the goſpel to the *Scots* in *Britain*; but as the queſtion is here, of his miſſion and deſtination by pope *Celeſtine*, it appears by another paſſage of St. *Proſper*, who relates this miſſion, that *Palladius*'s miſſion regarded mainly the *Scots* in *Ireland*. For *Proſper* (*a*) ſeems viſibly to diſtinguiſh the iſland to which *Palladius* was ſent, as being a barbarous iſland, that is, in *Proſper*'s language, an iſland that had never been ſubject to, nor cultivated by the *Romans*, from *Britain*, which he calls a *Roman* iſland, becauſe the far greateſt part of it (and among the reſt, thoſe provinces of *Scotland* that lie

(*a*) Nec Segniore cura hoc ab eodem morbo [*Pelagianiſmi*] Britannias liberavit [*Celeſtinus*] quando quoſdam inimicos gratiæ ſolum ſuæ originis occupantes, etiam ab illo ſecreto excluſit oceani: & ordinato Scotis epiſcopo, dum *Romanam* Inſulam ſtudet ſervare catholicam, fecit etiam *barbaram* chriſtianam. *Proſper contra Collator. cap.* 41.

to

to the south of the *Friths*) had been civilized by the *Roman* discipline and polity.

But I add farther, that giving and not granting that this conclusion of *Fordun*, *ante cujus* [Palladii] *adventum*, *&c.* had been well drawn in the sense that *Fordun* meant it, the inference that the anti-episcopal writers draw from it, to wit, that before *Palladius*'s mission, there was during two hundred years in *Scotland*, a succession of pastors, or ministers of the word and sacraments, who had no episcopal ordination, and none but that of *Laymen* or simple presbyters; this inference is absolutely groundless, for neither *Fordun* himself, who knew that the doctrine of presbyterian parity was contrary to that of the church of all ages, and had been lately condemned in his own time, among the propositions of *Wickliff*, could ever entertain any such imagination; no more than *Major*, *Boece*, *Lesly*, *&c.* who copied after him: but all that *Fordun* and these other *Roman Catholick* writers understood, or could understand by the expression *ante cujus*, *&c.* was, that tho' the *Scots* had, as they believed, received christianity, *A. D.* 203. yet they had not a proper bishop sent to them, or residing among them, till the coming of *Palladius*, *A. D.* 431. and so the christian *Scots* had been obliged till then to content themselves with priests and monks, elevated to the dignity of priesthood by the neighbouring or foreign bishops. But to conclude from that passage of *Fordun*, as the

the anti-epiſcopal writers do, that becauſe (according to *Fordun*) theſe *Scots* chriſtians had no proper biſhop as yet ſent to them, till two hundred years after their firſt converſion; that therefore they had no other miniſters of the word and ſacraments but nominal prieſts or monks, who took upon themſelves the ſacred functions, without epiſcopal or any other ordination, but that of *Laymen* or *Preſbyters*, is no leſs ridiculous, than if one ſhould conclude, that the clergy or regular prieſts, who were the only miniſters of the word and ſacraments among the *Roman Catholicks* in *Scotland* for more than one hundred years after the reformation, had no other ordination, but what they gave to one another, becauſe, during all that time there was no biſhop of their communion reſiding in *Scotland*.

As to the expreſſion of *Proſper*, *ad Scotos credentes in Chriſtum*. That *Palladius* was ſent to the *Scots*, who believed in Chriſt, from which ſome conclude that the *Scots* were chriſtians before the coming of *Palladius*. But that no ways follows. That there were ſome chriſtians, or a beginning of chriſtianity among the *Scots*, whether in *Ireland* or in *Britain*, when *Palladius* was ſent, is very likely. They both dwelt in the neighbourhood of the *Britains*, who were early chriſtians, and either by commerce with them, or by chriſtian captives, which the *Scots* carried off frequently from among the *Britains*, there's all likelihood, that before *Palladius*'s coming there were ſeveral chriſtians among the *Scots* both in *Ireland* and in *Britain*: and it appears by eccleſiaſtical hiſtory, that it was the cuſtom of the zealous biſhops of the neighbourhood in ancient times, and more yet of the popes, to ſend in biſhops to countries where there was already a beginning of chriſtianity, or a diſpoſition towards it. And this is all that *Proſper*'s expreſſion imports. But all this will be more fully diſcuſſed in its proper place.

THUS far only, by the way, as to this famous paſſage of *Fordun*, which hath been made uſe of by the antiepiſcopal party in *Scotland*, as one of the chief arguments for presbyterain government, from the times of the reformation. So I return to *Fordun*, and to the particular account of his method of proceeding in the execution of his task, conſiſting of the ſeven above-mentioned heads.

As to the firſt head, or part of his undertaking, to wit, the reducing to fixed *Epochs*, and the digeſting into a chronological order the confuſed maſs of the materials he had to work upon, conſiſting chiefly of popular traditions, legendary accounts about the *Scotiſh* antiquities, and of all that had been till his time advanced in different ages, and on different occaſions, of what had paſſed among the *Scots* before the fourth and fifth ages of chriſtianity. As to all this, I ſay, we have (a)

(a) Supra, p. 207, 208, &c.

already ſeen that he reduced to a certain order of chronology both theſe high antiquities, and the more modern and certain accounts of the *Scots* digeſted into fixed *Epochs*, in the abſtract we have given elſewhere of the ſeveral books of *Fordun*'s chronicle.

We come therefore now to the ſecond and fifth part of *Fordun*'s task in the advancing the ſabrick of our remote antiquities, to wit, the fixing a certain *Epoch*, and preciſe year of the beginning of the *Scotiſh* monarchy before the incarnation, and the aſſigning the name of the firſt monarch and founder of it.

The tradition of the *Scots* ancient ſettlement in *Britain* was univerſally received among them long before *Fordun*; and this ſettlement was ſuppoſed to have begun above four centuries before the incarnation: but the firſt *Scotiſh* document we have now remaining of it, to wit, the ſhort chronicle in (*a*) *Latin* verſe or rythms, is poſitive that they had no kings in the *Scotiſh* line till *Fergus* ſon of *Erch.* This we have ſhewn elſewhere, from all the monuments remaining of our ancient hiſtory before the year 1291. And the firſt mention we have of ancient kings, before *Fergus*, was at the debates in king *Edward* I's time. Tho' 'tis not improbable, that there were ſome notions and

(*a*) Append. n. 6. c. 6.

uncer-

uncertain opinions begun to grow up and spread among the *Scots* before these debates: that seeming a natural consequence of their being persuaded that the *Scots* were settled in *Britain* so long before the birth of Christ: but till these debates, I find no certain testimony of it in any monument of history I have yet met with.

HOWEVER, the fact had been advanced, as we have seen, with great assurance, in the memorials given in to pope *Boniface* VIII. in the heat of the debate; and in the *Scots* nobility's letter to pope *John* XXII. and had now past current, and been generally received among the *Scots* from the beginning of the fourteenth century, till *Fordun*'s time. So when he set about to write the history, he was no more master to contradict so plausible, and so received an opinion, nor indeed disposed to call in doubt what he esteemed honourable to the nation, and so acceptable to his countrymen, as the opinion of so ancient a succession of kings. He made it rather his business to confirm it: and probably the chief end of his travels and searches was to find documents proper for proving that, and the other heads above-mentioned.

TO return then to the second and fifth heads, to wit, the fixing the *Epoch* of the beginning of the *Scots* monarchy, and the person of the first king or founder: hitherto we have seen nothing agreed on since the first mention of ancient kings. Neither

Neither the memorials, *A. D.* 1301, nor the letter to pope *John* XXII. *A. D.* 1320, fix any *Epoch* of the monarchy, nor so much as name the first king; and *Winton*, who according to the truth of history, named him *Fergus*, *Erch*'s son, as all *Scotish* writers, before *Fordun* had done, not being able to reconcile that with the vulgar opinion of the antiquity of the monarchy, falls in contradiction with himself, and at last leaves the matter in doubt, as we have seen, to be resolved by others.

FORDUN was the first, that we know of, who fixed the *Epoch* of the monarchy to the year 330, before the incarnation, and who places *Fergus* son of *Ferchart* the first king of the *Scots*, and founder of the monarchy.

As to his fixing the beginning of the monarchy to the year 330, before the birth of Christ, besides his vouchers, whom we shall just now consider, I conceive one of his chief motives to fix on that year may have been this plausible conjecture, that finding, as we have seen, the first settlement of the *Scots* in *Britain* fixed before his time to the year 443, or thereabout, before the incarnation, he thought it was natural to allow them about one hundred years to increase their number, and enlarge their bounds under the first leaders of their colonies from *Ireland*, before they got a king or monarch, to whom all were subject. So that placing the beginning of the monarchy, and of the

the reign of their first king, about one hundred and ten years after their entry to *Britain*, that is, about the year 330, before the incarnation, was very probable, on the supposition already received, that the *Scots* came first to *Britain*, about four hundred and forty years before it.

FORDUN was also the first, that we know of, who raised to the dignity of first monarch of the *Scots* in *Britain*, *Fergus* son of *Ferchart*, or *Feradach*, whose name had, till *Fordun*'s time, lain confusedly among the other names of the old genealogy of our kings, without any mark of distinction, or having ever been taken notice of, till *Fordun* added to his name, in the two copies he gives of the genealogy, the quality of *first king of* Albany; for none of the copies, antecedent to them, such as that in the appendix, *num.* 4. and that of *Ralph de Diceto*, both in the twelfth age, have that addition: nor even those that wrote after him, without copying his chronicle, such as *Winton* and *Gray*, &c. *Fordun* was determined to make choice of this first *Fergus*, and set him up for the founder of the *Scotish* monarchy, as a natural consequence from what he found already received and believed by the *Scots*, concerning these high antiquities; for that once supposed, nothing can be more plausible than the consequence he draws in favour of *Fergus* son of *Ferchart*.

For, 1°. The opinion of the *Scots* having had kings ſome ages before the incarnation, was generally received before *Fordun*'s time, and having been made uſe of by the apologiſts of the *Scots*, in the debate for the independency and dignity of the crown againſt king *Edward* I's pretenſions, it was no more to be called in queſtion in *Fordun*'s days. 2°. It was unqueſtionably more certain, and more univerſally received, that the name of the firſt king of the *Scots*, and of the founder of their monarchy in *Britain*, was *Fergus*. All the *Scots*, till the fourteenth age, had believed that it was *Fergus* ſon of *Erch*, as we have ſeen; but this could not agree with the monarchy's beginning ſome ages before the incarnation, ſince this *Fergus* ſon of *Erch* is placed, in the genealogy univerſally received, only ten generations or deſcents before *Keneth Mac-Alpin*, who lived in the ninth age. This was a labyrinth out of which *Winton* could not extricate himſelf.

FORDUN, who ſeems to have had more genius and learning, as well as more application, than *Winton*, found means to reconcile this contradiction; for, by looking back more attentively into the old genealogy, he diſcovered another *Fergus*, the ſon of *Feradach*, whom *Winton*, and all *Scotiſh* writers till *Fordun*, had paſſed over, without taking any more notice of him than of the reſt of the old names in that genealogy:

nealogy: whereas *Fordun* finding this first *Fergus* in the series of that genealogy, about forty-five generations or descents before *Keneth Mac-Alpin*, which, according to the vulgar reckoning of thirty years for each generation, amounted to a number of years sufficient to place this first *Fergus* at the beginning of the *Scotish* monarchy in his account, that is, three hundred and thirty years before the incarnation: upon this discovery, *Fordun* naturally concluded that this *Fergus* son of *Feradach*, was the *Fergus* first king and founder of the *Scotish* monarchy; and by this means reconciled the then current tradition of the monarchy's beginning some ages before the incarnation, with its having had a *Fergus* for its founder, and first king.

But because, by all the remains of the ancient history of the *Scots*, it appeared that the *Scots* had always held *Fergus* son of *Erch* for their first king, it was necessary that *Fordun*, in order to have his new scheme received with less difficulty, should in the first place bring some authorities to prove, that the first king of the *Scots* was *Fergus* son of *Ferchard*, and that the monarchy began three hundred and thirty years before the incarnation. 2dly, That he should find some means to answer the objection drawn from the ancient monuments, in which *Fergus* son of *Erch* is called in express terms the first king of the *Scots*. We are then in the first place to hear his proofs for beginning the *Scotish* monarchy three hundred and thirty years before Christ, and *Fergus* son of *Ferchart* his being their first king. We shall afterwards relate the means he makes use of, to obviate or explain the ancient testimonies of *Fergus* son of *Erch*, his being the first king of the *Scots*.

His vouchers for the first are, 1°. these four *Latin* verses.

Albion (a) *in terris rex primus germine Scotus*
Ipsorum turmis rubri tulit arma leonis
Fergusius fulvo Ferchard rugientis in arvo
Christum trecentis ter denis præfuit annis.

Fordun doth not tell us whence he had those verses, whether from any former writer or chronicle, new or old: but tho' I will believe he found them made to his hand, yet it must be own'd, that the author of them, be who he will, must have been very little skilled, if he intended that they should pass for ancient, since king *Alexander* II, in the thirteenth age, is the first of our kings, in whose seal we find the lyon rampant on his shield. For there are no arms on the seals of his predecessors *Duncan*, *Edgar*, *Alexander* I. *David* I. *Malcolm* IV. nor on that of king *William*, and the blazoning, 'tis like, is yet posteriour. So these verses

(a) Fordun. edit. Hearne, l. 2. c. 12. p. 85.

are

are probably no older than the fourteenth age, when, as we have observed, these ancient kings before *Fergus* son of *Erch* were first mentioned, or rather these verses are only the productions of *Fordun*'s own time, since he is the first who calls *Fergus* son of *Ferchart* first king of the *Scots*.

FORDUN's second voucher is a legend of St. *Congal* an *Irish* saint, which, he says, relates (*a*) that *Fergus* son of *Ferchard* brought with him the famous chair from *Ireland* to *Scotland*, and was crowned in it the first king of the *Scots*. It will no doubt at first appear a little surprizing, to find an account of this nature in the life of a saint. But it must be considered, that it was no unusual thing among the *Irish*, to set down stories of their remote high antiquities, or other parts of their history, in the preface to some of their saints lives. Thus we have in the preface to the life of St. *Abban* (*b*) and in that of St. *Cadroe* in *Colgan*'s collections, rude draughts of the *Irish* remote antiquities.

AND if *Colgan* had continued his collection till the twelfth of *May*, the feast of *Congal*, we might perhaps in the preface to it, have met with some word of a *Fergus* king of *Scots*; for I can scarce doubt, but that in *Fordun*'s time, there was ex-

(*a*) Fordun, l. 2. c. 12. edit. Hearn. p. 86.
(*b*) Colgan. Act. SS. Hybern. tom. I. p. 494, & 610.

tant something of this kind, in the life of that famous abbot of *Banchor* in *Ireland*, in the sixth age. But in case there was, no doubt it was to be understood of *Fergus* son of *Erch*, for this was the *Fergus*, who according to the old *Latin Rythmical* chronicle above-mentioned, brought from *Ireland* the famous-stone, and made himself first king over the *Scots*, in the beginning of the sixth age, in which S. *Congal Abbot* lived. And so 'tis not unlikely, that such a famous transaction which happen'd near the saint's time, and which was so honourable to the *Scots*, both of *Ireland* and of *Britain*, might have been mentioned in the preface to this saint's life.

But 'tis like, *Fordun*'s mistake lay, in supposing the *Fergus*, mentioned in this life, was the son of *Ferchart*, and in applying to him here, as he doth elsewhere, what he found said of a *Fergus* first king of the *Scots*, that brought over the famous stone; because for the reasons already given, he looked on *Fergus* son of *Ferchart*, as the first founder of the *Scotish* monarchy: tho' the original writer of S. *Congal*'s life, no doubt meant *Fergus* son of *Erch*, whom all ancient writers, till the fourteenth age, looked upon as the first king of the *Scots*. So that legend of S. *Congal*'s, tho' we could find it, would prove of no more service towards *Fordun*'s system, in favour of *Fergus* son of *Ferchart*, than the *Latin* verses he brought for his first voucher.

I HAVE

I HAVE found at last the life of this S. *Congal.* It was published by *F. Fleming*, among the works of St. *Colomban.* But there's not a word of *Fergus* son of *Ferchart* in it, or any thing relating to *Fordun*'s narration.

BUT there remained as yet the hardest and most essential part of *Fordun*'s task, in order to support the new scheme of the *Scotish* kings, before *Fergus* son of *Erch.* He had to find a plausible answer to the objection drawn from the remains above-mentioned, of the ancient chronicles or histories of the *Scots*; in all which *Fergus* son of *Erch* is constantly reckoned first king of the *Scots. Fordun* was too diligent in his searches, to let such pieces escape his knowledge, and he was too ingenuous to deny their authority, how much soever they seemed opposite to his scheme of our antiquities: nay, he is so sincere as that he mentions, and even sets down, almost *verbatim* one of the most precise of them, as we have seen (*a*) elsewhere, and observed the turn which he gives the passage, by the adding a few words, to take off the force of it.

BUT that was not enough, nor like to satisfy those, in whose hands those ancient pieces should fall. They are all very formal, that Fergus *son of*

(*a*) Supra, *p.* 672, 673.

Erch *was the first king of the* Scots *in* Britain. The consequence seemed plainly to overturn *Fordun*'s system of forty-five kings, or indeed of any soveraign kings at all, before this *Fergus* son of *Erch*. *Fordun* was aware of this consequence, and being, I suppose, at the same time fully perswaded of the truth of what he had advanced, he finds a distinction to evade the objection, to take off the force of the consequence; and to reconcile to his new system, the expressions of the ancient extracts of the chronicles, where *Fergus* son of *Erch* is constantly called first king of the *Scots*.

In order to that, he found a very natural expedient to rid himself of that difficulty, and this was to suppose, that there must needs have been a second beginning and new founding, or rather a restoration of the kingdom of the *Scots* in *Britain*, by *Fergus* son of *Erch*, which gave sufficient ground to ancient authors, to call this *Fergus* the first king of the *Scots*, to wit, after the restoration of the monarchy. Now a restoration necessarily suppos'd a dissolution; and therefore *Fordun* is at so much pains to find vouchers for a dissolution or destruction of the kingdom of *Scots*, in the times immediately preceding the fifth age, where he places the restoration of *Fergus* II. He quotes for that a passage of *Sigebert*, who had copied *Tiro Prosper*, or *Gregory* of *Tours*. But all that the passages of these two writers import, is, that *Maximus* having usurped the empire, did beat o

the

the *Scots* and *Picts*, who were making incursions upon it. But that was usual in those ages, and imports neither that the *Scots* had any kingdom then in *Britain*, nor that *Maximus* destroyed it, and indeed the bulk of the story that *Fordun* gives of *Maximus*, his martial feats in *Britain*, is originally owing to *Geoffrey*, who calls him *Maximian*, and makes him a *Britain*.

UPON the whole, *Fordun* seems to have argued or reasoned thus with himself, tho' he doth not express his argument in formal terms. *Fergus* son of *Erch* was indeed first king of the *Scots* in *Britain*, as the ancient *Scotish* writers call him; but that is to be understood, that he was their first king after their re-entring *Britain*, and restoration of the monarchy: but it doth not follow, that this *Fergus* was absolutely their first king, or founder of the monarchy. There must needs then have been a dispersion of the *Scots*, and a destruction of their monarchy in *Britain* in the fourth age. *Fordun* continues: this dispersion of the *Scots*, and dissolution of their monarchy, lasted about forty years; during which time, all the *Scots* of *Britain*, princes, and people were dispersed and banished into foreign countries. At last, *Fergus* son of *Erch*, descended of the ancient kings of the *Scots*, having gathered them together from several places, entered *Britain* at their head, conquered anew their ancient territories; and having set up again, and restored the monarchy, became a new founder

founder of it, and deserved to be called by the title of *first king of the* Scots, to wit, after this new erection or restoration of the kingdom. Thus *Fordun* must have reasoned, in order to reconcile his system of the forty-five kings, with the remains of the ancient chronicles of the *Scots*.

As to the grounds or vouchers that *Fordun* had for this expulsion of the *Scots* out of *Britain*, all that he brings, as we observed above, is a passage of *Sigibert*, and the feats of *Maximus* from *Geoffrey*, who calls him *Maximian*. But if *Fordun* had lived after the times of the restoration of literature in the sixteenth or seventeenth age, when many ancient *Roman* writers (which in *Fordun*'s time lay unknown in the corners of ancient libraries) were published and made common, he would have met with proofs of a defeat and expulsion of the *Scots* and *Picts* out of their possessions by the famous general *Theodosius*, father to the first emperor of that name, during the reign of *Valentian* I. and of their being forced to retire at least to the northern extremities of *Britain*. All this he would have found in (*a*) *Ammian* and (*b*) *Claudian*, two famous writers of the time: and that it happened near about the time in which he fixes the expulsion of the *Scots* by *Maximus*.

(*a*) Amm. Marcel. ed. Vales. in 4to. l. 27. p. 346, &c.
(*b*) Claudian. Panegyr. in III. & IV. Consulat. Honor.

I SAY

I SAY *near about the time*; for this expedition of *Theodosius* against the *Scots* and *Picts* happened at soonest, *A. D.* 367, whereas *Fordun* fixes the expulsion of the *Scots* by *Maximus* precisely to the year 360; and to confirm it, he brings verses which import that the exile of the *Scots* out of *Britain* lasted forty-three years, which ending in his account by the restoration, *A. D.* 403, determines the year 360 for their expulsion. But as this calculation agrees not fully with the expedition of the general *Theodosius*, so it disagrees entirely with the usurpation of *Maximus* by twenty-three years; since he was not proclaimed emperor till *A.D.* 383. And the writers *Severus Sulpitius*, *Zozimus*, and others that lived in or near the time, ascribe no command to *Maximus* in *Britain*, nor so much as name him till he took the purple; and are positive, that immediately after he was proclaimed emperor by the soldiers, he passed suddenly over to the *Gauls*, with all the forces he could make, and surprized the emperor *Gratian* unawares. This leaves no room for his expedition against the *Scots* and *Picts*, either before or after his usurpation, much less for his making a long war against them.

BUT besides that, neither these *Roman* writers, nor any other before the fourteenth age, give any ground to suppose that the *Scots* had any kingdom in *Britain* in the fourth age, we may surely reckon that *Fordun* had never seen these writers that gave

gave an account of the expedition of *Theodosius*, nor perhaps ever heard of them. Accordingly in the forty-fourth, forty-fifth, and forty-ninth chapters of his second book, and first and second chapters of his third book, in which he gives an account at length of the expulsion and restoration of the *Scots*; whosoever will compare his narration with the fourth chapter of the second book of *Geoffrey*'s history of the *Britons*, will easily perceive whence *Fordun* took the story of *Maximus*'s atchievements in *Britain*. And nothing that we have hitherto met with in *Fordun*, looks like a tolerable proof of a destruction or restoration of a *Scotish* monarchy in *Britain* in these times.

HOWEVER, to confirm it by a new argument, *Fordun* gives us another *Latin* piece of poesy, beginning with these words, (*a*) *Agmine condenso ventis*, &c. *Fordun* doth not tell us whence he had

(*a*) Agmine condenso ventis velamina pandit:
Et ratis æquoreos atque galea petunt
Fluctus: in his acies juvenum phalerata superbo
Principe congreditur. Nec mora, turba potens
Ad natale solum properat; relevare jacentes
Rex fasces regni cespite sospes adit
Intrepidus patrio, pandens vexilla Leonis,
Terruit occursu quem fera nulla ferox.
Ocius advenit, fuerat quæ turbine diro
Subdita plebs, annis X quater & tribus; hæc
Congaudens patrio regi servire parata,
Ad libertatem quicquid ut orbe volat.

Fordun. l. 3. c. 1. p. 171. edit. Th. Hearne.

these

these verses; but the lion placed in king *Fergus* II's banner, at the head of his troops, and the stile of the verses, can give us no better opinion of the author, and of the antiquity of this composition, than of the other verses already (*a*) mentioned, in which the entry of *Fergus* I. to *Britain* is described So, upon the whole, it appears, that the chief ground *Fordun* had to go upon, for a dissolution and restoration of the *Scotish* monarchy in the fourth age, were not drawn from the authority of ancient writers, but that his chief motive was to reconcile, by that means, the formal expressions of the extracts or abridgments of the old *Scotish* chronicles, such as we have set them down, with the persuasion that he was in, that the *Scotish* monarchy was begun many ages before *Fergus* son of *Erch*.

As to his placing the beginning of *Fergus* son of *Erch*'s reign in the year 403, instead of 503, and thus anticipating the date of it a full hundred years, as we have (*b*) shewn, I see no other reason for this, than that looking on the beginning of this *Fergus*'s reign, rather as the restoration of an ancient kingdom, dissolved by oppression and invasion, than as the setting up a new one, and finding in such histories, as he had occasion to meet with, no more proper person to become the author of

(*a*) Supra, p. 740.
(*b*) Ibid. p. 690. &c.

the

the *Scotish* overthrow, than the tyrant *Maximus*; as he is described by *Geoffrey*, towards the end of the fourth century, he found it necessary to place the restoration about the beginning of the fifth century, lest if he had deferr'd it, and by consequence the beginning of *Fergus* II's reign, till the sixth century, the interval of about one hundred and forty years would have been too long, and the monarchy restored by *Fergus* II. would rather have looked like the setting up of a new kingdom, than the continuation or restoration of an ancient one.

BUT it happened here to *Fordun*, what usually falls out to those that build upon a crazy foundation, the building they erect must necessarily be tottering, and full of crevices, so that no sooner one chink or crevice is filled up, but another breaks out. This anticipating the reign of *Fergus* II. about one hundred years (besides that it is contradicted by all the remains of our ancient history, and by the common way of allowing three generations to a century) threw *Fordun*'s system into another inconveniency, and discovered a new flaw in it, by making three generations fill up two centuries, against the constant course of descents, and succession of the race of our kings ever since; as I have (*a*) shewn elsewhere.

(*a*) Supra, p 690, 691.

As

As to the number of the ancient kings preceding *Fergus* II, there was nothing certain till *Fordun:* we have (*b*) seen the uncertainties and contradictions under which our countrymen labour'd, when the story of these ancient kings was first advanced. The first account we have of their number from an unknown (*c*) hand in these dark times, is absolutely incredible: and I have seen a *Scotish* writer (*d*), in the time of king *James* III. or IV. that reckons the number of these kings six score, beginning at *Simon Brek*, who, this writer supposes, came in Person to *Scotland*. The *Scots* nobility's letter to pope *John* XXII, *A. D.* 1320, reduces them from that exorbitant number, and fixes the number of these ancient kings to that of fifty-seven. *Fordun* lays aside about a dozen more, and reduces them to forty-five. *Boece*, and his followers, takes off five or six more, and fixes the number of the kings before *Fergus* II. at thirty-nine; by all which, we see the *Scots*, in former ages, were not so scrupulous as some of our modern writers, who make it a crime to alter the number of those ancient kings, as they are set down by *Boece*. But to return to *Fordun*, he gives us no account of the grounds he went upon, for this number of forty-five, nor so much as the names of these kings, except three or four, or

(*b*) Ibid. p. 709, 710.
(*c*) Ibid. p. ibid.
(*d*) Biblioth. Reg. Lond. ad calcem Chron. And. Winton.

such

ſuch as may be ſuppoſed to be in the old genealogy, without diſtinguiſhing who of thoſe were kings, or who were not.

As to their lives and actions, we are left almoſt quite in the dark by *Fordun*. He gives us a touch of the beginning of his *Fergus* I's reign, applying to him as the firſt king, what belonged to *Fergus* ſon of *Erch*, who was truly the firſt king; and, after adding ſomething of *Rether*, whom he ſuppoſes all one with *Beda*'s *Reuda*, all the reſt of his ſecond book deſigned to contain the hiſtory of his forty-five kings, is filled up, moſt part, with parcels of the general hiſtory, ſacred or prophane, of theſe firſt ages; and particularly of the *Romans*, *Britons*, *Scots* and *Picts*, taken from *Eutropius*, *Bede*, *Jeffery* of *Monmouth*, &c. from ſome legends and traditions of the vulgar, and without ſo much as naming any one more of theſe forty-five kings. *Fordun* concludes their whole hiſtory in theſe few words: (*a*) *A primo hujus Regni Rege Ferguſio filio Ferechard ad* [hunc] *Regem Ferguſium filium Erch incluſive quadraginta quinque Reges ejuſdem gentis & generis, in hac inſula regnaverunt. Sed & horum, ſingillatim diſtinguere tempora Principatuum, ad præſens omittimus, nam ad plenum ſcripta non reperimus*. This is indeed but a ſorry account of theſe his ancient kings: however, in theſe laſt words, *Fordun* inſinuates, that he had found ſome

(*a*) Ford. l. 3. c. 2. edit. Hearn. p. 173.

account

account of them, but not full enough to be ſet down.

THE truth is, *Fordun* had the old genealogy, containing the ſeries of the deſcents, from *Fergus* ſon of *Ferchard*, called *Fergus* I, till *Fergus* II. the ſon of *Erch*. This was indeed ſome account, being about thirty-two names: but though they had been all kings of *Scots* in *Britain*, which was to be proved, yet there were ſtill wanting twelve or thirteen more to make up the number of forty-four or forty-five. So he had reaſon to ſay, that he had not as yet found a full account of them.

IF *Fordun* had left any other account of the forty-five kings than this, it would, no doubt, have been preſerved with a yet greater care than the collections, it is believed, he left towards continuing down his chronicle after the firſt five books. Theſe collections have been preſerved, and perhaps may be a part of what M. *Hearne* hath printed, beginning *p.* 499 of his edition of *Fordun*, A.D. 1722. Now any collections left by *Fordun* of the forty-five kings, had been much more precious than thoſe of modern times, and had been, no doubt, preſerved by thoſe who had the care and keeping of his chronicles, and his other collections, or by ſome or other of his many continuators in the fifteenth age, who were all in queſt of materials for ſupplying the deficiency or gap in the story of the forty-five kings left imperfect in his second book.

THE words of *Fordun*, *A primo hujus Regni Rege*, &c. above-cited, craved that of them, and made a natural impression of the want of a supplement upon those that read or copied that passage: as we see by an addition to *Fordun*'s text, in the MS. (*a*) chronicle of *Couper*; where, after these last words of the above-cited passage, *ad plenum scripta non reperimus*, the writer adds, *præterquam*, *l.* 3. *c.* 9. by which it would at first appear, that the writer sends us to a place, where we will find, at least, some farther account of the forty-five kings preceding *Fergus* son of *Ercb*: but when we come to this place, all we meet with is a part of the old *Latin* chronicle in rythm, beginning *Primus in Ergadia Fergus rexit tribus annis*, and so continues down the rest of the series of the kings successors to *Fergus* II. son to *Ercb*, instead of those of *Fergus* I, which the reader was put in hopes of. But this shews the lively impression that passage of *Fordun* made on that writer, of the want of a supplement to the forty-five kings. Most of the other continuators of *Fordun* have made additions to his text; but none of them give us any farther account of the forty-five ancient kings of *Scots* before *Fergus* son of *Ercb*.

(*a*) Chron. Cupri MS. l. 3. c. 2.

THE

The first I have met with that attempted it, is one *Gremond Domate*, whose MS. history is in the library of St. *Genoveve* at *Paris*. Of this author, and of his essay on the kings before *Fergus* son of *Erch*, I have (*a*) elsewhere given a full account, to which I refer the reader. I have only here to add, 1°, That this writer, for a further account of the forty-five kings, sends us to the old books of *Ireland:* for, in his translation of *Fordun*, he gives this version, or rather paraphrase, in his old *Gaulois* of *Fordun*'s famous passage, *A primo hujus Regni Rege, &c.* *A* (*b*) *present laissons de parler* [de ces 45 Rois] *qui touts furent d'ung mesme sang & genre comme plainement appert aux anciens Livres d'Hybernie (sic) car a present n'avons trouvé a plain de leur antique origine dignifique (sic).* 2°. That *Domate* wrote and dedicated his translation of this chronicle of *Scotland* to *John* duke of *Albany*, A.D. 1519, that is, about five or six years only before *Boece*'s history appeared in print, and about the very time that *Boece*'s famous vouchers were said to have been discovered with an ample account, as *Boece* tells us, of the first forty kings.

(*a*) Supra, p. 633.

(*b*) Grem. Domate, MS. liv. 3. chap. 2. fol. 50.

CONCLUSION.

§. 6. *Sixth and last step of the growth of our high antiquities by* Boece *and* Buchanan.

It only remains to treat now, 1°. of *Boece*'s own labours, and of his bringing the fabrick of our high antiquities to its full height and dimensions, by giving us, on the credit of his vouchers, besides other embellishments, a detailed account of the lives and actions of the forty kings before *Fergus* son of *Erch*, which *Fordun*, and his continuators, had left so lame and imperfect. 2°. Of the polishing and adorning this fabrick by *Buchanan*, a more polite writer, and more skilled architect, who, removing the rubbish of palpable fables, and reforming the irregularities that *Boece*'s unskilful hand had left in that fabrick, reduced it to a more perfect symmetry, and varnished it all over, to render it more taking and agreeable to his countrymen, and more proper to support the cause in which he was imbarked.

But having given elsewhere a full account of the labours of both these writers of our history in its proper (*a*) place, I need only refer the reader to it.

(*a*) Supra, p. 214, &c. and p. 305, 361, &c.

But to do justice to *Hector Boece*, I cannot but add here to what I have (*a*) elsewhere observed, that as to the motives he had in writing our history, I cannot see the least ground to suspect that he himself had any view or design to support any party or faction against the soveraign, or to justify the rebellion against king *James* III, but quite the contrary, in the catalogue which *Boece* left of our kings, in which he gives a short character of each of them, and continues it down till king *James* V; he gives a quite contrary character of king *James* III. from what *Buchanan* gives him, and from what he himself had given of the wicked kings from his *Veremund*; and speaks with indignation of the conspiracy of a part of the nobility against him, and of the manner of his death that ensued upon it. And no wonder; for he had his information from the great and loyal bishop *Elphinston*, who remained stedfast in his fidelity to his soveraign king *James* III. to the last moment. All this is a new confirmation that *Boece*'s simplicity was imposed upon by the pretended histories of *Veremund*, &c. which he took for genuine copies of ancient pieces, though, as as it hath been shewn elsewhere, they were forged after the act passed to justify the rebellion against king *James* III, and most probably by some of those concerned in that rebellion, or by dependers

(*a*) Supra, p. 365.

on thoſe who had a hand in it. But enough of that in its proper place.

As to *Buchanan*, his motives in writing our hiſtory, are demonſtrated by his own actions and writings; of which enough alſo hath been ſaid.

And now, after all that I have ſaid in this chapter, and the account that I have given of the ſeveral ſteps and additions, by which our high antiquities grew up through the ſeveral ages and hands they have paſſed, the learned and judicious reader will be now pretty well ſatisfied, that at the bottom all the ſtory of theſe remote antiquities, that is, of the forty kings of the *Scots* in *Britain* before *Fergus* ſon of *Erch*, are, if not abſolutely fabulous, at leaſt entirely uncertain and groundleſs, notwithſtanding all the details of facts, ſucceſſions of kings, attended with genealogies, and chronological dates, and all the other characters (except that of ſufficient vouchers) of ancient authentick hiſtories, in which they are dreſſed up, and of the air of aſſurance with which they are preſented by *Boece* and *Buchanan*.

But, at the ſame time, I hope that the learned among my countrymen will eaſily obſerve, that the freedom that I have taken to lay open the uncertainty of thoſe remote antiquities, as they are delivered by our modern writers, doth in no manner derogate from the real honour of our country: for, besides that, there can be no real honour, but what is grounded upon truth; what hath been said in the first book of this essay, particularly of the descent of the present Inhabitants of *Scotland*, from the most ancient, or first known inhabitants of the northern parts of *Britain*; to wit, partly from the *Mæats*, or *Midland Britains*, partly from the *Caledonians* or *Picts*, as well as from the *Scots*; and of the antiquity of the monarchy of *Albany*, and number of kings in the *Pictish* line, doth abundantly compensate the loss of the first forty kings; as the honour of the pretended martial atchievements, attributed by *Fordun*, *Boece*, &c. to the *Scots*, under the reigns of *Julius Cæsar*, *Augustus*, and the following first *Roman* emperors, without any authority, is fully counterballanced by the noble opposition that the *Romans* met with from the *Caledonians*, and their maintaining their ancient possessions to the north of the *Friths*, and their liberty, during so many ages, against all the *Roman* forces in *Britain*, whilst all the other inhabitants were brought under the *Roman* yoke. And all this supported by the testimony of the best contemporary *Roman* writers.

To conclude now this essay; I hope the reader will have met with in it as distinct an account, as the few remains we have of these first times do furnish us, of the several ancient inhabitants of the northern parts of *Britain* (so well known these many ages by the name of *Scotland*) to wit of the *Romans*, *Britains*, *Caledonians* or *Picts*, *Scots*, &c. I have endeavour'd to trace each of these people down, from the first appearance they make in these parts of *Britain*, till they disappeared under their proper names, either by retiring elsewhere, or by being, by degrees, incorporated into one body of people, and under one government, with the *Scots*, become to be the ruling people, they came all, at last, to be known by the common name of *Scots*.

THE view I have given of the situation of these several ancient inhabitants, especially in the earliest times of christianity in those northern parts, will appear with more advantage in the second or chronological part of this essay, if I live to continue it, and will help to discover to the reader the occasions of the first entry of the light of the gospel, and of the progress that the doctrine and discipline of the christian church made among these northern nations. All these dispensations of the mercies of God having often, in the common course, a certain connexion with the civil state and circumstances of a people on whom it pleases God to bestow them, according to his infinitely wise providence.

APPEN-

APPENDIX
OF
ANCIENT PIECES.

HAVING already given an account of the ſeveral pieces contained in this APPENDIX, and there being before each of them a reference to the page of this eſſay, where they are deſcribed, it would be unneceſſary to ſay any thing further here.

BUT the names of the firſt forty-two kings of the *Scots*, from *Fergus* till *Malcolm Keanmore*, which frequently occur in theſe pieces, being all of them originally *Gælick*, or *Iriſh*; from thence it hath happened, that moſt of our writers, being *Lowlanders*, ignorant of that ancient language, there hath enſued ſo great a variety in the pronouncing, ſpelling, and writing thoſe old names in the different writers, MS. or printed; and our modern hiſtorians have at length ſo altered ſome of them, that they appear quite different names; and no more like to thoſe which we meet with in the ancient chronicles or catalogues of our kings: ſo that without ſome knowledge of the more ancient forms of writing theſe names, it is not poſſible

3 to

to underſtand ſome important paſſages concerning *Scotiſh* matters, that occur in ancient pieces.

WHO could, for example, by conſulting only the names of our kings, ſuch as our modern writers repreſent them, underſtand by which of our kings theſe ancient laws and ſtatutes were at firſt made, which according to the ſecond piece in the appendix, *n.* 2. are ſaid to have been renewed by king *Donald Mac-Alpin*, in an aſſembly of the *Scots* at *Forteviot ? In hujus* [Domnalli R.] *tempore jura ac leges Edi filii Ecdach fecerunt Goedeli* [i. e. Scoti] *cum rege ſuo in Fothuir-tabaicht ?* For in the modern catalogues of our kings, ſuch as thoſe of *Fordun*, *Boece* and *Buchanan*, we find no ſuch names; whereas in ancient chronicles or catalogues, we meet with *Eda* or *Edus*, whoſe ſurname was *Fion*, i. e. *White*, the eighteenth king of the *Scots*; called by the moderns, in one word, *Etſinus*, who was ſon to *Eochoid Rinneval*, called otherwiſe *Echdach* or *Echadach*, the thirteenth king, whom our moderns miſcall *Eugenius quintus:* ſo of theſe ancient laws made about the beginning of the eighth age, we ſhould know nothing, by conſulting our modern writers, tho' they muſt have been very famous in ancient times, ſince they are taken notice of by this *Iriſh* writer (for ſuch I take him to have been, till I can meet with farther light concerning him.)

FOR

For these, and such like reasons, especially to help to understand any other ancient pieces of our history that may yet be discovered, at home or abroad, I conceived it would be an useful curiosity to give here, by way of introduction to this *Appendix of Ancient Pieces*, a catalogue of these first forty-two kings, according to the order of their succession, as I find it uniformly set down in all the more ancient chronicles or catalogues of them, taken from our genuine annals, together with all the various forms in which I have observed these names written in ancient or modern authors; and, in the first place, those names, as they are originally written in *Gælick*, upon which all the rest, by different pronunciations, corrupt reading, ignorance of the language, *&c.* have been formed or derived from them. In the last place, I shall set down the names given to these kings by our modern historians.

Mean time, the reader may find, *p.* 131, *supra*, where I have treated of the names of the *Pictish* kings, some remarks upon the occasion of these alterations in ancient names, to which I refer. I shall only here observe, that the letter C in *Gælick* or *Irish*, is always pronounced K; and the letters BH and MH, are pronounced V; and GH W: that in the notes on the pieces of the appendix, these abbreviations F, signifies *forte* or *forsitan*; and L, *Lege*.

The letters [a b c], *&c. placed over the various names in the following catalogue of the first forty-two kings of the* Scots, *mark the chronicles or writers whence they are taken, according to this Index.*

- a Appendix, num. 3.
- b Appendix, num. 4.
- c Genealogia in Append. n. 4.
- d Append. n. 5.
- e Append. n. 6.
- f Winton's Chronicle.
- g Fordun's Chronicle.
- h The two Genealogies in Fordun.
- i Boece.
- k Buchanan.

Cata-

Catalogue or Series of the names of the first forty-two kings of the Scots, *according to the true order of their succession with the various forms of their names, as they are found in ancient and modern writers.*

1 FEARGUS fil. Erc, Erch [d], Eric [b], Erth [f].

2 Domangard, Domhangard [b], Dovenghart [d], Donegart [e], Dongard [g], *or* Dongardus [k].

3 Comgall, Congal, Congel [b], Congallus [k].

4 Gabran [c], Gabhran, Gauran [d], Gouren [e], Goveran [b], Gonranus [k], Conranus [i].

5 Conall, Convallus [g].

6 Aodan, Aidan, Edan [b], Edain [h], Edhan [d], Aidanus [g].

7 Eochoid-buidhe, Eochod-flavus [b], Heoghed-bude [d], Eoghed-bod [e], Hecged-bud [f], Echac-buidhe, Ochabind [h], Eugenius IV. [g k].

8 Connadh-cearr, Kinat-kerr [d], Kinat-sinister [b], Keneth-ker [i].

9 Fearchair [d], Fercar [b], Ferquarth [e], Ferquardus [k].

10 Domnall-breac, Domhnal-breac, Dovenald-varius [b], Downald-brec [f], Donaldus IV.

11 Malduin, Maldowny [f], Malduinus [i].

12 Fear-

12 Fearcair-fada, Fergar-longus [b], Ferchar-foda [d], Ferquardus [k].

13 Eochoidh-rinnemhail, Eochol-habens-curvum-nasum [b], Heoghed [d] Rinavel-Echdac-Echadach [a h], Eoghed [e], Hecged-ronaval [f], Eugenius V [g k].

14 Ainbceallach, Armchallach [e], Arinchellac [b], Armkellech [d], Amrikelleth [g], Ambirkeletus [k].

15 Eogan [a], Eoghan, Ewan, Ewen [b], Heatgan [d], Eugenius VI. [g k]

16 Muireadach, Murdauch [e], Murechat [b], Murdochus, Murthec [f], Murdahu, Mordacus [i], Murdacus [g k].

17 Eogan [e], Heoghan [d], Ewan [f], Ewen [b], Eugenius VII.

18 Aodh-fionn, Ed-albus [b], Heth-fin [d], Hed-white [f], Eda[a]-find[c]-Ethafind[h], Etfinus [k].

19 Feargus, Fergus.

20 Sealbhach, Selvach, Selvac [b], Sealuanc [e], Sealuhanc[d], Sewald [f], Selwathius [g], Solwathius [k].

21 Eochoidh-anguibh, Eochal-annuine, Eochal-venenosus [b], Heoghed-annuine [d], Eogad-annuin [e], Echach, Ethacus [h], Eokal [f], Achajus [g].

22 Dunghal, Dunegal [b], Doughal [f], Dungallus [k].

23 Ailpin, Alpin.

24 Cionaodh, Cinacha [c], Kinadius [a], Kenaucht, Kinedus [b], Kinath [d], Kenethus [g].

25 Domhnal, Dunevaldus [a], Domnail [c], Dolfnal[b], Dovenald [d].

26 Conftaintin.

27 Aodh, Ed [d], Edus [a], Het [b], Eth, Ethus [k].

28 Gai-

28 Gairig, Girg [d], Giric [a], Greg [b], Gregorius [g].
29 Domhnal, Dovenald, Doneval [b], Donevaldus [a], Donaldus [k].
30 Constaintin.
31 Maelcoluim, Maelcolai [c], Malcolm [b], Milcolumbus [k].
32 Iondolbh, Indolf [b], Induff [d], Indulfus [k].
33 Dubhoda, Duf [b], Niger [a], Duffus [k].
34 Cuilin, Culin [b]; Culenrig [a], Culenus [k].
35 Cionadh, Cinadius [a], Cinada [c], Kinadius, Kinet [b], Kenethus [k].
36 Constaintin.
37 Grim-Macdubh, Chinet [b], Girgh [d]-mac-Kinath. Greg, Grimus [g].
38 Malcolium Milcolumbus.
39 Donnchadh, Donchath [d], Dunecan, Donuchada [c], Duncanus [i].
40 Macbeatha, Machetad, Macbethad, Macbeth [b], Machabæus [i].
41 Lulach [b], Lahoulan [e], Luthlath [l].
42 Malcoluim, Malcolm[i]-cean-more, Malcolm [b] Kenremore [e], Milcolumbus [k].

NUM. I.

NUM. I.

DE SITU ALBANIÆ QUÆ IN SE FIGURAM HOMINIS HABET: QUOMODO FUIT PRIMITUS IN SEPTEM REGIONIBUS (*sic*) DIVISA, QUIBUSQUE NOMINIBUS ANTIQUITUS SIT VOCATA, ET A QUIBUS INHABITATA. *Vide supra, p.* 601.

Ex MS. Bibliothecæ Colbertinæ, Cod. 3120.

1. OPERÆ pretium puto mandare memoriæ qualiter Albania, & a quibus habitatoribus primitus habitata, quibus nominibus nuncupata & in quot partibus partita.

2. LEGIMUS in historiis & in chronicis antiquorum Britonum, & in gestis & annalibus antiquis (*a*) Scottorum & Pictorum, quod illa regio quæ nunc corruptè vocatur Scotia (*b*), antiquitus appellabatur Albania ab Albanacto juniore filio Bruti primi regis Britannorum majoris Britanniæ. Et post multum intervallum temporis a Pictis Pictavia: qui regnaverunt in ea per circulum MLXX annorum: secundum quosdam MCCCLX. Nunc

(*a*) *Hinc patet extitisse annales Scotorum & Pictorum qui antiqui censebantur etiam sæculo* XII.

(*b*) *Ran. Higden Polychr. ex Giraldo, p.* 185.

vero

vero corruptè vocatur Scocia. Scotti (*a*) vero regnaverunt per spacium CCCXV annorum; anno illo quo Willelmus rex Rufus, frater Malcolmi viri honestæ vitæ & virtutis, regnum suscepit.

3. REGIO enim ista formam & figuram hominis in se habet. Pars namque principalis ejus, id est, caput est in *Arregathel* in occidentali parte Scociæ supra mare Hyberniæ: pedes vero ejus sunt supra mare *Northwagiæ*: montes vero & deserta de *Arregaithel* capiti & collo hominis assimilantur: corpus vero ipsius est mons qui *Mound* vocatur, qui a mari occidentali usque ad mare orientale extenditur: Brachia autem ejus sunt ipsi montes qui dividunt Scociam ab *Arregaithel*. Latus dexteræ partis ex *Murref*, & *Ros*, & *Mar*, & *Buchan*: crura enim illius sunt illa duo principalia & præclara flumina (quæ descendunt de monte prædicto, i. e. *Mound*) quæ vocantur *Tae* & *Spe*: quorum unum fluit citra montem, alterum vero ultra in mare *Norwegale*. Inter crura hujus hominis sunt *Enegus* & *Moerne* citra montem, & ultra montem aliæ terræ inter *Spe* & montem.

4. HÆC vero terra a septem fratribus divisa fuit antiquitus in septem partes: quarum pars principalis est *Enegus* cum *Moerne* ab *Enegus* primogenito fratrum sic nominata: secunda autem pars est *Adtheodle* & *Gouerin*: pars etiam tertia est *Stra-*

(*a*) *Polychr. ex Giraldo*, p. 185.

deern cum *Meneted:* quarta pars partium est *Fife* cum *Fotbreue:* quinta vero pars est *Marr* cum *Buchen:* sexta autem est *Murref* & *Ros:* septima enim pars est *Cathanesia* citra montem & ultra montem: quia Mons *Mound* dividit Cathanesiam per medium.

5. QUÆLIBET ergo istarum partium regio tunc vocabatur & erat: quia unaquæque earum sub regionem in se habebat. Inde est ut hi septem fratres prædicti pro septem regibus habebantur: septem Regulos sub se habentes. Isti septem fratres regnum Albaniæ in septem regna diviserunt, & unusquisque in tempore suo in suo regno regnavit (*a*).

6. PRIMUM regnum fuit (sicut mihi verus relator retulit, Andreas, videlicet, vir venerabilis Katanensis episcopus (*b*) nacione Scottus & Dunfermlis (*c*) Monachus) ab illa aqua optima, quæ Scotticè vocata est *Froth*, Britannice *Werid*, Romanè (*d*) vero *Scotte-wattre*, i. aqua Scottorum; quæ (*e*) regna Scottorum & Anglorum dividit & currit juxta oppidum de *Strivelin*, usque ad flumen aliud nobile, quod vocatum est *Tac*.

(*a*) *Cruithne primus Pictorum rex in Albania filios septem habuit reges, juxta Chron. Pictorum infra num.* 2.

(*b*) *Hinc patet autorem hujus libelli non fuisse natione Scotum.*

(*c*) *Obiit Andreas Episcopus Katanen. A.D.* 1185, *juxta Chron. Maylrossen.*

(*d*) *I. e. lingua vulgari.*

(*e*) *Hinc apparet autorem hujus libelli fuisse Anglum.*

7. SE-

7. Secundum regnum ad *Hilef*, ficut mare circuit, ufque ad montem aquilonali plaga de *Strivelin* qui vocatur *Athrin*.

Tertium regnum ab *Hilef* ufque ad *De*.

Quartum regnum ex *De* ufque ad magnum & mirabile flumen quod vocatur *Spe*, majorem (*a*) & meliorem tocius Scociæ.

Quintum regnum de *Spe* ufque ad montem *Bruinalban*.

Sextum regnum fuit *Muref* & *Ros*.

Septimum regnum fuit *Arregaithel*.

8. (*b*) *ARREGATHEL* dicitur quafi margo Scottorum feu Hybernenfium: quia omnes Hybernenfes & Scotti generaliter *Gaitheli* dicuntur a quodam eorum primævo duce *Gaithelglas* vocato. Ibi enim femper Hybernienfes applicare folebant ad dampna facienda Britannis. Vel idcirco quia Scotti (*c*) [*Picti*] ibi habitabant primitus poft reditum fuum de Hybernia; vel quia Hibernienfes illas partes occupavere fuper Pictos; vel quod certius eft quod illa pars regionis Scottiæ affinitima eft regioni Hiberniæ.

(*a*) *Sic.*

(*b*) *Vid. Ran. Ceft. Polyc. p.* 209 *ed. Gal.*

(*c*) *Vox* (Picti) *haud dubium hic redundat errore fcribæ.*

9. Fergus filius Eric ipse fuit primus qui de semine Chonare suscepit regnum Albaniæ, 1. A monte Brunalban usque ad mare Hiberniæ & ad Inchegall. Deinde reges de semine Fergus regnaverunt in Brunalban, sive Brunhere, usque ad Alpinum filium Eochal: Kined filius hujus Alpini primus Scottorum annis XVI. in Pictinia feliciter regnavit.

NUM. II.

(a) NUM. II.

,RONICA DE ORIGINE ANTIQUORUM PICTORUM (b).

Ex eodem Cod. MS. Bibl. Colbertin. *V. Supra, p.* 105.

PICTI propria lingua nomen habent a picto corpore eo quod aculeis ferreis cum atramento variarum figurarum (c) Stiugmate (*sic*) annotantur. Scotti qui nunc corruptè vocantur Hibernienses, quasi Sciti quia a Scithia regione venerunt, & inde originem duxerunt, sive a Scótta filia Pharaonis regis Ægypti, quæ fuit, ut fertur, regina Scot. (d).

SCIENDUM est quod Britones in tertia mundi ætate ad Britanniam venerunt. Scitæ autem, 1.

(a) *Quod spectat ad discrepantiam inter hoc vetus chronicon Pictorum & catalogos regum Pictorum (qui habentur apud scriptores Scotos) quoad nomina, numerum, chronologiam, &c. Vide quæ diximus, p.* 124, *&c.* 129, *&c. supra.*

(b) *Fragmentum hoc sive excerptum ex chronicis Pictorum hic exhibemus quale extat in Cod MS. nihil addito, dempto aut immutato præter titulos primæ & secundæ partis & numerales notas regum, quas majoris claritatis gratia, diverso charactere, adjecimus.* Vid. Supra, p. 602.

(c) L. Stigmate.

(d) L. Scociæ vel Scotorum.

Scotti in quarta ætate Scociam sive Hiberniam obtinuerunt. Gentes Scitiæ albo crine nascuntur ab assiduis nivibus: & ipsius capilli color genti nomen dedit; & inde dicuntur Albani: de quibus originem duxerunt Scotti & Picti. Horum glaucu oculis, i. picta inest pupilla, adeo ut nocte plus quam die cernant. Albani autem vicini Amazonibus fuerunt. Gothi a Magog filio Japheth nominati putantur de similitudine ultimæ syllabæ: quos veteres Græci magis Gethas quam Gothos vocaverunt. Gens fortis & potentissima, corporum mole ardua, armorum genere terribilis. De quibus Lucanus,

> Hinc Dacus premat, inde Gethis incurrat Hiberis.

(a) Daciam Gothorum soboles fuerunt & dicto; putant Dacos quasi Dagos, quia de Gothorum stirpe sunt: de quibus ille,

> Ibis Arcos procul usque Dacos,

Scithæ & Gothi a Magog originem traxerunt (b). Scithia quoque & Gothia ab eodem Magog Japhet fertur cognominata; cujus terra olim ingens fuit: nam ab oriente in die (c) a septentrione per pa;

(a) L. Daci.
(b) *Isidor. Hispal.* p. 120.
(c) L. Indiæ.

Iudes

ludes Mæotides inter Danubium & oceanum usque ad Germaniæ fines porrigebatur. Postea minor effecta est a dextra orientis parte quæ occanus Sciticus conditur (*sic*) usque ad mare Caspium quod est ad occasum: de hinc a meridie usque ad Caucasium jugum deducta est, cui subjacet Hircania ab occasu: habens pariter gentes multas propter infœcunditatem latè vagantes: ex quibus quædam agros incolunt, quidam (*sic*) portentuosæ ac truces, carnibus humanis & eorum sanguine vivunt.

SCITHIÆ plures terræ sunt locupletes, & inhabitabiles etiam plures. Nam quæ in plerisque locis auro & gemmis affluant, Griphorum immanitate accessus hominum rarus est. Smaragdis autem optimis hæc patria est. Cianeus quoque lapis & chrystallus purissimus Scithiæ est (*a*). Habet & flumina magna Oscorim, Fasidem, & Araxen. Prima Europæ regio Scythiæ inferior quæ a Mæotidis paludibus incipiens inter Danubium & oceanum septentrionalem usque ad Germaniam porrigitur, quæ terra generaliter propter barbaras gentes quibus inhabitatur, Barbarica dicitur. Hujus pars prima Alania est quæ ad Mæotidas paludes pertingit. Post hanc Dacia, ubi & Gothia: deinde Germania: ubi plurimam partem Suevi incoluerunt. In partes Asiaticæ Scithiæ sunt gentes quæ posteros se Jasonis credunt (*b*): albo crine noscuntur ab assiduis nivibus. De his ista sufficiunt.

(*a*) *Isidor. p.* 121.
(*b*) *Ibid. p.* 74.

Prima pars Chronici sive Catalogi Regum Pictorum.

1 CRUIDNE filius Cinge pater Pictorum habitancium in hac insula c annis regnavit. Septem (*a*) filios habuit. Hæc sunt nomina eorum: Fib, Fidach, Floclaid, Fortreim, Got, Cecircum, Circui.

2 Circui lx annis regn.

3 Fidaich xl.

4 Forteim lxx.

5 Floclaid xxx.

6 Got xii.

7 Ce xv.

8 Fibaid xxiv.

9 Gedeolgudach lxxx.

10 Denbacan c.

11 Olfinecta lx.

12 Guididgaedbrecach l.

13 Gestgurtich xl.

14 Wurgest xl.

15 Brude-bout, a quo xxx Brude regnaverunt Hyberniam (*b*) & Albaniam per cl. annorum spatium, xlviii an. regnavit. Id est, Brude-pant, Brude-urpant, Brude-leo, Brude-uleo, Brude-gant, Brude-urgant, Brude-guith,

(*a*) *Vide n. 5. de situ Albaniæ, supra in append. n. 1 de divisione Albaniæ in* vii *partes.*

(*b*) *Hinc apparet Pictorum aliquos in Hyberniam penetrasse & ibidem regnasse.*

Brude-

Brude-urguith, Brude-fecir, Brude-urfecir, Brude-cal, Brude-urcal, Brude-cuit, Brude-urcuit, Brade-fec, Brade-urfec, Brade-ru, Brude-eru, Brude-gart, Brude-urgart, Brude-cinit, Brude-urcinit, Brude-inp, Brude-urinp, Brude-grid, Brude-urgrid, Brude-mund, Brude-urmund.

16 Gilgidi ci an. regn.
17 Tharan c.
18 Morleo xv.
19 Deocilunon xl.
20 Cimoiod filius Arcois vii.
21 Deoord l.
22 Bliciblitirth v.
23 Deftoteric frater Diu xl.
24 Ufconbuts xxx.
25 Carvorft xl.
26 Deoartavois xx.
27 Uift l.
28 Ru c.
29 Gartnoithboc, a quo Gamait, iv regn.
30 Vere ix an. regn.
31 Breth filius Buthnt vii.
32 Vipoignamet xxx an. regn.
33 Canutulachama iv an. regn.
34 Wradech vechla ii an. regn.
35 Garnaichdi uber lx. an. regn.
36 Talore filius Achivir lxxv an. regn.

Secunda

Secunda pars.

37 Drust filius Erp c (*a*) an. regn. & c bella peregit xix anno regni ejus Patricius episcopus sanctus ad Hyberniam pervenit insulam.

38 Talore filius Aniel iv an. regn.

39 Necton Morbet filius Erp xxv an. regn. tertio (*b*) anno regni ejus Darlugdach Abbatissa Cillæ Darade Hibernia exulat proxime ad Britanniam. Secundo anno adventus sui immolavit Nectonius Aburnethige Deo & sanctæ Brigidæ præsente Dairlugtach, quæ cantavit Alleluja super istam hostiam. Optulit igitur Nectonius magnus filius Urup rex omnium provinciarum Pictorum Apurnethige sanctæ Brigidæ usque ad diem judicii cum suis finibus quæ positæ sunt (*sic*) a lapide in Apurfeirt usque ad lapidem juxta Cairfuil, id est, Lethfoss; & inde in altum usque ad Athan. Causa autem oblacionis hæc est. Nectonius in (*c*) uite iulie manens, *fratre* suo Drusto expulsante se usque ad

(*a*) Regnavit *seu* rexit *hic ponitur pro* vixit: *nam liber Pasltersis tribuit illi tantum* 48 *annos regni. Vide supra, p.* 136.

(*b*) *Prolixior hæc narratio fundationis celebris ecclesiæ de Abirnethy innuere videtur. Chronicon hoc breve extractum fuisse ex vetusto aliquo chronico ab alumnis ecclesiæ illius veteris de Abirnethy olim scripto.*

(*c*) F. in exilio manens, *fratre.*

Hiberniam, Brigidam sanctam petivit, ut (*a*) postulasset Deum pro se. Orans autem pro illo, dixit (*b*). Si pervenies ad patriam tuam, Dominus miserebitur tui, regnum Pictorum in pace possidebis (*c*).

40 Drest Gurthinmoch xxx an. regn.

41 Galanau Etelich xii an. regn.

42 Dadrest i.

43 Drest filius Gyrom i. Drest filius Udrost v, an. conregnaverant. Drest filius Gyrom solus v an. regn.

44 Gartnach filius Gyrom vii an. regn.

45 Cealtraim filius Gyrom i an. regn.

46 Talorg filius Muircholaich xi an. regn.

47 Drest filius Munait i an. regn.

48 Galam cum Aleph i an. regn.
cum Briduo i an.

49 Brides (*d*) filius Mailcom xxx an. regn. In

(*a*) L. postularet sive oraret.

(*b*) *Id est*, certe pervenies.

(*c*) *Ex Colgano de vitis SS. Hiberniæ patet Darlugdacham (de qua hic fit mentio) fuisse discipulam S. Brigidæ. Cæterum de antiqua hac ecclesia de Abirnethy hæc habentur in libro Paslet. desumpta, ut videtur ex chronico de Abirnethy.* In illa ecclesia [*de Abirnethy*] fuerunt tres electiones factæ, quando non fuit nisi unus solus episcopus in Scocia. Tunc enim fuit ille locus principalis regalis & pontificalis per aliqua tempora tocius regni Pictorum.

(*d*) *Hic ille est Brudeus rex, de quo Beda, lib. 3. cap. 4. De varietate seu discrepantia quæ reperitur in pronunciandis seu scribendis vetustis regum Pictorum & Scotorum nominibus.* Vide quæ dicta sunt supra, p. 129, &c.

viii (*a*) an. regni ejus baptizatus est a S. Columba.

50 Gartnaich filius Domelch xi an. regn.
51 Nectu nepos Verb xx an. regn.
52 Cineoch filius Luthrin xi an. regn.
53 Garnard filius Wid. iv an. regn.
54 Bridei filius Wid. v an. regn.
55 Talore frater eorum xii an. regn.
56 Talorcon filius Enfret iv an. regn.
57 Gartnait filius Donnell. vi an. regn. & dimid.
58 Drest frater ejus vii an. regn.
59 Bredei filius Bili (*b*) xxi an. regn.
60 Taran filius Entifidich iv an. regn.
61 Bredei filius Dereli xi an. regn.
62 Nechton filius Dereli (*c*) xv an. regn.
63 Drest & Alpin conregnaverunt v an.
64 Onnust (*d*) filius Urgust xxx an. regn.
65 Bredei filius Wirgust ii an. regn.
66 Ciniod (*e*) filius Wirdech xii an. regn.
67 Elpin filius Wroid iii an. & dimid.
68 Drest filius Talorgan iv vel v an. regn.
69 Talorgan filius Onnust ii an. cum dimidio.
70 Canaul filius Tarla v an. regn (*f*).

(*a*) *Deesse hic videtur literula seu num.* 1. *ut fiat* viiil. *errore scribæ.*

(*b*) *De hoc rege.* V. supra, p. 111.

(*c*) V. p. 112, supra.

(*d*) V. p. 113, supra.

(*e*) V. p. 114, supra.

(*f*) *Hi sunt septuaginta illi reges Pictorum usque ad Constantinum, de quibus* supra, p. 102, &c.

71 Castantin

71 Castantin (a) fil. Wrguist xxx an. regn.
72 Unnust fil. Wrguist xii an. regn.
73 Drest fil. Constantin & Talorgan fil. Wthoil iii an. conregnaverunt.
74 Uuen filius Unnust iii an. regn.
75 Wred fil. Bargoit iii an.
76 Bred uno anno regn.

(a) L. Constantin.

NUM. III.

NUM. III.

Excerpta ex veteri Chronico de regibus Scotorum a Kenetho Mac-Alpin ad Mac-Malcolm.

Ex MS. Codice Colbertino. *V. supra, p.* 603.

1. KINADIUS igitur filius Alpin primus Scottorum rexit feliciter istam annis XVI Pictaviam. Pictavia autem a Pictis est nominata, quos, ut diximus Kinadius, delevit. Deus (*a*) enim eos pro merito suæ malitiæ alienos ac otiosos hæreditate dignatus est facere: quia illi non solum Deum, missam ac præceptum spreverunt, sed & in

(*a*) *Ad ea quæ hic habentur de declinante apud Pictos religionis zelo, tanquam præcipua excidii causa monarchiæ, spectare etiam videntur quæ de oppressa a Pictis libertate ecclesiastica, continet epitaphium Gregorii regis ad calcem chronici Maylrossen & quæ de eodem rege habentur in Cod. MS. Bibl. Coton.* [Vitellius A. 24.] *& iisdem verbis in extract. registri S. Andreæ infra* n. 5. *Append. in* reg. 28. *his verbis. Hic* [Gregorius R.] *primus dedit libertatem ecclesiæ Scoticanæ, quæ sub servitute erat usque ad illud tempus ex consuetudine Pictorum. Hi tamen abusus videntur invaluisse apud Pictos sub postremis duntaxat regibus, nam celebris erat pietas & devotio erga ecclesiam, regum Constantini & Hungi qui regnaverunt apud Pictos ineunte hoc sæculo nono, vel labente octavo.*

jure

jure æquitatis aliis *æqui pariter* (*a*) noluerunt. Isti (*b*) vero biennio antequam veniret Pictaviam Dalrietæ regnum suscepit. Septimo anno (*c*) regni reliquias S. Columbæ transportavit ad ecclesiam quam construxit: & invasit sexies Saxoniam (*d*) & concremavit Dunbarre atque Malros usurpata (*sic*); Britanni autem concremaverunt Dulblaan, atque Danari vastaverunt Pictaviam ad *Duanan* (*sic*) & Duncalden. Mortuus est tandem tumore *an.* (*e*) id. Febr. feria tertia in palacio (*f*) Forthuir-tabaicht.

2. DUNEVALDUS frater ejus tenuit idem regnum quatuor annis. In hujus tempora jura ac leges regni Edi (*g*) filii Ecdach fecerunt Goedeli (*h*) cum rege suo in Fothur-thabaicht: obiit in palacio cum (*i*) Belachoir, id. April.

(*a*) F. æqui parari voluerunt.

(*b*) L. iste.

(*c*) *Servabantur ergo hactenus reliquiæ S. Columbæ in Scotia, secus ac narrant Hyberni aliqui scriptores.*

(*d*) V. *Ranulf. Higd. Polychron. p.* 210. *ubi ait.* [Kenethus] Sexies Saxoniam debellavit, &c.

(*e*) F. tumore ani.

(*f*) i. e. Forteviot. *Regia Pictorum, deinde Scotorum.*

(*g*) *Id est, Regis Ædi-albi sive Æth-fin filii Eochah sive Ecdach-rinneval qui regnare cœpit circa A. D.* 730. *De hisce vero juribus & regni legibus altissimum apud scriptores nostros silentium. Extitisse autem aliquando & celeberrima fuisse cum a vicino hoc Hyberniæ scriptore memorentur, haud dubitari potest. Perierunt tamen cum reliquis antiquis regni monumentis.*

(*h*) i. e. Scoti.

(*i*) F. suo Belachor. *de quo fit mentio apud scriptorem vitæ S. Cadroes-Scoti.*

3. CON-

3. CONSTANTINUS fil. Kinadi regnavit annis XVI. Primo ejus anno (a) Mael Sechnaill rex Hybernensium obiit & Aed (b) fil. Niel tenuit regnum: & post duos annos vastavit (c) Amlaib cum gentibus suis Pictaviam & habitantes eam a kal. Januar. usque ad festum S. Patricii. Tertio iterum anno Amlaib trahens cetum (d) (*sic*) a Constantino occisus est paulo post ab eo bello in XIV ejus facto in Dolair inter Danarios & Scottos: occisi Scotti in Coach-cochlum (*sic*): Normanni annum integrum degerunt in Pictavia.

4. EDUS tenuit idem uno anno. Ejus autem brevitas nil historiæ memoriæ commendavit: sed in civitate nrurin (e) est occisus.

5. (f) EOCHODIUS autem filius Ku (*sic*) regis Britannorum nepos Kinadi ac fil. regn. an XI. Licet

(a) Mael-seacluin rex Hyberniæ, *Obiit A. D.* 863. *successit ei.*

(b) Aodh-finliath fil. Niel.

(c) *Hic est ille Anlaphus Danus de quo in scriptoribus Scotiæ, Angliæ & Hyberniæ.*

(d) F. cœtum, i.e. exercitum.

(e) F. Inruri.

(f) *Quæ hic habentur de successore regis Edi sive Æthi obscura admodum sunt & apud Scotos omnino inaudita: nusquam enim mentio hujus Eochodii: & tam vetustorum excerpta annalium nostrorum, quam catalogi veteres & omnes nostri scriptores unanimi sententia referunt Gregorum immediatè Ætho regi successisse & cele-*

Licet *Giricium* (*a*) fil. alii dicunt hic regnaſſe eo quod alumpnus, ordinatorque Eochodio fiebat. Cujus ſecundo anno Aed fil. Niel moritur, ac in nono anno ipſo die cirici eclipſis ſolis facta eſt. Eochodius cum alumno ſuo expulſus eſt nunc de regno.

6. DONEVALDUS fil. Conſtantini tenuit regnum XI annis. Normanni tunc (*b*) vaſtaverun Pictaviam in hujus regno bellum fuit (*c*) *innisib collan* (*ſic*) inter Danarios & Scottos. Scotti habuerunt victoriam opidum (*d*) Fother occiſum eſt a gentibus (*ſic*).

7. CONSTANTINUS fil. Edii tenuit regnum XL annis: cujus tertio anno Normanni prædaverunt Duncalden omnemque Albaniam: in ſequenti utique anno Conſtantinus rex & (*e*) Kellachus epiſcopus leges, diſciplinaſque fidei, atque jura eccleſiarum, evangeliorumque pariter cum Scottis in

& celebrem fuiſſe ob victorias reportatas in Anglia, ſed præcipuè in Hybernia. An hanc ob cauſam ſcriptor hic rebus a Gregorio præclarè geſtis, obſcura hac & incondita narratione, detrahere voluerit, alii judicent. Videatur interea epitaphium ipſius ad calcem chronici Maylroſſenſis cum reliquis regum epitaphiis, editum, & quæ de eo narrantur in excerptis ex regiſtro S. Andreæ infra num. 5.

(*a*) F. Giric. Girgh. i. e. Grigor.

(*b*) t. MS.

(*c*) F. in urbe Cullen.

(*d*) L. Forres occiſus eſt.

(*e*) Kellach Epiſcopus S. Andreæ. *Vide quæ diximus ſuprà, p. 588, de concilio Scotico ſub hoc rege Conſtantino & Kellacho epiſcopo.*

colle credulitatis prope regali civitate Scoan devoverunt (a) custoditur. Ab hoc die collis hoc (nomen) meruit, i.e. collis credulitatis. Et in suo VIII anno cecidit excelsissimus rex Hybernensium & archiepiscopus apud Lagnechois, 1. Cormac (b) filius Culenan: & mortui sunt in tempore hujus Dovenaldus rex Britannorum & Dovenaldus filius Ede rex (c) elig. & Flanni filius Mael Sethnail & Nail (d) fil. Ede qui regnavit 3 annos post Flann. &c. Bellum Tinemore factum est in xviii anno inter Constantinum & Regnall & Scotti habuerunt victoriam: & bellum (e) Dumbrunde in xxxiv ejus anno; ubi cecidit filius Constantini; & post unum annum mortuus est Dubican fil. Indrechtaig Mormair Oengusa. Adelstan fil. (f) Aduarrig. Saxan & Eochod fil. Alpin mortui sunt. Et in senectute decrepita baculum cepit [R. Constantin] & domino servivit, & regnum mandavit Mael. filio Donmail.

8. Malcolm fil. Domnail xi. an. regn. Cum exercitu suo Maelcolam perexit in Moreb (g) & occidit Celach. in vii anno regni sui prædavit Anglos ad amnem Thesis & multitudinem rapuit ho-

(a) L. custodiri.
(b) *Auct:r Psaltorii Cassiliensis habetur Cormacus iste.*
(c) F. eligitur.
(d) *Lege* Nial, vel Niell. R. Hyb.
(e) *alias* Bruneburg, Brunford & Brunynfeld.
(f) L. Edward, vel Eadward.
(g) L. Moravia.

minum, & multa armenta pecorum quam prædam vocaverunt Scotti prædam Albudorum (*sic*) i. e. Nauuidisi. Alii autem dicunt Constantinum fecisse hanc prædam quærens a rege, i. Maelcolam regnum dari sibi ad tempus hebdomadis ut visitaret Anglos. (*a*) Un tn non Maelcolam fecit hanc prædam, sed instigavit eum Constantinus, ut dixi. Mortuus autem Constantinus in X. anno ejus sub corona pœnitenti in senectute bona. Et occiderunt viri na Moerne Malcolaim in Fodresach. i. in Claideom (*sic*).

9. INDULFUS tenuit regnum octo annis. In hujus tempore oppidum Eden vacuatum est ac relictum est Scottis usque in hodiernum diem (*b*). Classi (*c*) Sumerlidiorum occisi sunt in Buchan.

10. (*d*) Niger fil. Maelcolam regn. quinque annis. (*e*) Fothach episcopus pausavit: inter (*f*) iger caniculum (*g*) sr (*h*) dorsum crup (*sic*) in quo niger habuit victoriam, ubi cecidit Duchad Abbas Dulcalden, & Dubdou Satrapas Athochlach Expulsus niger de regno & tenuit caniculus brevi tempore. Domnall fil. Canill mortuus est.

(*a*) L. verumtamen.
(*b*) Vide pag. 624, supra.
(*c*) F. Danorum.
(*d*) i. e. Duff, sive Duffus R.
(*e*) Fothach Episcopus S. Andreæ.
(*f*) L. Nigerum, i. e. Duffus.
(*g*) F. Culen.
(*h*) L. super.

11. CULEN-RIG quinque annis regn. Marcan fil. Breodalaig occisus est in ecclesia S. Michaelis. Leot & Sluagadach exierunt ad Romam. Maelbrigd (*a*) episcopus pausavit. Cellach (*b*) fil. Ferdulaig (*c*) regnavit. Maelbridge fil. Dubican obiit. Culen & frater ejus Eochodius occisi sunt a Britonibus.

12 CINADIUS fil. Maelcolami regn. an. Statim prædavit Britanniam ex parte pedestres Cinadi occisi sunt maxima cæde in moni uacornax (*sic*) & ad Staugna (*d*) de rain. Cinadius autem vallavit ripas vadorum Forthin. Primo anno perexit Cinadius & prædavit Saxoniam & traduxit filium regis Saxonum. Hic est qui tribuit magnam civitatem Brechne domino.

(*a*) Episcopus S. Andreæ, dictus & Malisiur.
(*b*) Episcopus S. Andreæ successor Milisii sive Malbrigid.
(*c*) i. e. rexit seu gubernavit.
(*d*) L. Stagna.

NUM. IV.

NUM. IV.

CRONICA REGUM SCOTTORUM CCCXIV. ANNORUM.

Ex cod. MS. Colbertino. Vide p. 605, supra.

1 FERGUS filius Eric fuit primus qui de semine Chonare suscepit regnum Albaniæ i. e. a monte Drumalban usque ad mare Hiberniæ & ad Inche-Gall. Iste regnavit iii annis.

2 Domangart fil. ejus v an.

3 Congel fil. Domangrat xxxii (*a*).

4 Goueran frater Congel xxii. an.

5 Conal fil. Congel xiv an.

6 Edan fil. Goueran xxxiv an.

7 Eeohod flavus (*b*) fil. Edan xvi an.

8 Kinat Sinister (*c*) fil. Conal tribus mensibus.

9 Ferear fil. Eu (*d*) xvi an.

10 Dovenald varius (*e*) fil. Ecohid xiv an.

11 (*f*).

(*a*) *In plerisque aliis catalogis 22 aut 24. anni tribuuntur regno Congalli, cui hic dantur 33. errore, ut videtur, scribæ.*

(*b*) *Hic vocatur lingua montana sive Gælica Eacha-buydhe,* i. e. *Eacha-flavus.*

(*c*) *Hic patrio sermone vocatur* Connadh-cearr, *i. e.* Sinister.

(*d*) F. *Ewen ut in Catal. S. Andr.*

(*e*) *Lingua propria vocatur* Domnal Breach, *i. e.* varius.

(*f*) *Hic deest nomen Malduini Regis* XI. *oscitantia scribæ.*

 12 Fergar

12 Fergar longus (*a*) xxi.
13 Eochol habens (*b*) curvum nasum filius Douegarth filii Dovenal varii, tribus an.
14 Arinchellac (*c*) fil. Ferchar longi uno anno,
15 Ewen (*d*) fil. Ferchar longi xiii an.
16 Murechat (*e*) fil. Arinchellac tribus annis.
17 Ewen fil. Murcerdach tribus an.
18 Edalbus (*f*) fil. Eochal curvi nasi xxx.
19 Fergus fil. Edalbi tribus.
20 Selvac fil. Eogan xxiv.
21 Eochal (g) venenosus fil. Edalbi xxx.
22 Dunegal fil. Selvach vii.
23 Alpin fil. Eochal venenosi tribus.
24 Kinedus fil. Alpini primus rex Scottorum xvi.
25 Dolfnal (*h*) fil. Alpini iv.
26 Constantinus fil. Kinet xx.
27 Het fil. Kinet uno an.
28 Grig. fil. Dungal xii.
29 Doneval fil. Constantin. xi.
30 Constantin. fil. Hed xxv.
31 Malcolm fil. Doneval ix.
32 Indolf fil. Constantin. ix.

(*a*) *Lingua propria* Ferchar-fada, *i. e.* longus.
(*b*) *Lingua veteri propria* Eochoid-rinneval.
(*c*) *Alias* Armkelleth.
(*d*) Eogan & Heatgan.
(*e*) *Alias* Murdoch.
(*f*) *Alias* Eth-*fin*, *i. e.* Eth-albus.
(*g*) Eochal *alias* Eoka, Eokal, Achajus *nominatur. V. nomina regum supra.*
(*h*) Dosnal sive Dovenald.

33 **Duf** fil. Malcolm iv an. & vi menſ.
34 **Culen** fil. Indulf iv an. & vi menſ.
35 **Kinet** fil. Malcolm xxii an. & ii menſ.
36 **Conſtantin** fil. Culen uno an. & iv menſ.
37 **Chinet** fil. Duf uno an. & dimid.
38 **Malcolm** fil. Kinet xxx. Hic magnum bellum fecit apud Carrum. Ipſe etiam multas oblationes tam eccleſiis quam clero ea die diſtribuit.

39 (*a*)-
40 Macbeth fil. Findleg xvii an.
41 Lulach nepos filii Boide iv menſ. & dimid.
42 Malcolm fil. Duncan xxxvii an. & dimid. & iv mens.

Hic fuit vir Margaritæ reginæ: filiæ nobiliſſimæ Mathildis & Maria, ſui generis celſitudinem conjugio, morum ingenuitate, ſcientiæ magnitudine, rerum temporalium larga in pauperes diſpenſatione decenter ornaverunt.

Mathildis enim matrimonio juncta fuit *Henrico* Anglorum regi ſtrenuoſiſſimo, qui de Francorum excellenti regum proſapia duxit originem: quorum ſullimitas (*b*) prædicti, ſcilicet, regis & reginæ ad hoc uſque perducta eſt ut ipſorum ſoboles Romani imperii tenuerunt dignitatem. Eo-

(*a*) *Prætermiſſum eſt errore ſcribæ nomen* Duncani regis 39 *filii Beatricis filiæ* Malcolmi-mac Kineth.
(*b*) *L. Sublimitas.*

rum namque filia M. Prudencia, forma, diviciis digna imperio, imperatori nupſit Romano.

MARIA vero lege conjugii Euſtachio comiti Bolonienſi tradita; regina ſorore non minor extitit probitate, licet reginæ caruerit poteſtate. Hujus itidem filia ſtrenuum virum comitem Stephanum ſponſum accepit de regali ſimul & conſulari ſtirpe progenitam. Omitto filias adhuc viventes matres defunctas exemplo propono viventibus, quæ cum ſæculi pompa quod raro invenitur, divites ſanctis extitere virtutibus, pauperes utriuſque ſexûs, cujuſque condicionis eſſent, ac ſi membra coluerunt Chriſti; religioſos clericos, monachos, ſincero amore velud (*ſic*) patronos, & ſuos futuros judices cum Chriſto dilexerunt.

MATHILDIS regina Kal. Maij migravit de hac vita. A° ab Incarnatione Domini M.C.XVIII. ſepultaque eſt honorificè in eccleſia B. Petri Apoſtolorum principis Weſtmonaſterii juxta Londoniam Anglorum urbem nobiliſſimam.

MARIA autem comitiſſa 2°. Kal. Junii Anno ab Incarnatione M.C.XVI. apud Bermundſeiam, ex altera parte præfatæ urbis monaſterio S. Salvatoris in pace quievit; ubi a Domino Petreio admirandæ ſanctitatis viro tunc priore ejuſdem loci (*a*) Duniacenſis ſcilicet ad charitatem ſpeciali-

(*a*) L. Cluniacenſis.

pertinentis, gloriosè sepulta est. Tumulus vero marmoreus regum & reginarum ymagines habens impressas genus quiescentis demonstrat. In superficiem ejusd. tumuli titulus aureis literis sculptus nomen & vitam & originem breviter ita comprehendit.

Nobilis hic tumulata jacet comitissa Maria
Actibus hæc nituit, larga, benigna fuit.
Regum sanguis erat, morum probitate vigebat.
Compatiens inopi, vivat in arce poli.

EDMUNDUS vero frater earum vir strenuissimus, & in Dei servicio, dum vitam ageret præsentem, valde devotus apud montem Acuti in quadam videlicet cella, quæ ibi sita (est), requiescit humatus.

43 Dolfnal (*a*) frater ejus (Malcolmi R.) regnavit an. tribus & vii mensibus.
44 Dunchad fil. Malcolmi dimid. anni.
45 Edgarus fil. Malcolmi ix an.
46 Alexander frater ejus xvii an. & 3 mens.
47 David frater ejus xxx. Erat autem rex David vir piissimus in religione catholicus, in principes munificus, in (*b*) recuperandis basilicis studiosus, satis vigil, & orationibus in tantum studens ut plus supplicationibus ad

(*a*) L. Dofnal sive Dovenald.
(*b*) F. reparandis.

Deum

Deum profusis quam armis bellicis victoriam de inimicis optineret.

Rex vero piissimus David multa bona fecit, præcipuè tamen ædes sacras ubicunque in toto regno uectate (a) collapsas conscrat (b): pontificibus & patribus, ad quorum curam pertinebant, ut restaurarentur imperavit: adhibens curam per legatos ut imperata perficerentur. Unde sub ejus imperio multa sunt reparata, immò funditùs ædificata monasteria. Sed h^c (c) præcipuè monasterium puellare, & M. Puellare S. N. & multa alia puellaria & cætera plurima utriusque videlicet sexûs virorum & mulierum, quibus veluti quibusdam lychnis totum decoratur Scociæ regnum: quæ omnia piissimus David rex magnis auri & argenti ponderibus, gemmarumque pretiosarum muneribus, amplissimis etiam honoribus (d) dicau; & insuper, quod preciosius est, sanctissimis reliquiarum patrociniis insignivit.

Has omnes idem rex potens & piissimus honorabiliter multis excolebat muneribus: sed Melrossensem præcipuè inter omnes ecclesias & fideliter defensabat & dulciter diligebat, & suis opibus exornabat. Cæterum omnia ejus gesta quæ vulgo narrantur,

(a) F. vetustate.
(b) L. construxerat.
(c) Hocce.
(d) F. ditavit vel dicavit.

narrantur, non sunt hic propter vitandum fa[illegible] dium legentis pleniter explanata.

48 Malcolm filius (a) filii David xii an. vi men & xiii diebus.

49 Willelmus frater ejus.

Ab anno (b) 1°. Willielmi, regum Scottorum anni cccxv (c).

Willelmus rex Rufus filius Henrici, filii Malcolai filii Donuchada, qui fuit nepos Malcolai, f. Cinada, f. Maelcolai, f. Domnail, f. Constantin, f. (d) Ernacha, f. Alpin, f. Echach, f. Edafind, f. Echadach, f. Echach, f. Domongrat, f. Domnail-bric, f. Echach-buide, f. Edan, f. Gabran, f. Domangrat, f. Fergusa, f. Eirc, f. Echach-mirarcmuir, f. Oengus-saphir, f. Fedelinthe-aislingig, f. Oengusa-buiding, f. Fedelinthe-ramnaich, f. Seanchormaic, f. Cruith-linde, f. Find-fece, f. Achircir, f. Achach-antoir, f. Fiachrach-cathmail, f. Ecdach riade, f. Conare, f. Mogalande, f. (e) Luigdig, f. Ellatig, f. Corpre-crupchini, f. Dare-dornmoir, f. (f) Corbre-fadmoir, f. Co-

(a) supple Henrici.

(b) i.e. A.D. MCLXV.

(c) Scilicet ab unione regnorum Pict. & Scot. circa A.D. 850.

(d) L. Cinacha.

(e) Luigdig Ellatig.

(f) Corbre Findmore

nare-

nare-moir, f. Eterſceail, f. Eogam, f. Elela, f. Jair, f. Dedaid, f. Sin, f. Roſin, f. Their, f. Rothir, f. Roin, f. Arandil, f. Maine, f. (*a*) Forgo, f. (*b*) Feradaig, f. Elela-aramni, f. (*c*) Fachra, f. Firmara, f. Oengus-turmig, f. Firce-chairoid, f. Ferroid, f. Fir-anroid, f. Firatbrig, f. Labchore, f. Echachalt-letchin, f. Elela-caſſiacleg, f. Conliach, f. Erero, f. Moalgi, f. Coabtaig-coelbreg, f. Uganc-more, f. Eedaigluadaig, f. Duachlograich, f. Fiachraig-dualdach, f. Duachlograich, f. Fiachraig-tollgraich, f. Muredaich-bollgreich, f. (*d*) Simon, f. Brict (*e*).

(*a*) *Hic ille eſt qui a Forduno dictus* Ferguſius, *conditor regni Scotorum in Britannia conſtitutus eſt.*

(*b*) *Hic a Forduno & ſequacibus dictus eſt* Ferchardus ſive Ferquardus.

(*c*) Fiachra-Firmara.

(*d*) Simon Bric, &c.

(*e*) *Vide reliqua hujus genealogiæ nomina apud Radulſum* de Diceto *inter ſcriptores Angliæ, apud* Joan. Fordun *& alibi pregreditur ſeries genealogica, horum temporum* more, *uſque ad Noe.*

NUM. V.

NUM. V.

Ex Regiſtro Prioratus S. Andreæ, (a) *a folio 46, ad fol. 49.* (b)

NOMINA REGUM SCOTTORUM ET PICTORUM.

Series Regum Scottorum. fol. 46.

Summa Regum xxiii. annorum cccxxvii. & 3 menſ. (c)

1 FERGUS filius Erth primus in Scotia regnavit tribus annis ultra Drumalban uſque Sluagh (d) muner & uſque ad Inchegal.

2 Dovenghart fil. Fergus quinque ann. regnavit.

3 Congal fil. Dovenghart 24 an. regn.

4 Gauran fil. Dovenghart 22 an. regn.

5 Conal fil. Congal 14 an. regn.

6 Edhan fil. Gauran 34 an. regn.

7 Heoghedbude 16. an.

(a) *De excerptis hujus regiſtri.* V. *Supra*, pag. 606.

(b) *Hæc foliorum regiſtri tam accurata notatio, quæ & ſervatur in aliis hujus Regiſtri excerptis a V. Cl. D. Sybaldo ad me tranſmiſſis, probat primum exſcriptorem hujuſmodi excerptorum ipſum authenticum regiſtrum ob oculos habuiſſe: etſi ab aliquot annis ipſum autographum, neſcio quo caſu, diſparuerit.*

(c) *In hoc numero* cccxvii *annorum* xxiii *regum ab initio Ferguſii ad exitum Alpini manifeſtus eſt error ſive ſcribæ, ſive codicis ipſius; quemadmodum & ſæpiſſime alias erratum eſt in notis numeralibus annorum regni horum regum.*

(d) *L. Sluagh more.*

8 Kinathkerr fil. Conal 3 menſ.
9 Ferchar fil. Ewin 16 an.
10 Dovenald Brec fil. Heoghedbude 14 an.
11 Malduin fil. Dovenald Durn 16 an.
12 Ferchar-ſoda 21 an.
13 Heoghed Rinnavel fil. Dovenghart filii Dovenald Brec. 3 an.
14 Armkelleth fil. Findan. 1 an.
15 Heatgan fil. Findan 16 an.
16 Murdochus fil. Armkelleth 3 an.
17 Heoghan fil. Murdach 3 an.
18 Hethfin fil. Heoghed Rinnevale 30 an.
19 Fergus fil. Hethfin 3 an.
20 Sealuhanc fil. Eogagan 24 an.
21 Heoghed annuine fil. Hethfin 30 an.
22 Dungal fil. Heoghed annuine 7 an.
23 Alpin fil. Heoghed annuine. 3 an. Hic occiſus eſt in Gallewathia, poſtquam eam penitus deſtruxit & devaſtavit. Et hinc tranſlatum eſt regnum Scotorum in regnum Pictorum.

Nomina regum Pictorum. (a)

1 C*RUTHEUS fil. Kinne clemens judex accepit monarchiam in regno Pictorum, & regnavit* 50 *annis.*

2 *Gede* 101 *an. regnavit.*

(a) De diſcrepantia hujus catalogi a cronica Pictorum tam in nominibus quam in numero regum. Vide quæ dicta ſunt ſupra, pag. 124, 125, &c.

3 *Tharan*

3 *Tharan* 100 *an. regn.*
4 *Duchil* 40 *an. regn.*
5 *Duordeghel* 20 *an. regn.*
6 *Deootheth* 60 *an. regn.*
7 *Combust* 20 *an. regn.*
8 *Caranathrecht* 40 *an. regn.*
9 *Gernath-bolg.* 9 *an. regn.*
10 *Umpopnenet* 30 *an. regn.*
11 *Fiachua albus* 30 *an. regn.*
12 *Canatulmel* 6 *an. regn.*
13 *Dinornacht Netalec* 1 *anno*
14 *Feodak Finleg* 2 *an.*
15 *Garnat-dives* 60 *an.*
16 *Talarg fil. Keotber* 25 *an.*
17 *Drust fil. Urb.* 100 *ann. rexit* (*b*) & 100 *bella peregit*
18 *Talarg fil. Amil* 2. *an.*
19 *Nethan Thelcamot* 10 *an.*
20 *Drust Gormot* 30 *an.*
21 *Galam* 15 *an.*
22 *Drust fil. Gigurum* 5 *an.*
23 *Drust fil. Hydrossig* 8 *an.*
24 *Ganut fil. Gigurum* 6 *an.*
25 *Kelturan frater ejus* 6 *an.*
26 *Golorg fil. Mordeleg.* 12 *an.*
27 *Drust fil. Moneth* 1 *anno*
28 *Tagalad* 4 *an.*

(*b*) Exemplar Jacobi Gray ex iisd. S. Andreæ monumentis, ut apparet, descriptum, habet 100 ann. *vixit*, non autem *rexit*. De hoc v. notam p. 136. supra.

29 *Brude fil. Melchon* 30 *an. Hunc ad fidem convertit S. Columba*

30 *Garnat fil. Domnach* 20 *an.*

31 *Nethan fil. Ub.* 21 *an. Hic ædificavit Abernethyn.*

32 *Kinel fil. Luthren* 14 *an.*

33 *Nectan fil. Fottle* 5 *an.*

34 *Brude fil. Fathe* 5 *an.*

35 *Telarg fil. Fetobar* 11 *an.*

36 *Talargan fil. Amfrude* 5 *an.*

37 *Garnat fil. Domnal* 5 *an.*

38 *Drust frater ejus* 6 *an.*

39 *Brude fil. Bile* 21 *an. Hujus tempore floruit S. Adamnanus*

40 *Taram fil. Amfredech* 14 *an.*

41 *Brude fil. Derili* 31 *an.*

42 *Nectan frater ejus* 18 *an.*

43 *Garnath fil. Ferath* 24 *an.*

44 *Oengusa fil. Fergusa* 16 *an.*

45 *Nethan fil. Derili* 9 *mens.*

46 *Alpin fil. Feret* 6 *mens.*

47 *Oengusa fil. Brude* 6 *mens. Idem iterum* 36 *annis.*

48 *Brude fil. Tenegus* 8 *an.*

49 *Drust fil. Talargan* 1 *an.*

50 *Talargan fil. Drustan* 4 *an.*

51 *Talargan fil. Tenegus* 5 *an.*

52 *Constantin fil. Fergusa* 42 *an. Hic ædificavit Dunkelden*

53 *Hungus fil. Fergusa* 10 *an. Hic ædificavit Kilrymont*

54 *Du-*

canæ, quæ sub servitute erat usque ad illud tempus ex (a) constitutione & more Pictorum.

29 Dovenal Mac-Constantin 11 an. Mortuus est in Fores, & sepultus in Iona.

30 Constantin Mac-Edha 40 an. Hic dimisso regno sponte Deo in habitu religionis abbas factus Keledeorum S. Andreæ 5 ann. (b) & ibi mortuus est & sepultus.

31 Malcom Mac-Dovenald 9 an. interfectus in Ulurn a Moraviensib. (c) sep. in Iona.

32 Induff Mac-Constantin 9 an. interfectus a Norwagensib. in Inverculan sep. in Iona.

33 Duff Mac-Malcolm 4 ann. & 6 mens. Interfectus in Fores & absconditus sub ponte de Kinlos; & sol non apparuit quamdiu ibi latuit (d). Sepultus in Iona.

34 Culin Mac-Induff 4 an. & 6 mens. Interfectus ab Andarch filio Dovenald propter filiam suam in Laudonia.

35 Kinath Mac-Malcolm 24 an. & 2 mens. Interfectus in Fotherkern a suis per perfidiam Finellæ filiæ Cunechat comitis de Angus; cujus Finellæ filium unicum prædictus Kinath interfecit apud Dunfinoen.

36 Constantin Mac-Culin 1 an. & 6 mens. Interfectus a Kinat filio Malcolm I. in Rathveramoen, & sepultus in Iona.

(a) *Consuetudine* MS. Cot.
(b) *Servivit.* MS. Cot.
(c) *Per dolum.* Cot.
(d) *Et inventus est &* Cot.

37 Girgh

37 Girgh Mac-Kinat-Mac-Duff 8 an. Interfectus a filio Kinet in Moeghanard, sep. in Iona insf.

38 Malcolm Mac-Kinath rex victoriosissimus 30 an. Mortuus in Glamis, & sep. in Iona insula.

39 Donchath (*a*) Mac-Trini abbatis de Dunkeld & Bethoc filiæ Malcom-Mac-Kinat 6 an. Interfectus a Macbeth-Mac-Finleg in Bothgouanan & sep. in Iona.

40 Macbeth-Mac-Finleg 17 an. Interfectus in Lunfanan a Malcolm-Mac-Donchat & sepultus in Iona.

41 Lulach fatuus 4 mensf. Interfectus est in Essei in Strathbolgi, & sep. in Iona.

42 Malcolm Mac-Donechat 37 an. & 8 mensf. Interfectus in Inneraldan, (*b*) sep. in Iona. Hic fuit vir S. Margaretæ.

43 Donald Mac-Donechat prius regnavit 6 mensf. & postea expulsus est, &

44 Donekan Mac-Malcolm regnavit 6 mensf. hoc interfecto a Malpeder Macloen comite de Moerns in Monachedin: rursum Donald Mac-Donechat regnavit 3 annis. Hic captus est ab Edgar Mac-Malcolm, cæcatus est & mortuus in Roscolpin, sepultus in Dunkelden, hinc translata ossa in Iona.

45 Edgar 9 an. Mortuus in Dunedin, & sepultus in Dunfermling.

(*a*) *Mac trini.* C.
(*b*) *Juxta Alnwick.* C.

46 Alexander 17 an. & 3 menf. & dimidio. Mortuus in Crafleti, fep. in Dunfermling

47 David 29 an. & 3 menf. Mortuus in Carleolo, fep. in Dunfermling.

48 Malcolm fil. Henrici filii David 12 an. & 6 menf. & 20 dieb. Mortuus apud Jedword fep. in Dunfermling.

49 Willelmus 52 an. Mortuus in Strivelin, fep. in Aberbrothok, cui fucceffit

50 Alexander fil. Will. 34 an. & 8 menf. Obiit a° 1249 in expeditione in quadam infula Erregethal, & fep. apud Melrofs. cui fucceffit

51 Alexander filius puer feptem annor. coronatus apud Sconam 3 id. Julii a Davide Epo S. Andreæ 1251. Hic rex perexit in Angliam & honorificè fufceptus eft a rege Angliæ, apud Eboracum factus eft miles: & craftino die defponfavit regis filiam. Nefcio quo infortuito Zabulo feminante difcordiam inter magnates terræ hujus, cancellarius & jufticiarius Scotiæ apud regem Angliæ accufati, ab officiis deprivati, & alii eorum loco fubftituti.

NUM. VI.

NUM. VI.

Breve Chronicon Scoticum sive Chronicon Rythmicum (a).

Ad calcem Scoti-chronici MS. Collegii Scotorum Parisien. (b).

Prologus.

CUM hujus præcedentis voluminis prolixitas, hominum quoque memoriæ labilitas, & incerti temporis brevitas, non sinunt universa quæ inibi scripta sunt animo scire multa cupientis, similiterque semel (c) comprehendere; ideo mihi visum est pro ingenioli mei capacitate quædam inde extrahere; & in unius corpus codicilli quodam compendio, (d) scripto veteri metrico, & novo ad propositum respondente, quasi sub quodam epilogo

(a) *De hoc Chronico Rythmico vide quæ dicta sunt supra*, p. 608, &c. p. 677.

(b) *In hoc codice Parisiensi extat genuinum & minimè interpolatum. Habetur etiam hoc idem Chronicon sive in initio sive ad calcem Scotichronicorum MSS. Paslatyn. in biblioth. Regia Londin. Collegii Edinburgen. Panmuren. Cartusien. in bibl. Jurid. Edinb. Cuprensi & aliis: sed in plerisque cum multis interpolationibus & additionibus, quorum aliquas infra notabimus: sicut & varias lectiones alicujus momenti.*

(c) L. Simul & semel, *rectius juxta cod. Pasl.*

(d) Partim ex metris veteribus, partim ex recentibus ad propositum facientibus. *Cod. Paslat.*

ſummatim redigere, præcipuè quæ facere videntur ad noticiam inclytorum regum Scotorum; de qua ſtirpe, quave origine ad iſtas oras devenerunt; & quoto tempore, & quoto ante Pictos, cum iiſdem, & poſt eos viciſſim regnaverunt; & qualiter nunc ſtirps Scotigena miſcetur cum Saxonica, qualiterque Britannica ſtirpe multigena variatur, & quomodo rex Scociæ modernus de jure debito, debet tam Angliæ quam Scociæ præfici regnis (*a*).

PRIMA PARS CHRONICI.

CAP. I. *Quo tempore ante incarnationem Chriſti incepit Scota, a qua Scocia.*

Quiſque loqui gaudet validus de ſanguine puro
Quorumdam precibus de Scotis dicere curo:
Unde ſui generis ortus primævus habetur,
Quorum poſteritas trans tempora perpetuetur.
Quidquid narrabo per cronica ſcripta (*b*) probabo
De veterum geſtis: reliquorum ſum quia teſtis
Scribere nam volui mihi quæ præſentia vidi (*c*).

Adam primævum non incipiam numerare;
Quomodo nec dicam Noe cœpit generare.

(*a*) *Hic interſeritur in pleriſque Scotichronicis deſcriptio ætatum mundi.*

(*b*) L. priſca. *Cod. Paſlat.*

(*c*) *In cod. Paſlat. adduntur hic ſequentes duo verſiculi:*
Si verum ſcribam verum credo fore ſcribam
Scripſero ſi vanum, caput eſt quaſi non mihi ſanum.

Hoc

Hoc genus a Japheth ejus nato juniore
Quamvis descenderat, referam tamen a propiore
Per quem dicatur stirps hæc, & magnificatur.
Quingentis mille cum sexaginta monosque,
Annis ut reperi præcessit tempora Christi
Agnus sub lege primus mactatus in æde
Biblia testatur, quod tunc revocare paratur
Rex Pharao populum fugientem per mare rubrum
Cujus rex Pharao mergitur in medio.
Ex tunc Scotorum describam tempus, & horum
Progeniem referam per tempora continuatam.

CAP. II. *Gaithelos intulit lapidem.*

Postquam passus erat Pharao miserabile funus
Nobilis exierat ab Ægypto Schyticus unus
Exul qui lapidem Pharaonis detulit idem
Ut liber fatur, Gaithilglas ille vocatur.
Hic bis undenus fuit a (*a*) Japheth alienus
Ut sic credatis dat linea sanguinitatis,
Naufraga navigio qui plura pericula passus
Ad terram tandem venit sic (*b*) equite lassus:
Sed lapis hunc (*c*) erexit ipsum qui per mare vexi
Hic lapis, ut fatur, hæc anchora vitæ vocatur.

(*a*) *In veteri genealogia regum Scotorum sunt circiter* 22 *gradus seu generationes inter Japhet & hunc Gaskilglas seu Gaythelos*. V. Fordun lib. 5. c. 50. *In Hybernicis autem tantum quatuor: illi enim more solito veterem genealogiam reformarunt ob rationes supra notatas*. pag. 485, &c.

(*b*) F. Æquore.

(*c*) Rexit. *Cod. Pastat.*

Cumque locum petiit securus ad residendum
Pluribus hunc annis Hispania cœpit alendum.
Cujus progenies nimis augmentatur ibidem
Sicut scriptura testatur condita pridem.

Cap. III. *De eodem lapide* (*a*).

Post obitum regis Pharaonis mille duobus
Annis, ut recolo, tunc quidam nomine Milo
Rex Hispanorum, qui plures (*b*) magnos habebat
Natos, illorum tamen unum plus recolebat.
Scilicet is Simon cognomine Brek fuit unus:
Cui pater exhibuit quoddam prænobile munus,
Scilicet hanc Petram Gaizilglas quam tulit equam (*c*)
Perque fretum gessit ab Ægypto quando recessit.
Milo prophetavit nato (qui quem recreavit
Lætari cœpit hanc Petram quando recepit)
Quod sua regnaret stirps hanc quocunque locaret.
Ecce Deo dante; sicut (*d*) factum fuit ante
Sic fit in instante: Simon Brek quo mediante
Sic augmentante, Sobolis partem venientis
Ad se suscepit Hybernia: quo residentes
Annos per multos: horum quos vidit adultos
Quosdam deduxit validus (*e*) Lorimonie quidam

Primus

(*a*) De rege Milone. C. *Past.*

(*b*) Magnus. C. *Pest.*

(*c*) F, Secum. *Nam autor horum versuum numeros vel quantitatem parum videtur attendisse.*

(*d*) L, fatum. C. *Past.*

(*e*) Lori nomine quidam. C. *Pastat. Sed quisnam fuerit ille Lori qui primus deduxit Scotos ad Ergadiam nusquam reperi.*

Additur.

Primus ad Ergadiam : quo tempore concito dicam
Isti sunt ducti : dicuntur postea Scoti.
Nam velut a Githia Geticus, seu Gothia Gothi,
Dicitur a Sithia Sithicus, sic Scotia Scoti,
Quæ prius Albania sic fertur Scotia terra.
Scoti a Scota, de Scotis Scocia nota,
A muliere Scota vocatur Scocia tota.

Cap. IV. *Quot annis rexerunt Picti.*

Quod jam promisi tempus sic ecce relisi
(*a*) Bis bis centeno quater endeca, sed minus uno
Anno quo sumpsit primos Ergadia Scotos,
Ut referunt isti, fuit incarnatio Christi.
Annorum summa Pictis præoccupatorum
Hic dat Scotorum deca quinque centibinorum
Et annos quindecim, tres menses jungito quidem.
Tunc Scoti quærunt quot anni præterierunt
Postquam vicerunt Pictos qui tunc coluerunt
Albaniam citro Drumalban, sed minus ultra.

Additur tamen ad marginem libri Pastaten. alia manu : Lori fuit tertius a Simone Brek. *&* *alludere videtur ad nomen Loghraich quod pronunciatur* Loraich. *Fuit autem Duach Lograich tertius aut quartus in veteri genealogia a* Simone Brek.

(*a*) *Vide quæ superius,* p 703. *dicta sunt de Usserii interpretatione horum verborum. Sane ex tota hujus & præcedentis capituli serie patet per hos versiculos* Bis bis centeno, &c. *Autorem censuisse Scotos in Britannia quadringentis quadraginta tribus annis ante Incarnationem cæpisse habitare; sedesque in hac insula habuisse ante adventum Pictorum, quos & hic autor & omnes alii scriptores Scoti, ducentis saltem ante natum Christum annis, in has oras commigrasse sentiunt.*

Ut

Ut Scoti valeant memoratum tempus habere
Per Scociam totam quo cœperunt residere.
Qui Picti terram rexere mille ducentis,
Et pariter junctis viginti quatuor annis,
Ut verum renovem, mensibus atque novem.
Pictis amotis datur hæc responsio Scotis:
D. Semel & ter C. post X. ter & X. quater inde.
Istorum numeri monstrant quo tempore Christi,
Sed trans (*a*) Dun-Alban cœpit regnare Kenedus
Filius Alpini Pictorum fraude perempti
In bello pridem quos Alpin vicerat idem.
Sed cum septenis Kened regnaverat annis
Nititur in Pictos ulcisci funera patris,
Quosdam sternendo bello, (*b*) quoscunque fugando:
Ex tunc Albaniæ regnum totale regebat,
Quæ prius in parte regni dicta residebat,
Progenies cujus jus regni nunc tenet hujus.

CAP. V. *Primus rex regnavit in Argadia.*

Ex annis Domini qui continue renovantur
Apparet per quot annos Scoti dominantur:
Sic patet in genere de tempore sufficienter;
Reges nunc referam qui regnavere (*c*) frequenter.
In tamen Ergadia vixit per tempora multa
Hæc gens sub lege naturæ, sed sine rege,
Donec ad Ergadiam tulit audax nomine quidam

(*a*) L. Drum-albam. C. *Pastat.*
(*b*) L. Quosdamque fugando. *rectius cum* C. *Pastat.*
(*c*) L. Sequenter. i. e. Successive. *rectius cum* C. *Pastat.*

(*a*) Fer-

Fergusius (*a*) lapidem, de quo sit mentio pridem.
Hic primo rexit Scotos, lapidem quia vexit.
Quem Scoti lapidem sanxerunt ponere sedem
Regibus inde suis tantum, sed non alienis (*b*).

CAP. VI. *De continuatione regum usque ad Kenethum.*

R. 1. Primus in Ergadia Fergus (*c*) rexit tribus annis:
RR. 2, 3. Post Donegart quinis: Congal quater octo bis (*d*):
RR. 4, 5. Endeca bis Gouren: sed quatuor & deca Conal:

(*a*) *Hunc fuisse Fergusium filium Erch ex contextu chronici hujus totaque serie subsequentium regum sequenti capitulo, manifeste patet.*

(*b*) *In C. Paslat. Edinb. &c. hic additur versus sequens.*
Ut Scona testatur usque huc lapis iste locatur.

(*c*) *In hoc & sequentibus hujus chronici capitulis eadem omnino regum nomina, ordo & successio ac in duobus praecedentibus chronicis sive catalogis, quemadmodum & in chronico Wintonii infra posito, & in catalogo sive chronico Jacobi Gray; nec inter haec omnia chronica sive catalogos aliud reperire est alicujus momenti discrimen praeterquam in numeris annorum regni quorundam regum, in quibus frequenter ex more erratur, sive scribae, sive auctorum incogitantia, aut hallucinatione.*

(*d*) *Hic manifesta videtur transpositio numeri annorum regni Aidani pro annis regni Comgalli, & vicissim. Constat enim apud omnes Aidanum regnasse annis 34. sive* quater octo & binis *(ut hic habet Cod. Edingburg. collegii) qui hic tribuuntur Comgallo, quem ex aliis plerisque chronicis regnasse constat tantum 24, aut quatuor & deca bis annis, qui hic false tribuuntur Aidano.*

RR. 6, 7. Qua-

RR. 6, 7 Quatuor, & deca bis Edhan (a) x.
vi. Eoghedbod:

R. 8. Kinath-Ker per tres rexit tan-
tummodo menses:

R. 9. Sed Ferquarth annos per quatuor
& duodenos:

RR. 10. 11. Bis septem Donald: octo bis
Malduin annis:

RR. 12, 13. Ter septem Fercard: tredecim,
sed rexit Eoghed: (b)

RR. 14, 15. Armkellach uno: sed tred. (c)
regnavit Eogan:

RR. 16, 17. Rex Murdauch trinis: (d) Neo-
gan uno quoque bino:

RR. 18, 19, 20. Hetfin per deca ter: Fergus tres:
(e) sed Scaluanc

R. 21. Quatuor & deca bis: sed (f) Eo-
gad anuique tricenis:

RR. 22, 23. Dungal septenis: Alpinus sed tri-
bus annis:

24. Annis septenis Kenedus (g) filius
Alpin.

(a) *Jam observavimus hunc 24 annorum numerum congruere tantum Congallo.*

(b) Eogyn *C. Pastat.*

(c) L. tredecim.

(d) L. Heogan.

(e) Scalanvan. *C. Pastat.*

(f) L. Eogad annuinque.

(g) *Si Kenethus regnum inierit A. D. 836. & septem annis regnaverit super Scotos ante adjunctionem regni Pictici sedecim annis monarchiæ ipsius super tota Albania cæpisse oportet A. D. 843. Sed de his alias.*

Hi

Hi cum prædictis regnarunt tempore Pictis,
Quod trecentenos quatuor octoque continet annos,
His annis & tres debetis jungere menses. (*a*)
Christi transactis tribus annis atque ducentis (*b*)
Scotia Catholicam cœpit habere fidem
Roma victore primo papa residente.
C. quater & deca ter a carne Dei numerabis
In Scotia quando legem Christi renovabis:
Lex Christi colitur hanc Palladio renovante
Primus cælestinus Scotiæ quem miserat ante
Præcedunt Scoti quingentis Anglicis annis.
Quamvis & credit ante hos (*c*) *Brutus & obedit.*
(*d*) *Albion in terris rex primus germine Scotus*
Illorum turmis rubri tulit arma leonis
Fergusius fulvo Ferchardi rugieniis in arvo.
Christum tercentis ter denis præfuit annis
Lilifer ille leo rosidus nunc pingitur auro.

CAP. VII. *De continuatione regum*

R. 24. Et postquam Kenede Pictos omnino fugavit
Annos octo bis regnando continuavit:

(*a*) *Hic (ut superiùs monuimus pag. 677, 678.) inter hoc caput 6. & 7. in magnis plerisque Scotichronicis sequens inseritur interpolatio ex variis Forduni locis, & aliunde ineptè consarcinata, ut sola lectione manifestè pateat hanc additionem non esse genuinum autoris hujus chronici partum. Hinc in exemplari genuino codicis Collegii Scot. Paris. non habetur.*

(*b*) Fordun. lib. 2. cap. 35.

(*c*) i.e. antiqui Britones.

(*d*) Fordun. lib. 2. cap. 12.

R. 25.

R. 25. Donald Mac-Alpin post rexit quatuor annis

RR. 26, 27, 28. Sed (*a*) Constantinus: Ed. (*b*) uno: Greg. (*c*) duodenis:

RR. 29, 30. Donald undenis: Constantin bis quoque vicenis:

RR. 31, 32. Malcolmus primus, sic Induff quisque novenis:

R. 33. Sed Duff per senos menses & quatuor annos:

RR. 34, 35 Per tantum Culen: sed Kened sex quater annis

R. 36. Mensibus & binis: Constantinusque per annum

R. 37. Et menses senos: tunc Greg (*d*) octo per annos:

RR. 38, 39. Malcom per deca ter: Duncan sex: sed deca septem

RR. 40, 41. Macbeth: sed (*e*) Lahoulan per menses quatuor: atque

R. 42. Malcolm Kenremor (*f*) annos per ter deca septem

R. 43. Et menses octo: cujus frater Donevaldus
Annos complevit ternos regnando vicissim,

R. 44. Dum Duncan medio sex menses tempore vixit.

(a) i.e. Sedecim.
(*b*) Aodh sive Ethus dictus.
(*c*) Gregorius.
(*d*) *Alias* Grim. *Vide indicem sive catalogum nominum.*
(*e*) *Alias* Lulach.
(*f*) *Vulgo* Malcolm Keanmor.

CAP.

CAP. VIII. *De-hinc reges Scotorum processerunt de Stirpe tam Saxonum, sive Anglorum, quam Scotorum.*

Tunc ſtirps Scotigena Saxonum ſanguine mixta
Cœpit regnare, quod propono reſerare
Qualiter hoc eſſet, ut quivis dicere (*a*) poſſit.
De dicto nati Kenremor tres generati
Regnum rexerunt, quod ſucceſſim tenuerunt:
Quos Margarita peperit regina beata
Hæres Anglorum regum, regina Scotorum.
Ex (*b*) quo qui dubitat Anglorum cronica quærat:
Per quam (*ſic*) conjugium Scotis præbetur in uſum.
Non erat iſtorum generatio dico (*c*) duorum
Fratrum primorum: genuit tamen ultimus (*d*) horum
Per quem Scotorum generando continuatur (*e*)
Regia ſtirps, quorum ſucceſſio nunc reſeratur.
R. 45. Annis ter trinis & ternis menſibus Edgar
Primus regnavit de natis quos generavit
Malcolmus cum dicta Margarita beata.
R. 46. Hinc Alexander annis rexit deca ſeptem
Menſibus atque tribus, ſeptimaniſque duabus.
Iſte ſecundus erat fratrum: ſed tertius extat

(*a*) F. diſcere.
(*b*) F. De quo.
(*c*) *Silicet* Edgari & Alexandri.
(*d*) David.
(*e*) *Hic verſus oſcitantia ſcribæ deeſt in Cod. Pariſ. ſed habetur in reliquis Codicibus.*

R. 47.

R. 47. David vicenis regnans annisque novenis,
R. 48. Mensibus & ternis : tunc Malcolm fil. Henri
Annis bis senis & semis regna gerebat ;
Ut (a) rumor gessit hic Malcolm virgo recessit.
At Henricus erat natus regis quoque David,
Quem rex is David ex Matilda generavit :
Hæres qui fuerat Huntindoniæ comitatus,
Cujus sic esset si posset vivere natus :
Qui bello moritur de Cothon ; sed sepelitur
In abbatia nomine Calconia (b).
Hæc Matilda datur de Senlis, quæ tumulatur
In Scona cujus templum bustum tenet hujus.
R. 49. Quadraginta novem Willelmus rex erat annis :
Cujus Willelmi genitor dictus fuit Henri ;
Et pariter comitis de Dunde nomine David :
Tres sibi sorores fuerant : Britan. comitissa
Quæ Margarita Conano conjugi data
Hæc junior datur germana, sed altera vocatur
Nobilis Adissa : fuit hæc Holland comitissa,
Conjugioque datus erat huic de Ross comitatus :
Morte præventam Matildam dic & inuptam.

SECUNDA PARS.

CAP. IX. *De nobili politico Alexandro tertio.*

Hactenus hæc dicta novi per cronica scripta (c)
A modo quæ novi scriptis describere vovi

(a) Ut res se gessit. *Cod. Panmur. &c.*

(b) Abbatia de Calco, *vulgo* Kelso

(c) *Hactenus continentur quæ auctor ex scriptis sive priscis chronicis desumpserat. Hic incipit describere quæ vel ipse per se, vel ex coævorum relatione noverat : hinc addendum censuimus titulum hunc* Secunda pars.

R. 50. Altet Alexander, quem rex Willelmus habebat
Natum, ter denis annis & quinque regebat:
Hic Alexander alium fertur genuiſſe
Hunc alium ternum pro certo dico fuiſſe.
R. 51. Ternus Alexander ter denis rex erat annis,
Et ſeptem fere: væ Scotis qui caruere
Principe tam grato, largo, mitique beato,
Qui quinquagenus regum fuit ordine primus (*a*).
Hic princeps annos Domini poſt mille ducentos
Et novem novies, ſed quatuor his ſuper addes (*b*)
Kyngorn non rite perſolvit debita vitæ,
Scilicet Aprilis decimo quartoque Kalendas;
Quo decet exequias celebrari perficiendas (*c*),
Ne valeant obitum monachi ſervare ſopitum
A quibus incolitur Dunfermlin, ſed ſepelitur.
Tanti tumba viri ſtudio meliore poliri
Debuit, artificum ſi funus haberet amicum.

SECUNDA PARS.

(*a*) *Hinc nova confirmatur probatione ſive argumento Ferguſium filium Erch primum fuiſſe regum Scotorum juxta priſca chronica, unde deſumpta ſunt præcedentia capitula, cum Alexander tertius & in hoc metrico chronico & in aliis omnibus ante editum Forduni chronicon, quinquageſimus primus rex a prædicto Ferguſio numeretur.*

(*b*) *i. e.* A.D. 1285.

(*c*) *Hinc patet in more poſitum fuiſſe olim apud Scotos anniverſarias exequias regum celebrari in eccleſiis ſaltem ubi ſepulti erant.*

Post mortis morsum vertit dilectio dorsum (*a*);
Finita vita finit (*b*) amor, & ita
Corpus prædicti regis sine prole relicti
Post annos fere septem Scotis (*c*) (*sic*) doluere
Qui regem vere (*d*) aristis non habuere (*e*).

CAP. X. *De rege Roberto Brois.*

Andreæ festo, Domini post mille ducentos
Atque decem novies cum binis insimul annis
Servando morem (*f*) regis sibi sumpsit honorem;
R. 52. Quem quinquagenum regum facit ordo secundum:
Dehinc ex toto Johanne rege remoto,
R. 53. De Brois Robertus regum de stirpe repertus,
Suscipit in Scona regni Scociæ diadema:
Hæc in Aprilinas sexto sunt facta Kalendas.
Promittunt veteres quod erit hic belliger heros,
Qui sua rura novans regna sudabit ovans;
Stragibus immensis sudabit Scoticus ensis;
Corruet Angligena per eum gens non sine pœna.
Hactenus hi toti fuerant ut plebs sua Scoti;
Atque Deo dante sic amodo sie velut ante.
Est totum cœnum cujus caput est alienum
Sic populus quando fit rex alienus (*g*).

(*a*) *Quas querelas, quos gemitus edidisset antiquus hic scriptor, si omnium nostrorum regum priscorum monumenta non tantum in ecclesia de Dunfermlin, sed ubique per totum regnum coram vidisset disjecta subversa, solo æquata, aut etiam effossa!*

(*b*) L. Finitur.

(*c*) L. Scoti.

(*d*) L. Tot aristis. *Paslat.*

(*e*) *Hic in Paslat. & aliis multa addita.*

(*f*) *Intellige Johannem Bailol.*

(*g*) *Hic etiam nova additamenta in Paslat. &c.*

Cap. XI. *De Roberto Brois.*

De Brois Robertus regum de stirpe regali
Bis deca rex Scotos regnavit quatuor annis
M, semel & ter C, bis & X novem superadde,
Tunc rex Robertus bonus est de funere certus.
Ante suam mortem genuit similem sibi fortem,
R. 54. Magnanimum David rex Robertus generavit.
Hic rex regnavit deca terque novem simul annis (*a*):
Nullum superstes hæredem corpore gignit:
Mariora tamen soror ejusdem generavit
R. 55. Galtero Stewart Robertum rite secundum:
Qui regnando decemque novem feliciter annis
R. 56. Regem Robertum generavit denique ternum
R. 57. Hic XVI stetit annis, Jacobum quoque gignit
Primum, qui regit annis deca terque duobus,
R. 58. Et Jacobum nostrum genuit rex iste modernum
Tempore scripturæ: tunc lector sit tibi curæ
Quod fuit annorum septem decem numerorum (*b*)
Quem Deus exaltet, regnum regat, atque gubernet.

(*a*) *Regnavit revera David* II. *annis* 41, *mensibus* 8, *& diebus* 15.

(*b*) *i. e.* A. D. 1447.

NUM. VII.

Extract of the Chronicle of *Andrew Winton*, Prior of *Lochlevin*. *See page* 621, *&c.* & *page* 680, *&c.*

Ex Cod. MS. Bibl. Cotton. [Nero, D. xi.] fol. 30.

FErgus Erthsone fra him (*a*) syne
Down descendand evin be Lyne
Into ye 5 and 50 gre (*b*)
As evin recknand men may se,
Brought this stane within Scotland (*c*),
And first it set in Ycolmkil,
And skune yairefter it wes broucht til:
And yair it wes syn mony a day,
Quhen Edwart gert hail it away
King of England, and syne he
Gert it sett in Lundyn be.

(*a*) *I. e. Simon Breac*, who, according to the tradition of the *Scots*, first brought the famous stone from *Spain* to *Ireland*, and placed it there, says *Winton*, *as the charter of the kinrik*, from this *Simon* to *Fergus* son of *Erc*, there were, according to the old *Scotish* genealogy, about fifty-five degrees or generations.

(*b*) *I. e.* Degree.

(*c*) Furst quhen he came and wan yat lande, *Cod. Bibl. Reg. Lond.*

Ibidem, fol. 37.

Fergus Erthsone the first man
Wes yat in our land began
Befor yat time (*a*) yat ye Peythis
Our kinrik wan fra ye Scottis,
And syne ye Peythis regnand were
A thousand ane and sixty yheres;
And fra yis Fergus down be lyne
Descendand evin was be lyne
Kenaucht, yat wes aught hundred yhere
And thre and fourtie passit cleir
Eftir the blessit nativite,
Or regnand he begouth to be

(*a*) *Winton* supposes here, and all along, that the *Scots* were long settled in *Britain* before the *Picts*. This opinion had taken rise long before upon an emulation with the *Picts* (*V. pag.* 526, *supra*) and became, by degrees, common among the *Scots*, after the disappearance of the *Picts*, under their own name, by the destruction or dispersion of many of them, and by the incorporation of the rest into one body of people with the *Scots*. And we meet with a *Scotish* writer, in the time of king *James* IV, (*a short chronicle in prose at end of* Winton in Biblioth Reg. Lond.) who tells us, that *Simon Breac* himself came to *Scotland*; that the *Scots* came into *Britain*, even before *Brutus*; and that at last the *Picts* came in. In short, this writer tells us, that the number of kings of *Scots*, in his time, amounted to *near sax score of kings*. Thus we see the notion of an ancient settlement and monarchy, once it arose, went beyond all bounds.

Fra ye Peythis was put out.
The tend man without doubt (a)
Was Kenaught Malkalpyne
Fra yis Fergus even be lyne:
And swa ther ten should occupy,
Gif al were reckynit fullely,
Twelf hundred zheris and weil ma:
Bot I cannot consaif it swa:
Bot yat yis Fergus was regnand
Within ye kinrick of Scotland
And yai ten yat regnand were
Eftir yis Fergus zhere be zhere,
As yai yat ye Croniklis wrate,
In till number sett ye date,
Among ye Peythis wes regnand
Within the kingdom of Scotland,
And lissit in bargain and in weer
Quhyl Kenaucht rose wich his power.
Gif oyir of mair suffisans
Can fynd better accordance
Yis buke at likyn yai may mende:
Bot I now schortlie to mak ende
Thinkis for to sett yair date,
As Cornikles before me wrate, &c.

(a) *Winton* repeats this again (*fol.* 43.) that *Fergus Erthson* was first king of the *Scots*, and that before the entry of the *Picts*; but finding that there were but ten generations betwixt this *Fergus* and *Keneth-mac-Alpin*, which he acknowledges could not take up more than three hundred years, he concludes, at last, that the *Picts* were already settled in *Scotland*, when *Fergus Erthsone* came in; which, he says, he found by other sure authors.

Extract

Extract of *Andrew Winton*'s chronicle reviewed by himself, with additions and corrections. *Book* IV. *chap*. 8. (*a*).

Ex codice MS. Bibliothecæ Regiæ Londin. *See p.* 624, *supra*.

Four hundred winters and fifty (*b*)
And twa to reckyn our even likly
Before ye nativite, &c.
As in our storie written is
Yan in Scotland the Scottis
Begouth (*c*) to reign and to steir
Twa hundred full and fortie zhere
Five winters and monethis three
Gif yat all suld rekkonit be
Or the Peythis in Scotland
Came in, and in it were dwelland.
And now to thai (*d*) I turn my style,
Of yair lynage to speke a while:
As in the third buke (*e*) was before
From Simon brek till Fergus more
Is as the Scottis lynally
Come down of Irischery,

(*a*) I have met with this succession of the kings of *Scots* from *Fergus* in none of the other copies of *Winton*.

(*b*) L forty. *Cod. Colon*.

(*c*) *I. e.* began.

(*d*) The *Scots*.

(*e*) *Winton*, Book III. cap. 9. *Cod. Bibl. Reg. Lond.*

Quhar yen I left now to begin
Yair namis here I will tak in
He yat was callet Fergus more
In ye third buke ȝe hard before
K. 1. Was Fergus Erthson yat thre yhere
Maid him beyond ye Drum (*a*) to steir (*b*)
Oure all ye hychtis evir ilkane
As yai ly fra Drumalbane
Till Stanemore (*c*) and Inchegall
Kyng he mad hym (*d*) oure (*e*) yaim all;
K. 2. Dongart his swn yheris fyve
Was tyll his father successyve:
K. 3. Congal Dongarts swn twentye ȝheres
And twa was kyng withouttin weres;
K. 4. Gowran Dongarts swn alswa
Regnyt twentie ȝheris and twa:
K. 5. Conal nest (*f*) him Makcongal
Forteen ȝheres held yai landis all;
Thretty wyntyrs and four yan
K. 6. Edan regnyd Mak-Gowran:
K. 7. Hrocged bwd sex ȝheris and ten
Kyng was in yai landis yan:
K. 8. Kynat ker Mak-colnal
Three monethis held yai landis all:

(*a*) In the margin of the MS. is this note, *Drum Albain*, the back of *Albany*.

(*b*) To raign.

(*c*) F. Sluaghmore.

(*d*) Himself.

(*e*) Over.

(*f*) Next.

K. 9. Fercha

K. 9. Ferchar Mackcony sexten zhere
As kyng (a) couth all the landis stere.
K. 10. Donald-brek son Hucgedbuode
Kyng was fourtene zheres proude (b)
And eftir pat his dayis wes downe
K. 11. Maldowny Dolnald Doynyswn
Sexteen winters kyng was hale (c):
And nest tuke pat governale
K. 12. Ferchar fodys sune, and was pan
Twentie wynteris kyng and ane:
K. 13. Hecgede (d) monavele Mackdongat
Downad Brekswn after pat
Regnyd twelve zheris fullelie.
Here I suspend pis genealogy:
Bot I will speke mare parof swne
Quhen all pe (e) laive till pat is downe (f).

(a) Could.

(b) Powerful.

(c) Sixteen years whole.

(d) Eochod-rinavel.

(e) The rest.

(f) The names of the following kings are intermixed with *Winton's* chronicle, and in all the ordinary copies; so it were useless to set them down here.

NUM. VIII.

NUM. VIII.

INSTRUMENTUM (*a*) PUBLICUM, CONTINENS COPIAM ET EXEMPLAR DE VERBO IN VERBUM QUARUNDAM LITERARUM EDWARDI REGIS ANGLIE SUPER RENUNCIATIONE ET QUIETA CLAMATIONE OMNIUM OBLIGATIONUM, JURIUM, PACTORUM ET CONVENTORM FACTORUM INTER REGES SCOTIE ET ANGLIE, AUT SUORUM REGNORUM STATUS, SUPER SUBJECTIONE ET JURISCLAMIO REGIS SCOTIE ET IPSIUS REGNI. *Et res est bene notanda* (*b*).

Ex ipso authentico instrumento in collegio Scotorum Parisiensi. *Vide Præfationem*, num. xiv. *supra*.

UNIVERSIS sancte matris ecclesie filiis, ad quorum notitiam presentes litere pervenerint, *Henricus* (*c*) miseracione divina episcopus sancti Andree salutem in Domino sempiternam. No-

(*a*) *Hoc instrumentum servabatur olim in archivo sive tabulario ecclesiæ metropolitanæ Glasguensis; inde ereptum (dum universa ecclesiarum regni tabularia, prætextu religionis, conflagrarent) a Jacobo Beaton archiepiscopo cum aliis ecclesiæ suæ chartis & instrumentis in Gallias deportatum est.*

(*b*) *Hæc nota alia manu additur titulo ut majori cura servaretur hoc instrumentum.*

(*c*) *Henricus de Wardelau.*

verit

verit universitas vestra, quod nuper coram nobis pro tribunali sedentibus in capella juxta magnum pontem burgi de Perth nostre dioceseos, constitutus reverendus in Christo pater dominus (a) Gilbertus, Dei gracia, episcopus Abirdonensis, cancellarius Scocie, nomine, & ex parte trium statuum regni Scocie tunc congregatorum & consilium generale facientium in domo fratrum Predicatorum dicti burgi, quasdam literas recolende memorie domini Edwardi, Dei gracia, regis Anglie, principis quondam inclitissimi produxit, nobisque exhibuit & ostendit; quarum tenores de verbo ad verbum inferius describuntur. Quas quidem literas idem dominus episcopus & cancellarius transcribi petiit, & exemplari ac in publicam & attenticam formam ad futuram rei memoriam redigi authoritate nostra ordinaria, cum interpositione decreti, ne propter defectum probacionis eorum, que in ipsis literis continentur, dominus noster rex Scocie, qui pro tempore fuerit ac regnum & regnicole quovismodo inquietari vel perturbari valerent ipsis litteris originalibus perditis vel destructis. Nos igitur volentes probacionibus subvenire, ne veritate occultata justitia deperiret, visis, lectis, & diligenter inspectis litteris ipsis in nostra presentia, de verbo ad verbum, per notarios publicos infrascriptos, nobis veris absque suspicione reputatis, & cum originalibus examinatis, & sigillis in iisdem appensis integris, &, ut bene apparuit, veris. Ipsius

(a) Gilbertus de Greenlaw.

domini

domini episcopi & cancellarii petitioni, utpote rationabili, annuentes presatas litteras transcribi & exemplari mandavimus & fecimus per notarios publicos infrascriptos, tenore presentium decernentes quod transcripto hujusmodi sive exemplacioni deinceps per omnia plena fides adhibeatur, tam in judiciis quam extra, sicut originalibus literis prelibatis: quibus omnibus & singulis nostram authoritatem interponimus & decretum. Tenores ipsarum literarum tales sunt. *UNIVERSIS presentes litteras inspecturis*, Edwardus, *Dei gracia, rex Anglie, dominus Hybernie, & Dux Acquitanie, salutem in domino sempiternam. Cum nos, nonnullique predecessores nostri, reges Anglie, jura regiminis dominii, seu superioritatis regni Scocie conati fuerimus obtinere, ob hocque motarum dira guerrarum discrimina Anglie & Scocie regna diutius afflixissent, nos attendentes cedes, occisiones, scelera, ecclesiarum destructiones, & mala innumerabilia, que hujusmodi occasione guerrarum regnicolis utriusque regni multipliciter contingebant, bonaque quibus regnum utrumque mutuis compendiis habundaret, perpetue pacis stabilitate connexum, ac per hoc contra conatus noxios rebellare vel impugnare volentium interius vel exterius majori firmitate securum, volumus, & concedimus, per presentes, pro nobis, heredibus, & successoribus nostris, quibuscunque, de communi consilio, assensu, & consensu prelatorum & procerum, comitum & baronum, ac communitatum regni nostri in parliamento nostro, quod regnum Scocie per suas rectas marchias prout temporibus bone memorie Alexandri* [illegible] regis Scocie ultimò defuncti fuerunt habite & ser-[illegible] magnifico principi domino Roberto, Dei gracia, regi Scotorum, illustri confederato ac amico nostro [illegible], suisque heredibus & successoribus divisum [illegible] a regno Anglie integrum, liberum & [illegible] in perpetuum, absque qualicunque subjectione, servitute, clameo vel demanda. Et si quod jus nos, vel antecessores nostri, in regno Scocie retroactis temporibus petierimus, vel petierint quoquomodo, prefato regi Scocie, heredibus & successoribus suis, renunciamus, & dimittimus, per presentes. Omnes autem obligaciones, convenciones & pacta, initas, vel inita qualitercunque cum nostris predecessoribus quibuscunque, quibuscunque temporibus, super subjectione regni Scocie, vel incolarum ejusdem, per quoscunque reges vel incolas clericos, vel laicos ipsius regni Scocie, pro nobis, heredibus & successoribus nostris, remittimus penitus & omnino. Et si que litere, carte, munimenta vel instrumenta, reperiantur de cetero ubicunque super hujusmodi obligacionibus, convencionibus & pactis confecte vel confecta, pro cassis, irritis, inanibus & vacuis habeantur, nulliusque valoris esse volumus vel momenti. Et ad premissa omnia plene, pacificè & fideliter perpetuis temporibus observanda, dilectis & fidelibus nostris Henrico de Percy consanguineo nostro, & Willielmo la Zousch de Assheby, & eorum alteri, ad sacramentum in animam nostram inde prestandum, per alias litteras nostras patentes, plenam dedimus potestatem ac mandatum speciale: in cujus rei testimonium, has litteras nostras fieri fecimus patentes. Datum apud

Ebor.

Ebor. primo die Martii, anno regni nostri secundo: PER IPSUM REGEM ET CONSILIUM IN PARLIAMENTO. Item; Edwardus, *Dei gracia, rex Anglie, dominus Hybernie, & dux Acquitanie, dilectis ac fidelibus suis Henrico de* Percy, *& Willelmo de la* Zousche *de* Assheby *salutem. Cum per cartam, sive litteras nostras patentes, concesserimus magnifico principi Roberto, Dei gracia, regi Scotorum, quod habeat regnum Scocie per suas rectas marchias, prout temporibus bone memorie Alexandri regis Scocie ultimò defuncti fuerunt habite & servate; & jus, si quod nos, vel antecessores nostri in regno Scocie retroactis temporibus petierimus, vel petierint quoquomodo eidem domino regi Scotorum renunciaverimus. Nos de fidelitate vestra & circumspectione provida plenius confidentes, ad firmandum & vallandum omnia & singula in dictis carta sive litteris contenta per juramentum in animam nostram prestandum, vobis & alteri vestrum tenore presentium, committimus potestatem ac speciale mandatum. Et hoc omnibus, & singulis, quorum interest, vel interesse poterit, innotescimus per presentes litteras nostras patentes sigilli nostri munimine roboratas. Datum apud Ebor. primo die Martii, anno regni nostri secundo*: PER IPSUM REGEM ET CONSILIUM IN PARLIAMENTO. Sigillabantur autem dicte litere sigillo magno & rotundo de cera alba, in cujus una parte erat forma cathedre in qua erat ymago regis sedentis, induti quasi regalibus vestibus, cum corona in capite, & sceptro in manu dextra, & ex utraque parte cathedre flos lilii; & in circumferentia

ntia scriptum erat litteris legibilibus. EDWARDUS, DEI GRACIA, REX ANGLIE, DOMINUS HYBERNIE, DUX ACQUITANIE. Ex altera autem parte sigilli erat ymago regis armati sedentis super equum, gladium ferentis evaginatum elevatum in manu dextra, & super humerum sinistrum erat scutum in quo erant tres ymagines leopardi gradientis; & in circumferentia erat scriptum litteris legibilibus: EDWARDUS, DEI GRACIA, REX ANGLIE, DOMINUS HYBERNIE, DUX ACQUITANIE. In quorum omnium & singulorum testimonium presentes litteras, sive presens publicum instrumentum, per notarios publicos infrascriptos scribi & publicari mandavimus, nostrique sigilli fecimus appensione muniri. Datum & actum in capella supradicta, sub anno Domini millesimo quadringentesimo quintodecimo, mensis Martii die decima septima, indictione nona, pontificatus sanctissimi in Christo patris ac domini nostri domini Benedicti divina providentia pape XIII. anno vicesimo secundo, presentibus reverendis in Christo patribus & dominis dominis Willelmo Glasguensi, Henrico Moraviensi, Waltero Brechinensi, Thoma Candide-Case, Fynlao Dunblanensi, Alexandro Rossensi, & Alexandro Cathinensi, Dei gracia, episcopis; Willelmo de Dumfermlyne, Waltero de *Abirbrotbok*, Joanne de *Balmurinach*, Willelmo de *Kinlosse*, Joanne de *Culros*, & Patricio de *Cambuskyneth*, Dei gracia, Abbatibus, cum multis aliis testibus ad premissam publicationem viden-

videndam & audiendam vocatis specialiter & rogatis.

Et ego Ricardus de *Crag*, presbyter Sancti-Andree diocef. publicus imperiali authoritate notarius de mandato dicti domini mei episcopi Sancti-Andree, & ipso auttoritatem prestante, dictum instrumentum in publicam formam redegi, manu propria totum scripsi, nihil addito vel diminuto quod sensum mutet vel vitiet intellectum, & in presentia judicis & testium, cum magistris Patricio de *Huyston* canonico Glasguensi, Ricardo *Knyth* rectore ecclesie de *Connetb*, & domino Waltero *Ra* rectore ecclesie de *Garvalde* notariis publicis, diligenter & fideliter cum ipso attentico ascultavi, & ipsas originales litteras vidi, & testibus ostendi, & perlegi, non vitiatas, non cancellatas, nec in aliqua sui parte abolitas seu suspectas neque in castâ, neque in scriptura, neque in sigillo; premissisque omnibus aliis, & singulis, dum sic ut premittitur fierent & agerentur presens fui, & ideo hic me subscripsi, signumque meum solitum apposui, rogatus & requisitus in fidem & testimonium omnium premissorum (*a*).

Et ego Ricardus *Militis*, clericus Sancti-Andree diocef. publicus imperiali auttoritate notarius,

(*a*) Signum Notar.

tarius, premissis omnibus & singulis, dum sic ut premittitur coram prefato domino meo episcopo Sancti-Andree fierent & agerentur, una cum prenominatis testibus, presens interfui, eaque sic fieri vidi & audivi, & cum subscriptis notariis in notam recepi, & presens publicum instrumentum aliena manu scriptum de mandato dicti domini episcopi *similiter* publicavi, illudque una cum appensione sigilli dicti reverendi patris, signo & subscriptione meis solitis & consuetis signavi in testimonium premissorum requisitus & rogatus (*a*).

Et ego Robertus de *Ferny*, clericus Sancti-Andree dioces. publicus auttoritate apostolica & imperiali notarius, omnibus & singulis suprascriptis, dum sic ut premitittur & coram prelibato domino episcopo Sancti-Andree fierent & agerentur, una cum subscriptis testibus presens interfui, eaque ut prefertur sic fieri vidi & audivi, una cum subscriptis notariis, presens publicum instrumentum aliena manu suprascriptum de mandato prefati domini episcopi publicavi, ac signo meo solito & consueto, una cum sigilli predicti reverendi in christo patris munimine signavi: ideo me hic manu propria subscripsi, rogatus & requisitus coram testibus notariisque supradictis in testimonium veritatis omnium & singulorum premissorum (*b*).

(*a*) *Sign. Notar.*
(*b*) *Sign. Notar.*

 Huic

Huic instrumento appensum est sigillum magnum Henrici de Wardelau *episcopi S. Andree.*

ADDITION.

The printer wanting matter to fill up this sheet, I thought nothing could be more proper than some authentick pieces that I have quoted, and referred to in this essay, upon occasion of the rebellion against king James III. *and of his murther ensued upon it* (a). *The first is the act of* The Proposition of the Debate of the Field of *Striveling*, *which is the first precedent of any act made in* Scotland, *to justify the rising in arms against the soveraign, and which hath ever since been referred to by all those that have imitated the example of the authors of it. The second is a Bull of pope* Innocent VIII. (b) *granted at the instant supplication of those that had any hand in that rebellion, empowering the abbots of* Pasly *and* Iedword *to absolve them from that crime, and from the excommunication they had incurred by it, upon their hearty repentance, and promise to do, for expiation of it, whatever penance should be enjoined them. Both these acts are quoted and referred to in the relation of this tragedy, and serve to give light to the subject.*

(a) V. p. 253, & p. 279, &c. supra.
(b) V. p. 280, supra.

NUM. IX.

NUM. IX.

The Proposition of the Debate of the Field of Striveling.

From the Acts of Parliament, commonly called the Black Acts, printed by Lekprevik, fol. 82.

Parl. K. James the IVth. 6 Octob. 1488, cap. 14.

ITEM, in yis present parlament our soverane lord beand present together with his thre estaitis of the realme, was proponit the debait and cause of the field of Striveling, in the quhilk unquhile James king of Scotland, quhom God assolize, father to our soveraine lord happenit to be slane, and the cause and occasion thairof commonit, openit and arguit among the lordis of the thre estaits, John lord Glamis presentit and schew certane articlis subscribit with the said unquhile K. James hand, the tenor of the quhilk followis, &c. The quhilkis beand read and schawin that the said articlis was diverse timis grantit to, and brokin be perverst counsal of diverse personnis beand with him for the tyme: quhich counsalit and assistit him in the inbringing of Englishmen, and to the perpetual subjectioun of the realme, and under desait and colour maid and refusit, and that our soveraign lord that now is ever consentit for the gude of the realme and the profit thairof. (For the quhilk the earl of Huntlie, the earl of Errol, the earl Marshal, the lord Glamis, and utheris diverse barons, and utheris the kyngis true liegis left him, and his desaitfull and perverse counsale, and adherit to our soveran lord that now is, and his true opinion for the common gude of the realme) the quhilk mater being schawin examinat and commonit, and understanding be the thre estaitis and haill bodie of the parlament, they ryplie avisit, declarit and concludit, and in thair lauteis and allegeance ilk ane for himself, declarit and concludit: that the slauchter done and committit in the field of Striviling, quhair our soveran lordis father happenit to be slane, and utheris divers his baronis and liegis, was alluterlie in their default, and culourit dissait done be him and his perverst counsale diverse tymes before the said field: and that our soveran lord that now is, and the trew lordis and baronis that wes with him in the samin field, war innocent, free, and quyte of the said slauchters done in the said field, and all pursute of the occasioun and cause of the samin: and that part of the three estatis forsaidis, prelatis, bischopis, great baronis, burgessis, gaif thair seillis heirupon, together with our soveran lordis greit seill, to be schawin and producit to our H. Father the pape, the kingis of France, Hispanzie, Denmark, and uther realmis, as sall be sene expedient for the tyme.

NUM. X.

NUM. X.

Rescriptum Innocentii papæ VIII. *quo facultatem impertit absolvendi eos qui in Jacobum regem* III. *insurrexerant & de perpetrato crimine ab intimis se dolere protestabantur, &c.*

Ex Collect. C. de Panmure.

INNOCENTIUS episcopus servus servorum Dei dilectis filiis de Passleto & de Iedworth Glasguen. diocef. monasteriorum abbatibus & cancellario ecclesiæ Glasguensis salutem & apostolicam Benedictionem. Exuberans apostolicæ sedis clementia recurrentium ad eam post excessum cum humilitate personarum statui libenter consulere, eisque se propitiam exhibere consuevit atque benignam. Exhibita siquidem nobis nuper pro parte nonnullorum regnicolarum regni Scotiæ petitio continebat, quod olim, postquam per nos intellecto quod nonnulli domini tam spirituales quam temporales dicti regni adversus claræ memoriæ Jacobum tertium ipsius regni regem, illiusque statum insurgere, imo & regem ipsum a dicti regni regimine expellere intendebant & moliebantur: nosque per quasdam literas nostras, nonnullas sententias, censuras & pœnas ecclesiasticas, etiam privationis dignitatum & beneficiorum ecclesiasticorum; necnon ad illa inhabilitationis, contra ipsum regem insurgentes, & eorundem insurgentium fautores promulgaveramus: quæ post modum in partibus illis promulgatæ fuerunt, nonnulli regnicolæ ejusdem

regni

regni cariſſimo in Chriſto filio noſtro Jacobo quarto ejus filio moderno regi, tunc principi Scotiæ, qui pro ſalute & utilitate defuncti regis & regni prædictorum, ſtatum & conſilium ipſius regis reformare, & quoſdam regis prædicti conſiliarios vi & potentia expellere deliberaverunt, adhæſerunt, & illius fautores extiterunt: ac pro parte tam defuncti quam moderni regum prædictorum, exercitus parati fuiſſent & inter ſe manus conſeruiſſent, præfatus rex defunctus in conflictu cum diverſis aliis perſonis occubuit, nonnullis ex præfatis exponentibus in dicto conflictu præſentibus; & alias aliquotiens ipſi regnicolæ qui prætextu duntaxat dicti conflictus contra ipſum regem defunctum inſurrexerant. Unde tam præſentes quam abſentes adhærentes, & alias contra dictum regem defunctum inſurgentes præfati, dubitant ſententias, cenſuras, & pœnas incurriſſe. Cum autem, ſicut eadem petitio ſubjungebat, *Exponentes præfati de præmiſſis ab intimis doleant, cupiantque pro commiſſis pœnitentiam agere ſalutarem*, pro parte ipſorum nobis fuit humiliter ſupplicatum, ut ipſos a ſententiis, cenſuris, & pœnis præfatis in ipſis litteris noſtris quomodolibet contentis abſolvere, ac alias ipſis & eorum ſtatui in præmiſſis opportunè providere de benignitate apoſtolica dignaremur. Nos igitur attendentes quod præfatæ ſedis clementia ad eam recurrentibus poſt exceſſum cum humilitate perſonis, ſuæ pietatis gremium favorabiliter aperire conſuevit, ac volentes prædictos, apud nos alias de probitatis & virtutum meritis commendatos, horum intuitu favo-

ribus

ribus profequi gratiofis, eorum in hac parte fupplicationibus inclinati, difcretioni veftræ per apoftolica fcripta committimus & mandamus quatenus vos, duo, vel unus veftrum omnes & fingulos qui in dicto conflictu interfuerunt, ac abfentes qui illis adhæferunt, & auxilium, confilium affenfum & favorem verbo vel facto quoquomodo præftiterunt, nec non qui alias quam prætextu duntaxat dicti conflictus contra ipfum regem defunctum infurrexerunt, & contra dictas noftras litteras quovifmodo devenerunt, ac fi eorum nomina & cognomina præfentibus infererentur, fi hæc humiliter petierint, ab omnibus & fingulis cenfuris & pœnis in dictis noftris litteris quomodo libet contentis, & per eos præmifforum occafione qualitercunque & quotiefcunque incurfis, quas ac fi litteræ prædictæ de verbo ad verbum infertæ forent præfentibus habere volumus pro expreffis, auctoritate noftra hac vice duntaxat abfolvatis in forma ecclefiæ confueta, injunctis ipfis & eorum cuilibet, pro modo culpæ pœnitentia falutari, & aliis quæ de jure fuerint injugenda; eofque & eorum fingulos unitati fanctæ matris ecclefiæ, & facramentorum ecclefiafticorum participationi, communionique fidelium, eadem auctoritate reftituatis. Non obftantibus præmiffis, ac conftitutionibus & ordinationibus apoftolicis, cæterifque contrariis quibufcunque. Datum Romæ apud S. Petrum anno incarnationis Dominicæ millefimo quadringentefimo nonagefimo primo 5to kalend. Julii pontificatus noftri anno feptimo.

FINIS.

Lightning Source UK Ltd.
Milton Keynes UK
UKHW020611230123
415808UK00007B/1458

9 781018 352862